Holy Spirit Tours

Winter Excursion I

By Bob Garvey

Holy Spirit Tours

Winter Excursion I

By Bob Garvey

Home Crafted Artistry & Printing
New Albany, Indiana
USA

ISBN-13: 9 780 9827621 7 2
ISBN-10: 0 98276 21 7 8

Home Crafted Artistry and Printing
1252 Beechwood Avenue
New Albany, IN 47150
HomeCraftedArtistry@yahoo.com

Cover design by Mary Dow Bibb Smith
Home Crafted Artistry & Printing

Dedicated to
all of the
Catholic charismatic
brothers and sisters
I have prayed with since
November, 1970.

CONTENTS

Preface

"How sweet are your words to my taste, sweeter than honey to my mouth." (Ps 119:103)

Imagine this! God's words are sweeter than honey. This is like saying God's words taste better than donuts.

What if a store offered free donuts and pastries every morning, do you think it would be a popular place? You bet. The Church serves God's word every day and it is free. Besides it tastes better than the richest of pastries. Is this the world's best kept secret?

Isaiah, speaking for God, said: "Listen, listen to me, and eat what is good, and your soul will delight in the richest of fare." (Is 55:2) God has set a banquet for us. He wants to feed us with the best that is available because we are his children. And how few step up to the table and eat the meal God provides daily.

About two years ago, inspired by the daily reader that was originated by Father Al Lauer of Cincinnati, I decided to read daily the Scripture passages offered to us by the Church. To improve my spiritual taste buds, I began to write personal reflections on this Word and share them by email with friends in the charismatic renewal. Now, about five hundred and seventy-five days later, I am continuing on this project. While I send the writings out to friends, my main purpose is to get a generous helping from God's banquet table for myself.

I can testify, as a donut lover, that God's words are sweeter than sugar. I have become so attached to the daily readings served us by the Church, that reading them and reflecting on them has become the highlight of my day.

The Holy Spirit has inspired the program of readings that the Church presents to us, and they fit together as a beautiful mosaic set in the liturgical rhythm of the Church. Staying in tune with these readings gets us caught up in the symphony of God's song to his people. This daily bread raises us up to a new level of union with God and the Church and gives us added strength for our journeys.

As with most rich foods, it takes some time and perseverance to develop a taste for the food of God's Word. Spending regular time each day munching on what comes off God's banquet table, brings us to a place where we can't do without it. And since the Church prepares the menu and the meal each day, all we have to do is show up. We don't have to figure out what to read each day; the Church has done this work for us.

I have been encouraged by friends to put some of my reflections in book form. I hope this inspires many to develop a taste for God's Word as it is served daily in the Church. I hope that it helps priests and religious educators gain new insights that will help them in their teachings and homilies.

Since most of us like bus tours where we sit back and let the driver take us to new and exciting places, we can view this set of writings as a trip through God's Word. It can be looked upon as a vacation with the Holy Spirit. So I call his book, *Holy Spirit Tours,* and this season is the "Winter Excursion". Each day the bus lands in a new and enriching place and the food gets better every day!

Acknowledgement: Special thanks to Presentation Ministries for permission to use quotes from "One Bread, One Body" (daily reader)

Holy Spirit Tours

Winter Excursion I

*And so,
let us begin our journey . . .*

. . . "Come Holy Spirit,
fill the hearts of Your faithful.
Enkindle in them the fire of Your love.
Send forth Your Spirit and
they shall be created and
You will renew the face of the earth!"

Lovely Feet

"How lovely on the mountains are the feet of him who brings good news." (Is 52:7) also quoted in today's epistle (Rom 10:15). When the troops were out to battle, the people anxiously awaited the news of what happened. They didn't have internet in those days; they depended on a runner to bring them news. Seeing the "herald" appear, coming across the mountains, was the most beautiful sight imaginable when he had "good news" to report. Even his dirty feet looked "lovely".

Here we are talking about mountains again. This time we join the "runner" as he bolts across the mountain with the good news of victory. People look with fear at the "signs of the times" and wonder how things are going to turn out. God sends the "runners" ahead of Jesus as "evangelists", which means "bearers of good news". We are those evangelists to the people of our day.

At the outset of Advent the Church introduces us to a St. Andrew, the first evangelist. We have just stepped forward into our journey, and the Church is already exhorting us to run across the mountains proclaiming the good news of victory. When things look bleak and dark in the world, people look for a "runner" who has a message of Good News.

Today's Gospel reading (Mt 4:18-22) tells the story of the first apostles leaving their nets to follow Jesus. Their profession was changed from catching fish to catching men. Jesus anointed them as evangelists. They eagerly accepted the call. Matthew says *"at once*

19

they left their nets and followed him."

Do we have this "at-once" attitude when we hear Jesus call, or do we have an "I'll think about it" approach? Let's watch Andrew show us what wearing "the shoes of eagerness" (Eph 6:15) is all about.

In John's Gospel (1:35ff) we learn that Andrew was a disciple of John the Baptist. He was a seeker of God who not only went to the Jordan to be baptized, but attached himself to John the Baptist as a disciple. When John pointed to Jesus, Andrew immediately followed Jesus to find out where he was staying. Jesus said "come and see", and he did. Now what do you think was the first thing Andrew did after finding Jesus? *"The first thing Andrew did was to find his brother Simon and tell him 'we have found the Messiah'. And he brought him to Jesus."* Andrew knew how to jump on an opportunity. He jumped on the opportunity to be a disciple of John the Baptist, he jumped on the opportunity to follow Jesus, and he jumped on the opportunity to tell his brother, Simon, the Good News. In fact this was the greatest news the world was ever or will ever hear.

Little did Andrew know that he was introducing the first "pope" to Jesus. God was, at that moment, planting a seed for church leadership that would last for over 2000 years. What if Andrew had been "possessive of his salvation", and kept the news to himself?

Paul tells us that *"the word is in you; it is in your mouth and in your heart"* (Rom 10:8) and that *"everyone who calls on the name of the Lord will be saved"* (Rom 10:13). Paul makes it clear that "everyone" includes both Jews and Gentiles. No longer would people have to go through the gyrations of meticulously obeying the Law to be saved. Now all they had to do was to hear the Good News and say "yes" to Jesus. What a message we are privileged to bear. Salvation is free, not earned. What better news could there be?

We are people, like Andrew, who left our nets and eagerly followed Jesus. Let us, like Andrew, be quick to tell others the secret that we have found. There is a "Simon" in our lives waiting for us to come and say "guess, what, I've found the Messiah". Have we forgotten about that?

"Jesus, let us be so overflowing with good news that when people see us approach, even our feet will appear lovely to them. Through St. Andrew's intercession may a new spirit of 'eagerness' overtake us and the fire of evangelization stir once again within us."

Pep Talk

We have barely started Advent and the Church calls "time out" to give us a "pep talk". Knowing how human we are and how we may be having a tough time with the "Advent climb", the Church calls on Isaiah to give us a motivational talk. He visits us and speaks eloquently of what to expect at the top of the mountain. Through the words of this prophet, the Holy Spirit stirs up within us a vision that will keep us climbing enthusiastically.

Isaiah (25:6-8) tells us what God has prepared for us further up the mountain. He speaks of the "messianic" age that is coming. There will be a feast of rich foods and aged wines for "all" the people, not restricted just to the Jews. God will remove the shroud that keeps people from seeing him. On the mountain death will be "swallowed up", tears of grief will be taken away, and all disgrace will be taken from His people. "The hand of the Lord" will be on the mountain to protect his people from their enemies—nothing more to fear.

Then in the Gospel (Mt 15:29-36) we see the fulfillment of this messianic age in Jesus. What Isaiah foretold actually happens on the "mountainside". Those who chose to leave their daily routines behind and walked up the side of the mountain with Jesus got to taste the messianic banquet that day. Miracles exploded in their midst.

"Great crowds came to him bringing the lame, the blind, the crippled, the mute, and many others and laid them at his feet; and he healed them." Imagine the

excitement as the blind suddenly began to see, the lame began to walk, and people began to proclaim their healings. Death, grief and disgrace were removed miraculously. Then, moved by compassion, Jesus created a spontaneous banquet for the crowd. With but a handful of bread and fish he fed over 4000 people. *"They ate and were all satisfied."* And seven baskets were left over. The number 7, as I recall, symbolized completion. This was another sign that the messianic age had arrived. The meats, the rich food, the aged wine were experienced more within than without. It was a banquet in which God's love so saturated the people that they were totally satisfied.

This was the beginning of the "end times", the messianic era. The fulfillment of prophecy was seen in Jesus. The mountain of Isaiah had appeared. We know, of course, that at the end of that glorious day, people went back home and Jesus moved on to his next destination. The completion of the "end times" had not yet taken place.

The Church reminds us that today the "end times" are here; we are living right smack in the middle of the "messianic age." We, during Advent, are taking time out of our busy lives to spend a day on the mountainside with Jesus. He will work miracles for those we bring to him; he will provide a banquet for us "in the sight of our foes". He will feed our hearts with the richest foods, the best meats, and the aged wine. Isn't this available every time we participate in the Eucharist? Even before we reach the top of the mountain we are saturated and satisfied with God's love.

When we open our hearts to Jesus, we get carried along

by the Holy Spirit. During Advent he is carrying us to a new place, a place where we will be set free from our burdens and feast on God's great love. What better motivation to re-commit ourselves to the Advent climb, and to get excited about the surprises God has planned for us in the days ahead.

Thank you, Holy Spirit, for the "pep talk". We needed it.

"Holy Spirit, intervene in our lives at this moment and awaken again the desire to leave all and follow Jesus. With great anticipation we climb the mountain so we can taste of the wonders God has already prepared for us. Praise Him that we are privileged to be part of the messianic age."

Construction Work

So the Church doesn't slight those who are not into "mountain climbing", it shifts its image today and talks about "building houses". (Mt 7, 21, 24-27). Today, instead of thinking about our Advent challenge as climbing a mountain, we think of it as building a house.

During our time on earth we are given the task of "building a house"; the house is ourselves. At the end of life, we will look back and see what kind of job we have done. As builders know, the first and most important step is creating a solid foundation. Jesus spoke about foundations today in the gospel.

To help understand Jesus' image, here's an experiment to try. Get a 4-foot broomstick and hammer it about 6 inches into the ground. Next to it hammer a second broomstick about 3 feet into the ground (if you are strong enough). People will be more impressed with the first broomstick because it is so much taller. Then try to push the first broomstick over. There is some resistance, but it quickly falls over or breaks. Next, try to push the second broomstick over. It is impossible, because its foundations are too deep.

As long as no one pushes on the broomstick, who cares how deep it is? It is when the stick has to bear up against someone trying to remove it or push it over, that its foundation matters.

Our lives are like the broomstick. If we are shallow in our foundations, it doesn't take much to push it over.

That's why Jesus tells us today, to examine, our foundations closely. At this time in Advent we do a "building inspection" of the foundations of our lives. Jesus tells us that a house built on sand may go up quicker and even be more attractive, but when the flood comes it goes down the river with the rest of the debris. A house buildt on rock withstands the worst of disasters.

Floods always come. We just don't know when. And when the flood comes, it's too late to shore up our weak foundations. Jesus wants us to be prepared now, for He sees ahead and He knows when the flood is coming. How deep is our relationship with the Lord?

We know, of course, that the only foundation to our lives that is "rock" and will hold us up when the flood comes is Jesus. It is easy to give mere lip service to this truth and in reality buy into the "sand" foundations that the world holds before us: money, career, position in life, human relationships, even alcohol, recreation, and fun. For the most part these foundations are popular, and we get the impression that they work. Are there parts of our lives still built on the "cheap sand" presented to us by the world?

Remember the unnerving story of Ananias and Sapphira (Acts, chap 5). They professed Jesus as the foundation of their lives, yet in case Jesus didn't work out, they had a back up plan. They kept a store of money, just in case they wanted to "quit" the Jesus trip. In spite of calling themselves Christians, their real foundation was money. You can read the story to see what happened to them.

As we examine our foundations before the Lord and notice that we are leaning too much on one of the foundations promoted by the world, let us repent. Then we expose that weak part of our lives to the Holy Spirit and ask Jesus to shore it up with Himself.

Isaiah, today, also talks about building. (Is 26:1- 6). He says that the city of God is built on the "Rock eternal", and those who dwell in that city can *"trust in the Lord forever"*, whereas, in time God will lay "the lofty city low". That is, the city built on pride and human effort alone will not stand.

And the responsorial psalm today (Ps 118) reminds us that *"it is better to take refuge in the Lord than to trust in man"*, and that *"the stone rejected by the builders (Jesus), has become the capstone"* of God's house on earth (the Body of Christ).

"Holy Spirit, thank You that Jesus is the foundation stone of our lives. Show us any way we have compromised this foundation and weakened our spiritual lives. Today, we let go of any "sand" foundations that have crept in and invite Jesus into our hearts again as our only Lord There is no other."

Wait a Minute

We are told that Advent is a time of "waiting". Americans do not like to hear this word. We don't want to wait in line, wait for the red light to turn, wait until we have enough money to buy something, or even wait for Santa Claus. Today's psalm (Ps 27) ends with the exhortation, *"wait for the Lord"* (vs.14).

Have you ever become tired waiting for something to go on sale, given up, and bought something else instead? Then a few days later you see the item is now on sale? "If only I had waited a little longer", we say to ourselves. When we choose not to wait, we sometimes settle for less than what really satisfies us. Are we willing to wait for Jesus or will we jump out and buy something else instead?

Isaiah keeps reminding us that "that day" is worth waiting for. Today's reading (Is 29:17-24) begins with the phrase "in a very short time." He says that the waiting time is shorter than we think. Then what will happen? Forests will turn into fertile fields, and fields will turn into forests. Deaf will hear God's word, and blind people will see. The humble and the needy will rejoice because the days of their oppression by the wicked will be over; they will no longer be ashamed and will once again "acknowledge the holiness of the Lord".

What a day that will be! If Isaiah's words are true, there is nothing better worth waiting for.

In the Gospel (Mt 9:27-31) we see that the "very short

time" is over. That great day that was prophesied by Isaiah had now come. Jesus was turning things around, just the way forests turn into fertile fields, and oppressors become the oppressed. Jesus touched the eyes of two blind men and their sight was restored. "That day" had arrived!

Reading the story closely, we see that Jesus made the blind men "wait" to be healed. As Jesus went out from the place where He had brought the young girl back to life, the two men followed Him. He could have stopped, turned around and healed them on the spot. Instead He kept on walking and didn't pay attention to them until after *"He had gone indoors"* (vs 28).

Do you think He had walked several miles before He came to the house and went inside? Jesus kept the door open and the blind men followed him right up to the door. It was only after this "waiting" period that Jesus began to talk to them. They had been pleading for mercy and acclaiming him as Son of David (the Messiah king). In effect they believed that the time foretold by Isaiah had come. Jesus still kept them waiting. He asked, *"Do you believe I am able to do this?" Without hesitancy they said, "Yes Lord".* Only after they had waited did He ask them to make an act of faith.

Why did Jesus do it this way? Why does He make us follow persistently, almost ignoring our pleas, before He turns and responds to our needs? For one thing, we value what we have to wait for. And in "waiting" we surrender our own wills little by little and become more ready to accept God's plan for our lives.

Then there is a surprising turn in the story. The men disobey Jesus. He tells them to keep "waiting" instead of broadcasting what had happened to them. The day of fulfillment had begun, but the outpouring of the Holy Spirit had not yet come. Jesus was not the kind of Messiah king that they imagined. Matthew says that Jesus "sternly" said *"See that no one knows about this."* We read *"But they went out and spread the news about him all over that region."* Jesus knew they would do this, I'm sure. How could they keep such a miracle quiet?

We can get too much into the "waiting" mode as we climb the Advent mountain and wistfully wonder about what will happen when we reach the top. There is a time, when we have to "let loose" and proclaim who Jesus is and what He wants to do for the world. If we keep seeking Him and let him touch us, we, like the blind men, will be so filled with wonder and joy that we won't be able to wait even another minute to "spread the news about Him" over the "regions" in which we live. And, remember, we live in the days of the Holy Spirit when we are told to "go out' and tell the good news, not to keep it hidden under a bushel basket. Jesus' words to us are "See that everyone knows about this".

"St. Francis Xavier, on this your feast day, pray that we will have a share of your zeal in proclaiming the good news of who Jesus is. You were not afraid to leave all that you had, travel to a strange land, risk your life and your health so that a part of the world that never heard about Jesus could be touched by Him. We need that kind of love."

Broken Hearts

Today the Church sings Psalm 147, and in verse 3 we praise God who *"heals the brokenhearted and binds up their wounds."* Yesterday we heard Isaiah talk about God healing the blind and the deaf. Today, a deeper kind of healing is being described. God is healing broken hearts.

In Isaiah (30: 19-21, 23-26) God addressed the grief of His people. Speaking to the inhabitants of Jerusalem who had lost everything because of their infidelity to God, He said the day is coming when *"you will weep no more."* In time, their days of grief would be over, and prosperity would return. This new day would so far surpass the glory of days past that *"the moon will shine like the sun and the sunlight will be seven times brighter"*.

Then Isaiah said that in that day the Lord will bind up the "bruises of His people" and heal "the wounds He inflicted". He was talking to a people who had been broken because of their sins and could be healed only by the gracious hand of God. There is a deeper healing involved here than physical healing.

The grace of God's favor runs deeper than we can imagine.

Then Matthew (9:35, 10:1, 5-8) tells of Jesus as He went through the towns and villages teaching, preaching, and healing people. Once again we are reminded that though we wait for Jesus' return in glory, He is already here proclaiming the kingdom of God and pouring out his healing power.

Matthew takes us a step further. We read that Jesus shared His charisms with the apostles and sent them out to preach the nearness of the kingdom, to heal, and beyond that to "raise the dead, cleanse those who have leprosy, and drive out demons". The power of Jesus' ministry goes much deeper than healing, and, to their surprise, I'm sure, He extended this power (for a limited time) to His apostles. It was unheard of that a man like Jesus could work such miracles, and even more unheard of that He would extend this power to 12 simple, untrained men. After Pentecost Jesus extended His charisms to the whole Church, and He continues to fulfill the "glorious day" prophesied by Isaiah, through us - each of us.

How is Jesus appearing and continuing to bring about a "new day" at this moment in the Church? I believe the great work of Jesus today centers on "healing the brokenhearted". Is the great epidemic of our age blindness or deafness? Or is the great epidemic wounded hearts, broken relationships and shattered dreams? We live in a prosperous society compared to other ages in history; in this country most material needs are taken care of, yet the inner needs of the heart are left unattended. And Jesus is more concerned about hearts than about bodies.

We, like the apostles, are being sent out to share the charisms of Jesus. We may not know many blind people; chances are we do know many who are lonely, hurt, or brokenhearted. The Holy Spirit within us has released in us the very power of love that came out of Jesus' heart when He walked the earth. What a thought - we have the power to heal the brokenhearted of our world. Isn't this the Christmas gift that Jesus wants us to give this year? Isn't this His priority?

We can easily miss Jesus when He comes, just as many of the people did 2000 years ago. They were expecting something different - a David-like king. Instead Jesus appeared as the embodiment of the compassion of God. He appears this season in the same way through the loving touches of His people. This may not be what people are expecting, but it is what people of today need.

"Jesus make my heart like yours, overflowing with God's love for the world. Let me be awake to the brokenhearted whom You put in my path. Use me as a vessel of Your healing love to as many people as possible as You return and visit the earth."

Branches and Fire

Today John the Baptist joins us in our mountain climb. He was a rather striking figure with his garb of camel hair and a leather belt, eating a handful of locusts dipped in wild honey. His rugged appearance was matched by the toughness of his message. He was not intimidated by the religious people in the group as he called them a "brood of vipers", and let them know he was not one bit impressed with the pride they took in being "sons of Abraham". God could make children of Abraham out of dirty rocks if he wanted to. John the Baptist was not afraid of what people thought about him as was indicated by his apparel, his diet, and his straight-forward words. (Mt 3:1-12)

He spoke of a day of reckoning accompanied by fire. Even at that moment, the lumberjack was laying his ax to the "root of the trees", giving them no more chance to survive. It was not just a matter of trimming or pruning; the trees would be destroyed. And the trees that had not borne good fruit would be thrown into the fire - they wouldn't even be saved to make furniture or fences.

John the Baptist's time was almost up and the one coming after him was already emerging on the scene. He would be as a strong farmer cleaning up the threshing floor. Wheat and chaff would be separated - the wheat for his table, the chaff for the fire. A day of reckoning was already beginning.

John's words catch our attention and probably make us shudder. We all want to be the wheat and not kindling wood for the fire.

Then John spoke about the one "more powerful" than himself ministering a twofold baptism that would go beyond that of John. Repentance was not enough. The one coming would baptize in the Holy Spirit and with fire. Beyond repentance, we will receive the Holy Spirit into our hearts and a new fire within us.

In the charismatic renewal we know from experience what it is to be baptized in the Holy Spirit. The very Spirit that was in Jesus and came upon Him at the Jordan, now comes into the center of our beings. And beyond that, there is a third baptism—the baptism of fire. We are not only filled with the Holy Spirit but the very fire that stems from the heart of God is planted in our hearts. This fire is the fire of His love. It takes us beyond a "feel good" love to a burning love for God that moves us to go forth and proclaim with John the Baptist to, *"prepare the way of the Lord"*. And this fire also disturbs us for it takes the "trees" in us that do not bear fruit and the chaff that is useless and burns them up. This fire purifies us so we can be holy vessels of God's love and power in the world.

And where does this "more powerful" One come from? Isaiah (11:1-10) tells us He is the branch that grew out of the root of tree stump. Unimpressive. Babylon had leveled Jerusalem and chopped God's people down to a mere, powerless stump. Yet God took what seemed dead and rescued a branch to bring new hope to His broken people. And this insignificant Branch is raised up to, *"strike the earth with the rod of His mouth"*, and slay the wicked with the *"breath of His lips"*. He brings justice for the needy and the poor of the earth. And in Jesus we see this branch of Jesse's root reach full stature. The day of reckoning has come - it is here!

Fr. Lauer, today, makes an interesting application of today's Word. "No matter if whole branches (of our lives) have been sawed off through divorce, abuse, rejection, failure, or injustice...there's still hope". If God can raise Jesus out of the root of a tree stump, think of what he can do for us even if our lives have seemed almost destroyed through tragic experiences. Paul tells us today (Romans 15:4-9) *"Everything that was written in the past was written to teach us, so that through endurance and the encouragement of the Scriptures we might have hope."* As attention-getting as John the Baptist's message is, it is a message of great hope for the "poor and needy" regions of our hearts and of the world.

Listen as Paul steps in and prays a blessing over us today. *"May the God of hope fill you with all joy and peace as you trust in Him, so that you may overflow with hope by the power of the Holy Spirit."*

"John the Baptist, intercede for me today that the fire of the Holy Spirit will burn away the chaff of my life. Pray that the "poor and needy" of the world, and the "poor and needy" parts within me find hope in Jesus as we continue our Advent ascent."

Progress Report

We are one-fourth the way through Advent, and it is time for a quarterly progress report. How are we doing so far? How have we responded to the grace of this season that purifies us, makes us holy, and gives us an eagerness to receive Jesus as he comes in a new way? It is worth spending some quiet time today with the Lord and reviewing how well we've been doing so far.

John the Baptist like a lion roared out a call to repentance yesterday. We can't miss his message. Today is a good time to reflect and repent. I find that it is discouraging trying to maintain an Advent spirit as the world kicks into high gear fulfilling all the obligations it has imposed on itself. Our economy, like a tyrant, screams out its demands. Even in the Church while there may be lots of activity doing the decorations and preparing liturgies, how much fervor of heart is there?

Though we may be a remnant, we respond to the call of the Holy Spirit to repent, to pray, and to prepare a way in our hearts for the Lord. Our faithfulness does not hinge on what we see everyone else doing. It is built on our love for Jesus and desire to follow Him at any cost.

I listened with amazement as a family member described her pursuit of a Christmas gift that was difficult to find. Phone calls, checking out different store locations, and car trips around town finally helped her land her prize catch. Do I have that same zeal in preparing my heart for the coming of Jesus?

Today's Gospel story shows us two heroes who would let nothing get in the way of finding Jesus. (Luke 5:17-26). Their paralyzed friend was in a hopeless condition. Good chance he was depressed and maybe even resistant to seeking God's help. The two heroes picked up their friend, ignoring his resistance, and came to the house where Jesus was teaching. Even there, it was an impossible situation. The crowd was too thick to navigate through. Rather than turn around and head home, they carried the paralytic to the roof, removed the tiles, and lowered him to the feet of Jesus. Impressed by their faith, Jesus said "friend, your sins are forgiven." A wave of freeing grace swept over the man, and he felt his inner paralysis cease. At last he was right with God again. It was to deliver hearts that Jesus came. The physical healing was a confirmation of the real healing that had been rendered.

What if the two friends were only half-hearted in bringing their friend to Jesus? As they met obstacle after obstacle, they would have surely given up. Instead they sought Jesus with all their hearts until they landed their friend in front of his feet.

Are we as zealous to receive the touch of Jesus as were these men in the Gospel? Will we make it to confession this Advent, or will we let our crowded schedules stand in the way? Will we spend extra time in prayer and fasting to help break down our resistance to preparing a way for the Lord? If we have lost desire to do our part in getting ready for the coming of Jesus, then that's where our prayer needs to begin. Holy Spirit come and "kindle in me the fire of Your love"; awaken a new desire in my heart.

Isaiah stirs the captive people with an exciting vision. (Is 35:1-10) *"The wilderness will rejoice and blossom"*. *"Water will gush forth in the wilderness and streams in the desert."* Looking at the practical steps that had to be taken, Isaiah knew the journey would not be easy. So he said: *"strengthen the feeble hands; steady the knees that give way; say to those who are fearful of heart 'be strong, do not be afraid; your God will come…"*. Can we hear the Holy Spirit speak this same word to us today… *"be strong, do not be afraid"*, continue to pursue your goal. Then we will qualify to walk the "highway" that God has prepared for the redeemed. It is called the "Way of Holiness."

"Holy Spirit, stir new fire in our hearts that we may have the eagerness and persistence of the two men in the gospel story. If we have fallen short this week, give us the strength and courage to get up again, and continue to seek with all our hearts the Way of Holiness that we have already begun."

The Shepherd Comes

Today's Gospel (Mt 18:12-14) is the parable about the lost sheep.

I remember many years ago when our oldest daughter was about 3 years old, Linda and I lost her in a shopping mall. I thought Linda was watching her, and she thought I was. When we realized that no one was watching her, we both panicked. I remember running frantically through the store and then down the mall searching for her. There was nothing else important in my life at that time - money, cars, the rest of the family - all I cared about was finding the "lost sheep". Isn't this the way the Father feels when one of his sheep strays? The loving shepherd in the story forgets the 99 on the hillside, and goes off searching for the lost sheep...nothing else matters to him.

And then I remember when we found our 3-year-old hiding in a rack of dresses, how relieved and elated I was. Winning the lottery would have meant nothing compared to finding our little girl who was worth more to us than everything in the world combined. Multiply this many times and we get a glimmer of God's joy when he finds one of his lost sheep.

There are many images that the Church puts before us to awaken our expectations of the coming of Jesus. This one, Jesus as tender shepherd leaving everything to find one lost sheep is one of the most endearing images of Jesus in the gospels.

Now let's turn the gospel story around a minute. Let's think about how the lost sheep felt. Imagine being a sheep lost in the dark and dangerous wilderness, vulnerable to any hungry lion or wolf that might walk by. Confused, the sheep does not know which way to go. Panic sets in as the sheep sinks into feelings of hopelessness. Then the little sheep hears the voice of the shepherd calling his name. Soon he sees the shepherd working his way through the brush coming to him. Imagine the joy that the sheep feels at the coming of the shepherd. At last, the he knows he is safe again.

Listen to this beautiful image of God that Isaiah sings about today. (Is 40:1-11) *"He tends his flock like a shepherd. He gathers the lambs in His arms and carries them close to His heart; He gently leads those that have young."* Can we stop a minute and see this same tender Shepherd gathering us in His arms even at this moment? Isaiah is told by God to *"speak tenderly to Jerusalem and proclaim that her hard service has been completed."* After He gets our attention, sometimes through unpleasant life experiences, God takes us in His arms and speaks tenderly to us, and gently leads us in the direction He knows is best for us. This is our Advent grace.

Another powerful image that Isaiah embeds in this prophecy concerns the power of God's breath. *"The grass withers and the flowers fall because the breath of the Lord blows on them."* Imagine the power of God's breath to bring an end to life. Yet think of the other side of the coin. If God's breath can bring an end to life, it can be equally capable of bringing new life out of life's worst circumstances. God breathes on us and new life, new hope, new joy takes root in our souls. As we rest in His arms, let's allow God to breathe the Holy Spirit upon us and into us today. Let us absorb the power of His breath that restores us to life, purifies us, and makes us holy. This is what Jesus does when He comes to us.

Most of us remember that there was a time in our lives that we were lost sheep. We know we had no hope unless the Shepherd loved us enough to seek us out. We remember the relief we felt as the tender Jesus appeared on the scene, picked us up and breathed the life of the Holy Spirit into our hearts. We keep singing "I once was lost, but now I'm found." Imagine the joy of the Father's heart when this moment occurred in our lives.

When we stop and become still before the Lord in our Advent preparation, we may notice an inner part of ourselves that still feels "lost". We may long for the coming of the Shepherd in a new way to comfort us as He did His people of old.

As we get closer to Jesus, our hearts begin to grieve over the lost sheep of our day, especially those family members who have strayed from Him. And in our grief we pray that the Shepherd will search after the lost more than ever before, as "the day of His coming nears."

"Good Shepherd, thank you for rescuing me from darkness. Let me never tire of being scooped up in Your arms and held close to Your heart. May my heart be one with Yours in grieving over the lost of today, and join You in bringing them back to Your flock."

The New Eve

Today there is an unexpected "peak" in the Advent mountain climb. We are taken to one of the mountain tops of the Church year, the feast of the Immaculate Conception. Almost as an early Christmas present, God scoops us up and takes us to visit Mary.

To appreciate the gift of her immaculate conception, the Church revisits the Genesis story (Gn 3: 9-15, 20). Eve was one of the central characters. Having disobeyed God, for the first time she and Adam experienced shame; they hid themselves when God approached. They fell into satan's trap, lured by his false promises and forever disconnected themselves from God. They were now under the rule of the "prince of this world". When one is disconnected from God there is no hope.

Yet God in his mercy promised a day when He would reverse their sin and its effects. He spoke directly to the serpent and prophesied a day when a woman and her offspring would crush his head. Meantime He was merciful to our first parents. Though they deserved death and deprivation, He allowed them to have descendants with the stipulation that Eve would experience pain in child-bearing; and rather than let them starve to death, He promised them food with the stipulation that Adam would have to work and fight the soil to get it to produce.

The Gospel (Lk 1:26-38) tells of the fulfillment of the Genesis prophesy, as the Angel Gabriel announced to Mary the unheard of truth, that God himself would become man within her womb. The "woman and her offspring" now appear.

Today's feast takes us to a time before the Annunciation. It takes us back to the moment of Mary's conception. This is when the greatest miracle since the fall of Adam and Even took place. Mary was conceived without any effects of sin. All of Adam's descendants, including us, inherit the "separated" state of our first parents. Mary became the only exception. In her conception a new Genesis takes place. A new Eve is created by a miraculous intervention of God. She is as pure and holy as the first Eve was, yet goes beyond Eve, for from the moment of her conception God was preparing her to be the home of his incarnate Son Jesus, the new Adam. The significance of today is that it represents the first act of God to reverse the effects of sin, and to bring hope for those who live in the kingdom of darkness.

So the Church lets out "all the stops" today as she leads us to sing Psalm 98: *"sing to the Lord a new song"* for He *"has made His salvation known." "Shout for joy all the earth, burst into jubilant song with music." "Let the sea resound and everything in it"..."Let the mountains sing together for joy"..."for He comes."* In Mary there is a total break with the old creation; in her God came to earth in a most spectacular intervention. He came through Mary, and today He comes to us through Mary again.

So where do we fit into this picture? Paul lets us know the answer to this question in his letter to the Ephesians (Eph 1:3-6,11-12) that what God did for Mary, He has done for us. In our baptism He allowed us to enter into the "new Genesis", becoming part of the "new Adam", and receiving the "new Eve" as our mother. Paul praises God who has *"blessed us in the heavenly realms with every spiritual blessing in Christ"..."He chose us before*

44

the creation of the world to be holy and blameless in His sight. In love He predestined us to be His adopted children through Jesus Christ." Even before Adam and Even were born, God had each of us in mind to be His daughters and sons. We are "blessed", "chosen", "sons and daughters". We have been brought into the glorious new creation with Mary, made possible by the death and resurrection of Jesus. In a way our personal "immaculate conception" took place at our baptism.

Unlike Mary we still deal with the effects of Adam's sin. Part of us is what we inherited from our first parents. We still have a strong inclination to sin; we still have to work out our salvation *"in fear and trembling."*

As we draw close to Mary and take advantage of our relationship with the "new Eve", it makes the "working out" of salvation, so much easier and more effective.

"Father we rejoice in the great work You did at the moment of Mary's conception. We rejoice that at the moment of Baptism You set us free from the kingdom of darkness and brought us into the kingdom of Your son. Help us to draw close to Mary and get full benefit from her example, her intercession, and her motherhood in our lives."

"O Mary conceived without sin, pray for us who have recourse to thee."

Greater Than John

Yesterday we heard the angel remind Mary that "nothing is impossible with God". When God decides to step into the picture, changes begin to take place that boggle our imaginations.

First we listen to another of Isaiah's prophecies (Is 41:13-20). He spoke to a beaten-down Israel who had little hope. His words were not exactly flattering. *"Do not be afraid, O worm Jacob, O little Israel."* Worm? Can you imagine a more powerless, insignificant creature on earth? It has no feet to run, no hands to fight, no mouth to scream or to hiss. A worm is vulnerable to the first bird that spots it or to the first fisherman looking for bait. And the word "little" does not exactly make people feel good, much less confident, about themselves. Yet the Lord tells them repeatedly, *"do not be afraid, I will help you"*. He lets them know that He has a firm grip on their right hand, the way a parent squeezes the hand of a toddler when they cross the street together.

Now comes the amazing part of the prophecy. *"I will make you* (the worm) *into a threshing sledge, new and sharp, with many teeth. You will thresh the mountains and crush them..."*. What kind of power can take a defenseless worm and turn it into such a powerful sledge that it is able to crush mountains? God will not only rescue Israel from their captors but make them mighty beyond comprehension. "Nothing is impossible" for Him.

Then we read Matthew's passage. (11:11-15). The great

John the Baptist appeared on the scene again; this time John was in prison just a short time away from martyrdom. Jesus, in speaking of John, said that, *"among those born of women, there has not risen anyone greater than John the Baptist."* Jesus proclaimed John even greater than Moses, Elijah, Jeremiah, Daniel and the rest. Could anyone ever rival the holiness of John? He lived a life of extreme poverty depending on God for everything. He gave up family life, work, money, and social status to dedicate all of his time to doing the Father's will - calling people to repentance and baptizing them. Thousands were converted through John's preaching. Then he stepped aside in a remarkable gesture of humility to make room for Jesus; there was no "ego" in John - *"He must increase, I must decrease".* Finally he made the ultimate sacrifice by shedding his blood for the cause of God's word. Could anyone outdo John the Baptist in the "holiness" arena?

The answer is "yes".

Jesus stuns his disciples by saying, *"yet he who is least in the kingdom of heaven is greater than he* (John).*"* How could this be? We are among the least in the kingdom of heaven; how could it be possible that we could come close to John much less greater than he was?

At Pentecost when the first disciples were "baptized in the Holy Spirit", they entered into a new realm, a new level of existence that even John the Baptist did not experience. Never before had the Trinity lived in the heart of mere men, except with Jesus and Mary. Can we imagine what has happened to us when we surrendered to "Pentecost" in our lives? Do we realize that we have been transported to a level of union with God beyond what the holiest people of the Old Testament were able to experience? This transformation of mere men into Temples of the Holy Spirit goes beyond even the "worm to sledge" transformation. Our personal testimonies bear witness to the fact that "nothing is impossible with God." If He has already accomplished these miracles, what are the even greater ones that are yet in store for us?

It is fitting that today is the feast day of St. Juan Diego. An illiterate peasant, the least of the least, was so used by God after his experience of Mary that over 8 million Mexicans were converted from their "culture of death" to faith in Jesus Christ. And the influence of Juan and Our Lady of Guadalupe has multiplied so many times that every country in our hemisphere has been affected by the grace God poured out through him.

Do we have a mighty God or what? Now that we are in the "greater than John the Baptist" realm, is there any limit on what God can do through us if we say "yes" to Him and allow Him to use us as He used the ordinary saints in the Church's history?

"Jesus help me believe that nothing is impossible with God. Use me, an earthen vessel, to help bring the wine of Your love and mercy to the world in which I live. Today as I await Your coming, I say "yes" again to You and rededicate my life to Your service."

Spoiled Children

Jesus compared the people of his generation to spoiled children. I wonder what He would say about the people of our generation?

Today's Gospel (Mt 11:16-19) is an "editorial" that summarizes Jesus' opinion of the people of His time. He said that they were like children in the market place refusing to play whatever game was suggested - spoiled and unwilling to cooperate. God went to extremes to win the people to Himself. He sent an austere religious man, John the Baptist who fasted, prayed, and lived a life of hardship. The people sat around and criticized him for being such a religious fanatic, claiming he must be possessed by a demon to live this way. So busy judging, they had no time to be touched by his message. Then the gentle, human Jesus is sent whose compassion embraced even the tax collectors and the sinners. Maybe this would capture the people's attention. No, they sat in the market place and criticized Jesus as well. How could this man be of God, why He even befriends the outcasts of our society? Religious people are not supposed to act this way. No matter what God did, this spoiled people, refused to dance with Him. They didn't like festive music; they didn't like mournful music. God couldn't reach them no matter who He sent or what approach He took.

Yet in spite of their response, God was faithful to His plan and followed through with what He had promised. His faithfulness did not hinge on the fickleness of their response.

In Isaiah's prophecy (Is 48:17-19) we get a little of the same message. *"If only you had paid attention to My commands"*, writes Isaiah, you would have had peace flowing like a river, righteousness as steady as the waves of the sea, descendants as numerous as the sand, and a name that would endure forever. "If only" Israel would have responded to God's call, the horrors of the Babylonian captivity would not have been necessary. Instead, like spoiled children, Israel ignored God's call, persecuted His prophets, and in the end had to learn the hard way. Yes, God would follow through with His promises; first, though, they would have to experience His judgment. Being humbled and purified they would come to their senses and realize what a mistake they had made in ignoring God's word to them.

What is God saying to the people of today? Are we listening to His voice and joining in His dance? Or is God saying to this generation, "if only you had paid attention" to those I sent you, including My own Mother and heeded their advice. Are we surprised that a world who chooses to stay disconnected from God by sitting back in complacency judging those He sends, will suffer extreme consequences for their choices? If our world starts falling apart at the seams, isn't this what we would expect of a society that chooses to separate itself from God?

It seems in every age the majority of people are like the children in the marketplace refusing to respond to God's voice. Yet throughout the Church there has always been a remnant that revered God and joyfully obeyed Him no matter what the price of doing this might be. I want to think that we are part of the faithful "remnant" today who have dedicated ourselves to being faithful to God's call. Realizing that the world ignores the Advent journey and continues to do "its own thing", we have hope because together we choose to go God's direction, even if our numbers are few. Remember God's promise to Lot, that if a remnant of just 10 righteous people could have been found, He would have spared Sodom?

Mary, Joseph, Elizabeth, John the Baptist were members of the "remnant of Israel" (see Zeph 3:12,13) in Jesus' time. And God needed only this small remnant to bring about the greatest act of love the world has ever known. Let us be the faithful remnant of today who warms the heart of God, keeping our eyes on Jesus and not on the spoiled children sitting in the market place of our day. Let us be the people who "delight in the law of the Lord and meditate on His law day and night." (Ps 1)

"Jesus forgive us for the times we've acted like spoiled children, expecting God to serve our needs and accommodate Himself to our whims. Today we turn ever more attentively to Your voice, and want to make the best of these days of preparation, so we will be alert and ready to receive You when You come."

Three Comings?

The Church seems a little mixed up today. We are in the middle of Advent, awaiting the coming of the Lord, and the Church tells us to "rejoice", as though Jesus has already returned. Purple vestments are put away for a moment, and rose-colored ones - a spring like color - come out of the closets. It is as though in the relative darkness of Advent, the clouds break and an unexpected ray of sunshine comes upon us. Traditionally this is called "Gaudete" Sunday, meaning "Rejoice" Sunday.

How can we rejoice since Jesus has not yet returned? At Christmas we celebrate the past coming of Jesus on earth, and we wait in expectation for His future coming. Today the Church reminds us of the "now" coming of Jesus. St Bernard says there are "3 comings" of Christ. The first and the last are visible comings, the middle coming is an invisible coming - it is the road between the first and the last. St. Bernard explains that the first coming of Jesus was in weakness and poverty, His last coming will be in glory, and His present coming is in "spirit and power". Lest we get too much in a "nostalgic" mood about the Bethlehem coming, or in a "regretful" mood because Jesus has not yet returned, the Church says "rejoice" for He has come to us today.

Isaiah (35:1-6,10) spoke with excitement about a future day when, *"the eyes of the blind will be open, the ears of the deaf unstopped. Then will the lame leap like a deer, and the mute tongue shout for joy."* Yet the Psalm for today (146) talks in the present tense about what God is doing "now". *"He upholds the cause of the oppressed...gives food to the hungry...sets prisoners free...gives sight to the blind...lifts up those who are bowed down...watches over the alien, sustains the fatherless and widow..."* These words are set by the Psalmist within a song of praise... *"I will sing praise to my God as long as I live."* God is being praised now, not just for what He <u>will</u> do, but for what He <u>is</u> doing.

In the Gospel reading (Mt 11:2-ll) we hear Jesus giving instructions to John's disciples (note, not all of John's disciples followed Jesus the way Andrew did). He told them to report the facts - what they saw with their own eyes and heard with their own ears. *"The blind receive sight, the lame walk, those who have leprosy are cured, the deaf hear, the dead are raised, and the good news is preached to the poor."* In effect Jesus said, "we're not talking theology here, the Spirit and power of God is happening at this very moment. The day Isaiah foretold is now taking place."

Today we rejoice that we have accepted Jesus into our hearts, and we testify to the transformation that has taken place in our lives---Jesus is working miracles <u>now</u>. We don't have to wait until December 25 or until Jesus' return in glory. This is the day of His coming. This is the day that the power of God is available through Jesus Christ to heal, raise from the dead, and proclaim good news to the poor. If we don't recognize Jesus' presence and power today, how can we expect to be ready to meet Him in glory?

Isaiah drenches us with words of joy today. He spoke about the wilderness rejoicing and blossoming, *"it will rejoice greatly and shout for joy"*. Can we think of a place that has less reason to rejoice than the wilderness? What a day it will be if the bleak, dry, hopeless wilderness shouts for joy! And he says that the ransomed of the Lord will return entering Zion singing, with "everlasting joy" crowning their heads!

In our joy we don't want to overlook words of the practical, sober-minded James. His word for us was *"patience in the face of suffering"* (James 5:7-10). James was realistic; he knew that when we go through trials, we don't feel like rejoicing. So he called us to be patient, and not *"to grumble against each other."* In other words, don't take out your sufferings on the people you live with. He knew how difficult it is at times to live up to our commitment to Christ, so he told us to, *"stand firm because the Lord's coming is near."* He put everything in perspective by reminding us that the *"Lord is full of compassion and mercy."*

"Jesus we rejoice that we have already experienced your coming in 'Spirit and in power'. We have already seen the fulfillment of Isaiah's prophecy in our own changed hearts. Today as we pray, "Come Lord Jesus", awaken again in our hearts the joy of knowing You as Lord and Savior of our lives."

How Many Loaves Do You Have?

Today's Gospel story (Mk 8:1-10) sounds like a rerun of what we read a week ago when Jesus fed 5000 people with just a few loaves of bread and a few fish. This story is so similar that some think it was another version of the same event, with some differences in details. This time the audience was different, one commentator observed. In the first multiplication the Jews were the recipients of God's favor; this time the Gentiles were included.

In spite of the difference in details, some of the wording in the two stories is exactly the same. In both accounts, for example, Jesus asked the disciples for help, with the question "How many loaves do you have?" Why did He turn to them when He knew that all they would be able to come up with was "duh?"

We notice that Jesus did not ask "How many loaves do you think it will take to feed this crowd?" or, "How many extra loaves do you have, beyond what you yourselves will need?" He didn't address what they *didn't have*. He addressed what they *did have*.

As I understand it, the loaves were *"small round cakes made of wheat or barley" (commentary from Serendipity Bible)*. Seven such loaves would not begin to feed even the twelve apostles unless they rationed them into smaller pieces. It seems reasonable that they would have kept the seven loaves for themselves.

What did Jesus do after asking the disciples to inventory their food supply? He took all the loaves away from them! Now they had zero loaves for themselves. Though they had come up empty with a solution to feed the crowd, believing that the few loaves they had had not been worth donating to the cause, the disciples found out then, when Jesus was added to the mix, a little is all that was needed. Yes, the disciples were able to feed the whole crowd, with some left over, when they gave everything they had to Jesus for Him to work with.

Do we realize that our "seven loaves" of love, of money, of time, of charisms…can feed over 5000 people today? When we think "I don't have enough", or "I don't have the resources that stronger Christians have," we bend over in discouragement and hoard carefully our small bag of bread. When we think "I'll give all that I have to Jesus and let Him take charge from there", the power of God begins to explode in our midst and the world begins to be fed. I wonder what those "five minutes" of intercessory prayer that I hand over to Jesus are doing for the world today?

Back to the Gospel story. Jesus went through a "Eucharistic-type" rite that was surely meant to show the connection between that event and the "breaking of the bread' that Christians would do to remember Him.
> 1. He looked up to heaven (mentioned in the first multiplication story),
> 2. He gave thanks,
> 3. He broke the bread
> 4. He gave it back to the disciples
> 5. He told them to feed the multitude.

We see this same rite enacted every time we go to Mass. The priest "stands in for Jesus", takes our loaves, gives thanks, breaks them, and give them back to us in a transformed fashion so that we have something powerful to take with us to feed others. It is interesting that Jesus "broke the loaves" instead of creating a bunch of new "intact" loaves. When my bread is broken, that means part of it no longer belongs to me; it has been altered in such a way that now it can be given away to others. There is deep mystery here.

Let's take this "Eucharistic rite" and translate it to something we can do apart from Mass. Jesus is here at this moment and He asks each of us "How many loaves do you have?" What answer do we give Him? Maybe He is asking us to examine the contents of our hearts, or the few minutes of time we have available right now. Maybe I have a little love to give, maybe sadness about life, maybe trials that I am enduring, maybe some free time on my hands. Instead of clutching what I have, I let go so Jesus can take it all away. Then I join Him as He looks up to heaven, holding the small amount I've put in His hands, gives thanks to God for my meager gift, breaks the gift into parts, and then hands it back to me. "Now, go", He says, "feed the hungry people I send to you."

"For a thousand days in your sight are like a day that has just gone by or like a watch in the night." (Ps 90:4)

"Jesus I let go of all that is 'mine' so that it can become Yours. Transform these gifts so they can help bring the Father's saving love to the world."

Day of Wrath

Today the Church chooses two rather unpleasant readings which seems to me to be a strange follow-up to Gaudete Sunday. In both readings we get a taste of the "wrath of God". This is not too conducive to stoking our "Christmas spirit." On the other hand God is more interested in speaking the truth to us than in stirring up sentiments built on false hope.

Let's look at what the prophet Zephaniah had to say. (Zeph 3:1-2, 9-13). Zephaniah is sometimes seen as a "doom and gloom" prophet. He shouted out that *"the great day of Lord is near - is near and coming quickly."* (2:14). He goes on to proclaim *"That day will be a day of wrath, a day of distress and anguish, a day of trouble and ruin, a day of darkness and gloom, a day of clouds and blackness"….*(2:15).

If you want a full dose of Zephaniah's prophecy read the rest of chapter 2. He says that *"in the fire of His* (God's) *jealousy the whole world will be consumed, for He will make a sudden end of all who live in the earth."* (2:18) Sounds like the days of Noah.

In today's selection Zephaniah started out with a vision of Jerusalem's future. What did he say about the "holy city". *"Woe to the city of oppressors, rebellious and defiled. She obeys no one, she accepts no correction."* To spare us a case of spiritual indigestion the Church does not give us a full dose of Zephaniah's words about Jerusalem; this part is limited to just the first two verses.

Advent talks of the coming of Jesus; Zephaniah talked about the coming day of the Lord. What coming are we talking about today? - a day of wrath, or a day of glory - or both?

Then in today's Gospel (Mt 21:28-32) we can feel the wrath of God manifest in the words of Jesus. In the parable of the two sons, Jesus pointed out the fact that any father prefers a son who does what he asks than to one who gives him lip service only. Jesus took the two most despised groups of society, the prostitute who sells her body for money, and the tax collectors - those grimy men who extorted money from their own people to support the cause of its gentile oppressors and gain personal favor with them. He told the religious leaders that even these lowest of the lowly would enter the kingdom of God before they would. Not only did they reject the message of John the Baptist; they also rejected the magnificent work of God that brought even prostitutes and tax collectors to repentance.

Can you feel the anger that was stirred in Jesus as He presented this stark truth to those who prided themselves as observers of God's laws. Jesus was not exactly trying to win a popularity contest in this situation. He was exposing the fire of God's heart to those who rejected God's love to the point of conspiring against His very Son.

Is the Church trying to put a "wet blanket" on our holiday cheer? Is there any hope for us hidden in today's readings? The answer is "yes", if we are among the poor and lowly, that remnant, who surrender to the call of Jesus. If God's mercy extends even to prostitutes and tax collectors, then no one is excluded from His favor.

The Zephaniah selection ends with explosive words of hope! Though he speaks of the imminent judgment from God, he speaks also of a day of restoration after that. The "day of wrath" is a necessary cleansing, so that a purified Israel could be presented as a delight to God at a future time. *"But I will leave within you, the meek and the humble who trust in the name of the Lord. The remnant of Israel will do no wrong...and no one will make them afraid."* (3:12-13). As Noah was the link of hope between a corrupt world and a new beginning, so the "remnant of Israel" would be a link of hope during the "day of God's wrath" holding the torch of God's promise until the day of Jerusalem's restoration.

If we need the joy of "Gaudete Sunday" revived, let us read the consoling words of today's Psalm (Ps 34). *"...the afflicted will hear and rejoice"..."the poor man called...and the Lord saved him out of all his troubles"..."the Lord is close to the broken-hearted, those who are crushed in spirit He saves"..."and no one will be condemned who takes refuge in Him."*

Today we continue to prepare for Jesus by joining the "meek and the humble", the "remnant of Israel", the "afflicted, the poor, and the brokenhearted." We come not in the strength of religious righteousness but in our powerlessness as sinners ever in need of God's mercy. We do daily what the religious leaders of Jesus' day could not get themselves to do - repent and open ourselves to the love and mercy of God. It is our very sins and weakness that becomes a doorway of hope.

"Jesus, let my heart rest not on the false hopes of the world, but upon the truth of Your Word, even when this word is as a "two-edged" sword to me. Aware of my failings and my weakness I join the humble remnant in seeking Your mercy. Come Lord Jesus!"

A Better Deal?

When shoppers are presented a good deal, they wonder "is it best to buy now, or wait for a better deal?" They are not always sure that a better deal is around the corner; if they wait, they have the nagging thought that maybe they made a mistake.

This "buy now or wait" issue is what John the Baptist proposed to his disciples. (Lk 7:18-23) It is interesting how John the Baptist keeps resurfacing in the Church's Advent readings. In case we didn't catch his message the first time, we get hit again with the call to "repent" and turn to Jesus.

This time John was in prison, and his disciples must have wondered what to do in the event of John's execution. Rather than talk about Jesus, John sent his disciples to meet Jesus personally. Isn't this the model for us to follow? John tells them to ask Jesus "Are you the One who is to come, or should we look for another?"

Was Jesus one of many "Messiah" candidates in the picture, or was He, "the One" in whom the whole history of Israel culminated? This was not a theoretical question; it was a "now choice" that John's disciples had to face and would determine the course of the rest of their lives. John knew this, and he knew his whole purpose in life was to lead people to accept Jesus. Even in prison John continued to carry out his mission.

When individuals encounter Jesus, their hearts are deeply moved. If they are sincerely seeking God they know deep inside that Jesus is the One - there is no better deal later. While Jesus did not answer John's disciples' question directly, he pointed to the works of God that fulfilled Isaiah's prophecies. I believe the two disciples left Jesus "in wonder", for they not only saw the great messianic works of God, they also had a face-to-face encounter with His only Son. While they thought they were seeking an answer to a "religion question"; they later realized they had begun a life-changing relationship with the Son of God.

Our "personal Pentecost" experiences in the charismatic renewal convinced us that we had found "the One to come", and it was out of the question to look for another. Our inner experience of being baptized in the Holy Spirit was personal proof that we had found the "best deal" any human being could ever hope for. Yet when our initial hopes for the charismatic renewal began to collapse, prayer groups shut down, numbers declined, and pastors didn't seem much interested in "jumping on our band wagon", disillusionment set in. Maybe the charismatic renewal wasn't all it was cracked up to be? Maybe we'd better look for something else? It didn't deliver what we thought it had promised. And we might have heard that impy voice saying "give up and try something else."

For some reason Noah has been on my mind lately. Imagine building a triple-decker ship, 450 feet long with no power tools, and maybe little help. How many years do you think it took for Noah to put this together? And imagine his neighbors laughing at his project reminding him that they were nowhere near a large body of water. Imagine his wife saying, "Why can't you be like other men instead of being obsessed about that silly boat." Surely there were moments when Noah was tempted to give up; he must have felt alone and unappreciated much of the time. Yet, we are told, Noah *"did all that the Lord commanded him."* This was his one focus; he wasn't interested in "looking for another" plan for his life.

This is not the moment for us to give up the Ark we've been working on, or to quit cooperating with the "ark work" God is doing within our hearts and within our community. We have found the answer to life; we don't have to seek any other deal no matter what is going on around us. And, inspired by John the Baptist, we lead as many as we can to Jesus, so they, too, will be safe in His Ark.

Advent reminds us to keep our focus on one thing - Jesus and His coming. There will no other way out of the "floods" that are coming except Jesus and His Ark

This same message is repeated over and over again through Isaiah today: *"I am God there is no other...there is no God apart from me".* (Is 45:21-22 and surrounding verses).

"Jesus we rejoice that we have been brought into the safety of Your Ark. May the Holy Spirit lead us to share the "good news" with others - letting them know that there is a safe way through whatever raging waters might come upon the world. We pray for the grace of endurance."

Which Door?

Today (Lk 7:24-30) Jesus gives a "multiple choice " question to the crowd. *"What did you go out into the desert to see?"* Choices are: a) *"a reed shaken by the wind"*...do people go out to the desert to see beautiful displays of nature? If so, they'll be disappointed, because the best they'll find out there are "swaying reeds" b) *"a man dressed in fine clothes"*...if you're looking for people dressed in expensive clothes, you don't take a trip to the desert. c) *"a prophet"*. I have a feeling that the crowd answered this one correctly, opting for choice "c".

Jesus, in effect, says "good choice". Prophets were not always available to the people of Israel. Now and then, at a prize moment, God would send a holy prophet. (Of course there were always more than enough false prophets around to tell people what they wanted to hear.) So at a moment when God wanted to make a dramatic entry into history, He would raise up a prophet. When word of this got around, people flocked to listen to him; they wanted to hear the authentic word of God. John was such a prophet.

Then Jesus went further. John was "more than a prophet", in fact he was the "messenger", prophesied by Micah, who would prepare a way for the Messiah. And beyond that Jesus issued the greatest compliment ever given to a human being. *"I tell you, among those born of women, no one is greater than John."* History had peaked; the greatest era known to humanity was taking place. John was the prophet of prophets, for it was his task to awaken the people to the imminent coming of the Messiah.

65

During our Advent climb, the Church has been bringing John the Baptist along almost every day since two Sundays ago. By now, hopefully, John has done his job with us. He now disappears into the pages of our Bible. We have repented and are now ready to receive Jesus. (Incidentally, at our prayer meeting last night, we were exhorted to receive the Sacrament of Reconciliation before Christmas. The same word came through 4 different people! -- The Holy Spirit is rarely this emphatic in a message to us.)

Imagine, Jesus appears to us today to offer us a Christmas present. And suppose He gives us a "multiple choice" offering. Door "A" is 10 million dollars. Door "B" is a healing of family relationships and a perfect Christmas get-together. Door "C" is a "double-portion" of His love.

Our hands quickly grab the doorknob to the "A door". Then we think. If I have an endless supply of money, my children will start fighting over it. Then we will have to go through the hassle of getting a new house and cleaning out our messy basement. And imagine the sudden appearance of "new friends" who would want a piece of the pie. Hmm . . . better grab "door B" instead. With hand on the "B door", imagining the wonder of a family that is perfectly united with all relationships healed, we stop and think. Even with a loving family, there is still Peter who is unemployed...and there is Andrew whose heart is broken over a recent divorce...and James whose son is on drugs...and John who just lost a friend to suicide. Hmm, as my hand lets go and moves to "door C"...God's love is the only thing that really works. And the good news is: that is exactly what God is offering us, this very moment. If we get our eyes off the other doors and fix them totally on "door C", we will get all our Christmas wishes and more. "Seek ye first the kingdom of God and His righteousness, and all these other things will be given to you besides."

Today's reading from Isaiah is a "mountain top" reading in the Old Testament. Israel is represented as "a barren woman", a "desolate woman" with no husband, a young wife who was abandoned by her husband, and finally as a "widow". Each of these types of women experience deep grief beyond description. The prophet tells this people buried in grief to *"burst into song, shout for joy"*. Their day of disgrace is over, forever. *"Though the mountains may be shaken and the hills be removed (almost impossible), yet my unfailing love for you will not be shaken...."* Please read prayerfully the whole excerpt (Is 54:1-10)...it is one of the most powerful passages in the Bible. Then read slowly, in the Spirit, its "partner" Psalm that the Church proposes today. (Ps 30).

These readings have the power to get you immediately to the top of the mountain even before Advent comes to an end.

"Father in heaven I believe in your unbounded, unfailing love for us. Today we let go of all other desires, and ask in faith that You will fill our hearts with a 'double portion' of Your love. Thank You, for giving us a whole season to get spiritually conditioned to receive this greatest of all gifts. Lord Jesus, come!"

Joseph, the Law Breaker

In each reading today the Church talks about "righteousness". Jeremiah (23:5-8) prophesies the coming of a *"righteous Branch...who will reign wisely and do what is right and just in the land...He will be called the Lord, our Righteousness."* Our Psalm response (72) begins with *"Endow the king...with your righteousness."* So what a compliment that Matthew (1:18-25) calls Joseph a "righteous man", that is, bearing the qualities of the "righteous Branch" and the "righteous king."

Joseph joins us on our Advent climb today. He is a quiet man; unlike Mary, he does not utter a single word in the Gospel accounts. Fr. Don Halpin observed that being a "carpenter" Joseph was accustomed to creating things "right". As a holy Jew he was accustomed to doing what the Law required no matter the price. When he learned of Mary's pregnancy, he knew the will of God in the matter. Though it must have wrenched his heart to give up Mary, like Abraham climbing the mountain to sacrifice Isaac, he obeyed God and decided to divorce Mary. His plan was to do it in love by doing it "quietly." Then God crashed into human history in a most unusual way. An angel appears to Joseph and tells him to "break the law", and take Mary into his home. How confused, and at the same time overjoyed Joseph must have felt.

There was nothing greater than the Mosaic Law, and yet God trumped the Law in His message to Joseph. This was the beginning of the "New Covenant". Fr. Don pointed out to me that Joseph was the first one to live in both the Old and the New Testaments. Doing God's will was what a "righteous" man did, even if it conflicted with the provisions of the Law. And Joseph said "yes".

How seldom in the entire Bible does an angel break through to humanity and speak directly to a human being. It happens twice in this passage - Gabriel speaks to Mary about what the Holy Spirit is doing within her, and the angel speaks to Joseph as well. When God chooses to have the silence between the world of angels and the world of men broken, it is a spectacular and important moment. Though we stand exactly a week from Christmas, the Word has already "become flesh", and a miraculous intervention of God has taken place to provide for Mary and her child. With Mary, we are already "pregnant" with Jesus.

Only one accustomed to listening to the voice of God and seeking His will at any cost, can discern between the expectations of the Law and the "now" will of God. How important it is for us to spend so much time listening to the Lord, that we can easily recognize His voice when He chooses to speak to us.

Jeremiah points to Jesus, the righteous king who will "reign wisely." Psalm 72 explains what "wisely" means. *"He will deliver the needy who cry out, the afflicted who have no one to help. He will take pity on the weak and the needy and save the needy from death. He will rescue them from oppression and violence, for precious is their blood in His sight."* (vs. 12-14). Joseph, "the righteous man" had these qualities. That is why God chose him to look after Mary in her vulnerable condition and Jesus her unborn child.

Jesus today addresses the "needy and afflicted" in our

hearts. And through us, He brings healing and hope to the "afflicted" of our families and our world. Because of our baptism, we share in the kingship of Jesus, bringing His power and His love to the needy whom God sends our way. Let us, throughout this sacred time of year, be attentive to those moments when God wants us to be His righteousness for others. Let us be as tuned in and responsive to His will as were Joseph and Mary.

"St. Joseph pray for us that we have the courage to "break the laws" of fear and social expectations to say yes to God's will. Help us choose to serve Him each moment, and willingly pay whatever price this might involve. We want to be a righteous people."

Two Stories

If we read the genealogies of Jesus we run into a contradiction. Matthew's list (chap 1) and Luke's list (chap 3) match each other from Abraham to David, but after that they take off in two different directions. Heli, for example, is named as Jesus' grandfather by Luke, rather than Jacob, as Matthew states. What is going on here? Is the Holy Spirit confused?

Are their two "blood lines" for Jesus, or could it be that Luke's version is not meant to be a "blood line?" I am consulting a Bible expert to help clarify this for me; right now I don't know the explanation.

It does make me realize, however, that each of us Christians have "two different genealogies". In today's reading from Paul (Romans 1:1-7) the apostle talks about Jesus as the fulfillment of the Old Testament prophecies regarding God's Son, *"who as to His human nature was a <u>descendant of David</u>, and who through the Spirit of holiness was declared with power to be the <u>Son of God</u>..."* Jesus' "blood line" was from David; his "Spirit line" was from God. As Adam was the first "son of God" (see Lk 3:38) and all others who followed were "sons of Adam", so Jesus was a direct "Son of God" - in fact He is the "ONLY begotten son of God...God from God...light from light...true God from true God...begotten not made". All who follow, in a way, are children of Jesus.

So we have the teaching that there are in fact two creations in our history, one beginning with Adam and a second beginning with Jesus. That is why Jesus, in

71

speaking to Nicodemus (Jn 3:1-20), said, *"I tell you the truth, no one can enter the kingdom of God unless he is born of water and the (Holy) Spirit. Flesh gives birth to flesh and Spirit gives birth to spirit."* This confused Nicodemus. Was he to enter back into his mother's womb and become born a second time? No, of course, that is impossible; besides it would be just another "flesh" birth not a "Spirit" birth. Jesus went on to explain that the "second birth" would come for those who believed in Him. *"...the Son of Man must be lifted up, so that everyone who believes in Him will have eternal life."* The "flesh" life is temporary; the "Spirit" life is eternal.

When we were born, we became sons of Adam and received the "flesh" life. When we were born again at Baptism, we received the "Spirit" life. When we experienced being "baptized in the Holy Spirit", we chose to believe in Jesus and enter freely into the "new race" begun in Him. We are now children of the "new Adam" as well.

Today's Gospel reading (Mt 1:18-24) tells us about the act of God that began the presence of a second race on the earth. Adam was fashioned out of clay, Jesus was fashioned by a miraculous act of the Holy Spirit within the womb of the humble "virgin" of Nazareth (fulfillment of Isaiah's prophecy, 7:14).

Do we realize that having accepted Jesus as Lord and received the rebirth of the Holy Spirit, we now belong to "two races?"---the human race and the Jesus race. The first we had no choice about; the second we do. Every day we have the choice to follow in the footsteps of Adam or to follow in the footsteps of Jesus. The world is more than obliging to help nurture the "Adam life"; the Holy Spirit is with us at each moment to help us nurture the "Jesus life". Which do we listen to?

In a way our lives tell "two stories" as Neal Lozano puts it. The old story is as a womb from which emerges the new story of the "Jesus life" within us. Our flesh wants to go back to the old story and hang onto the messages of who we used to be. With a new Father, a new mother, a new family, and a new life source, we are set free to live the fullness of life available in our "new story" that began with our second birth. We, now have a brand new identity no matter what our "old story" might have been.

Christmas we celebrate the beginning of a new story on the earth; we also celebrate the beginning of our "bigger story" given freely to us by a miraculous intervention of the Holy Spirit.

"Jesus, thank you for being "lifted up" on the cross that I might be born again by the Holy Spirit into Your story. I believe that daily Your story is unfolding within me and is proclaiming to the world the good news that there is a "second life" available to all who will humble themselves and accept You into their hearts."

Ahaz or Mary

Today's first reading tells of a conversation between Isaiah and King Ahaz. Two enemies had conspired to overthrow Ahaz and destroy Jerusalem. We are told that "the hearts of Ahaz and his people were shaken as the trees of the forest are shaken by the wind." (Is 7:2) God sent Isaiah to Ahaz to prophesy a word of strength and encouragement. *"Be careful, be calm, and don't be afraid. Do not lose heart because of these two smoldering stubs of firewood."* Those whom Ahaz saw as mighty warriors who could destroy him, God saw as two old burnt-out loud mouths. Did these words give new heart to Ahaz? I don't think so. Because the next word given him by Isaiah was that he was supposed to ask God for a sign. Ahaz was afraid to deal with God and covered it up with the excuse that he did not want to put the Lord to the test. He didn't want to get run over by his enemies, but, on the other hand, he didn't want to get caught up in God's plan for Jerusalem. Isaiah lost his patience with the weak Ahaz, and in effect said, God is going to give you a sign like it or not. (Is 7:10-14).

Isaiah challenged Ahaz to ask for any sign he wanted *"whether in the deepest depths or the highest heights."* Ahaz refused. So God chose a sign, and strangely it was the prophecy that a baby would be conceived of a virgin. Babies are a sign of new beginnings and great hope. A new era was to begin for God's people, and small-minded Ahaz was happy if things kept creeping along as long as his two enemies left him alone. God's plan was a glorious one, as compared to Ahaz's anemic vision.

We now jump into Luke's story of Jesus' conception. (Luke 1:26-38). God's people were in another time of darkness and hopelessness. The Romans already held them captive; they were a captured people. Through the words of Angel Gabriel a sign is given. Another baby was going to be conceived, and this would be no ordinary baby. Gabriel prophesied a new beginning unlike any the world had ever experienced. This was the "beginning of all beginnings" even more significant than the creation of the world. *"Greetings, highly favored one, the Lord is with you...Do not be afraid Mary you have found favor with God."* Mary responded confidently and boldly to the angel and learned that just as at the start of creation when the Holy Spirit hovered over the waters to bring forth life, so now the Holy Spirit would hover over her and overshadow her womb with an act of "new creation". Mary, unlike the wishy-washy Ahaz, and knowing fully the possible consequences for conceiving a child outside marriage, responded boldly, *"May it be done to me as you have said."* This was the loudest "Yes" in human history...until Jesus gave his final "Yes" on the cross. And then, as though God wanted to give an "extra dip", Gabriel proclaimed another sign - again a surprise conception. Unbeknownst to Mary, her elderly cousin Elizabeth was pregnant. Another "impossible" event had taken place by a sovereign act of God for whom all things are possible.

Luke did the best he could to awaken within our hearts the wonder of this great moment. In a way, this was Christmas Day—for Jesus had come in flesh! Mary felt Him though she did not yet see Him. And, Luke let us know that God presents this word not just as something that did happen but as something that is now happening in the lives of his chosen ones.

In the stillness of prayer let us hear Gabriel speak to us: "you have found favor with God...the Holy Spirit will come upon <u>you</u> and a holy one will this day be conceived in your heart." In our hum-drum lives, interrupted by the noise of a commercialized season, we fall into the trap of "Ahaz thinking" and "Ahaz vision". God has a great and unique plan for each of us who has said "Yes" to Jesus and been filled with the Holy Spirit. Let us never doubt this no matter how old we are, how tired we feel, or how unmotivated our hearts have become. Today, Gabriel blows his horn in our ears with a wake-up call, to help us realize the significance of this moment in our history. Let us respond today with "Mary thinking", "Mary boldness", and "Mary vision"!

We are privileged to be part of a "new beginning" not just in the Church year, but in the history of the world. Our popes tell us to "wake up" and be part of the "new springtime" and the "new evangelization" that God is breathing forth into the Church.

"Mary, Isaiah, and Gabriel, pray for us that we wake up to the new beginning that God is ushering into our lives. Let us not be small-minded, but may our minds be renewed to capture the vision that God has for our lives and for the Church. Help us to say "Yes" to this new moment of grace."

First Day of Spring

Today is the darkest day of winter, the winter solstice. Besides, I've been told, the accompanying lunar eclipse will make today the darkest day in 400 years. Yet the Church thinks it's the first day of spring. *"See, the winter is past...flowers appear on the earth...the cooing of doves is heard...the fig tree is forming its early fruit."* (Song of Songs 3:8-14). This is the reading chosen for today. Is the Church mixed up again or is it reminding us that God's calendar does not match ours. In the deepest darkness God brings us the brightest light, and in the season of death God brings us the fullness of life.

Jesus is indeed coming! Our spirits begin to vibrate with excitement as our Lover can be seen "leaping across the mountains, bounding over the hills". And then, if we look carefully enough, we see Him "gazing through the windows." Jesus is now at the front door of our lives. Do we recognize Him?

Today's Gospel reading (Lk 1:39-45) brings another person to join our "Advent climb"; Elizabeth, Mary's cousin makes a surprise appearance. Elizabeth had the "first day of spring" experience when Mary appeared at her door. She was "filled with the Holy Spirit" and *"in a loud voice she exclaimed 'blessed are you among women and blessed is the fruit of your womb."* Jesus came to Elizabeth at a moment she did not expect Him, as a thief in the night. And even her unborn child, John, met Jesus and was filled with the Holy Spirit for he "leaped for joy" in the womb of Elizabeth. (Had Elizabeth been told that her prophetic word would be quoted billions of times by Christians throughout the centuries every time a "Hail Mary" is uttered, she would have "flipped out".

The Church is saying "Jesus is already here." He is not like Santa who stays cooped up in his North Pole house 364 days a year, then suddenly makes a miraculous appearance on Christmas Eve. Jesus comes "in stages." He was born within the womb of Mary, then, though He couldn't be seen, He touched the hearts of Elizabeth and John. His presence was getting stronger and stronger in the gospel story. The suspense mounts as we see Jesus leaping the mountains, gazing through the windows, and causing fig trees to bud.

Isn't this true of our own spiritual lives? Jesus keeps coming nearer to us and deeper within us. He is not a passive guest, but an active Lover who is always seeking deeper intimacy with His beloved. Today we are with Elizabeth experiencing the surprise visit of Jesus and Mary, and being filled again with the Holy Spirit.

There is a tendency for us to think of the "baptism in the Holy Spirit" as a one-time event. It happened, we rejoiced, and then it sort of lodged within us for the rest of life. In fact the "baptism in the Holy Spirit" is a dynamic experience that happens over and over to us at different points in our lives. It is not a thing of the past to be remembered nostalgically; rather it is a thing of today transforming us into Christ at a deeper level. Let us have expectant faith and be open to a new "baptism in the Holy Spirit" at this new coming of Jesus. Elizabeth is our model.

Let's listen more to what Elizabeth has to say. *"But why am I so favored that the mother of my Lord should come to me?"* Notice the breathlessness of her words, as she is filled with gratitude, wonder, and humility. How often have we been caught up in wonder when we realize that God has chosen us to be His beloved children. Think back to that moment when you accepted Jesus. There were hundreds of people just like you He could have selected - same age, same job, same background, same set of sins. Yet He put his finger on you, and on me. And it certainly wasn't because we were better than the rest; truth be told we were probably worse. What a mystery!

Today let's pray with Elizabeth, "why am I so favored?" Let us never take our "chosen-ness" for granted or become lax in our response to it.

"Jesus you are knocking again at the window. Why am I so favored that You've chosen to awaken a new springtime of love within me? May the Holy Spirit fill my heart with gratitude, wonder, and humility as I open the door of my heart again to receive You."

Mountain Ledge

Our mountain climb is almost over. The Church is not going to let us "coast home" in our journey. Those of us who are poised to welcome "sweet baby Jesus" may be upset by today's readings.

Malachi walks onto the scene to announce, in his own, non-diplomatic way, the coming of the Lord (Ma 3:1-4, 23-24). *"Suddenly he will come to the Temple, the Lord whom you seek...But who will endure the day of His coming, and who can stand when He appears? For He is like the refiner's fire, or like the fuller's lye...He will purify the sons of Levi."* And then Malachi ends his disturbing message by telling us that the day the Lord comes will be a *"great and terrible"* day. This does not sound like the little infant of Bethlehem. The prophet is talking about another kind of coming.

Now that Malachi has shaken us from our winter doldrums, there is a strange appearance of a priest, a son of Levi. He is silent but seems to want to tell us something. This man is Elizabeth's husband, Zechariah. Though Zechariah had prayed for a son many times, when his prayer was answered through the message of the Angel Gabriel, he didn't believe. Zechariah began to talk about how old he was, and that he didn't see how his wife could bear a child in her old age. (Lk 1:11-21). This "son of Levi" was struck dumb (remember Malachi's prophecy about purifying the sons of Levi?) by God to let him know that God meant exactly what He said, and this was not a time for a key player in God's plan to cave in.

Was Zechariah telling us to learn from his mistakes? If

we have slipped back into thinking as men think instead of how God thinks, now is the time to repent. We don't want God to have to use extraordinary means to get our attention, as He did with Zechariah.

When Zechariah wrote on the tablet "his name is John", the people were astonished! What was going on here? A priest, steeped in the tradition of Judaism, was going outside the box by naming his son "John", a name that did not exist among his relatives. It was as though God was taking John away from his family and designating him (as He did with Samuel) to be a full-time servant of God. John did not belong to Elizabeth, Zechariah, and their relatives; he belonged to God. In fact we know from Jesus' words that John was the "new Elijah" prophesied by Malachi.

And at the moment Zechariah obeyed the angel and named his son John, this act of conversion and faith brought about the restoration of his speech. What a dramatic reminder about the power of obedient faith. (Lk 1:57-66)

I see us standing on a ledge as we near the top of the Advent mountain. God is calling us to "conversion" as our final act of preparation. Last night in our prayer meeting the Holy Spirit spoke clearly to us that He wants us to "convert". Then we were led into about 10 minutes of silence as we each listened to the voice of the Holy Spirit within, letting each of us know the specifics about what God wanted. It reminded me of the tailor-made calls to repentance God gave each of the seven churches in the Book of Revelation. This time of silence and listening bore fruit. Many testified that the Lord spoke clearly to them what specific form of conversion He has in mind for them. Then we shared some of what the Holy Spirit gave us.

I want to encourage each of us to take 10 or 15 minutes of silence and listen to how God wants us to "convert". It may help to write down the specific area He is addressing in our lives. We want to take full advantage of this pause on the mountain ledge, so we are prepared for the last few days of our journey.

"Jesus, I stop now to listen to Your voice in my heart. Please speak to me of how I need conversion and let me have the obedient faith of Mary when she yielded to Your call."

Promises, Promises

Imagine this Christmas scenario. Bob had his hopes on getting a brand new, top-of-the-line BMW for Christmas. On Christmas morning he hurried out to his garage expecting to see the new car sitting there, and to his disappointment he saw only his old 12-year old Chevy with a note taped on the windshield. The note said: "Bob, your old car is just fine; instead of giving you a new car I promise to give your son a new car after you've died. Love, God." I wonder how Bob would take this?

This made-up story is similar to the story in our first reading this morning. (2 Sam 7:1-16). David's success had peaked; from a simple shepherd boy, he had become Israel's greatest king and even built a palace for himself. Feeling his oats, David decided on a new, grandiose project—he would build a temple for God. This would be the crowning moment of his reign. As he was getting excited about the idea, the Lord, speaking through the prophet Nathan, said in effect "no thanks, I'm happy with My tent." After God had scrapped David's plan, He then presented His plan. God was going to build a greater house than David could imagine. He promised that the kingdom of David would last forever; his name would be listed among the greatest men of the earth. And, David's idea of building a temple would come about after David's death under the supervision of one of his sons.

When God says "no" to one of our dreams or plans, He comes back with a promise that is hundreds of times greater than what we had in mind. While we may feel our bubble burst, if we listen to the Lord, He will replace our dreams with His promise. And His promises are always fulfilled. A promise of God is more than just a statement of what He will do in the future, it is a "now" event because in the communication of promise we experience such a deep encounter with God that we get a sense that the promise has already begun its fulfillment in us.

Let's look at how this worked for Zechariah (Lk 1:67-79). Zechariah had a dream of having many sons, one of whom would succeed him as priest and maybe even be elevated to be high priest of Israel. His dreams never materialized; his plans fell apart. Imagine Zechariah's disappointment and depression. Then in this moment of darkness, an angel gave Zechariah a surprise visit and said he would have a son, who would be greater than any prophet or priest of Israel. He would be the immediate forerunner of the Messiah!

After Zechariah finally conceded to the promise of God, he went into "ecstacy" as he sang out one of the most beautiful prayers ever written. His song of praise, prophecy, and blessing is still sung every night in every monastery throughout the world. Do you think Zechariah had any idea of the power of God's promise in his life? Do you think he had any idea that he was uttering, under the inspiration of the Holy Spirit, a word that would be sung and remembered in the Church till the end of time? How did this compare with the dreams that never materialized for him?

Zechariah emerges as one of the great levitical priests of the Bible. He breaks forth in unsurpassed praise, prophesies the mission of John, and gives a final prophecy of the coming of Jesus—*"the rising sun will come to us from heaven to shine on those living in darkness and the shadow of death."*

Where do we fit into all of this? Will God give us a BMW for Christmas? Or a promise about the future? Or the fulfillment of our dreams? I believe His gift to us will be more along the lines of what He did for Zechariah. He will give us each a special promise, and beyond that He will give us the gift of Himself. All else pales in comparison.

Let us remember the promise of Psalm 37:4—*"make the Lord your only delight and He will give you the desires of your heart."*

"Father in heaven, I let go of my plans and open my heart to Your plan. May I be touched by the Holy Spirit, as was Zechariah, and be filled with a new experience of Your love and Your promises. This is all that really counts."

(Homework: join Zechariah in singing his song today— the "Benedictus" Lk 1:68-79)

Ta Da!

Ta da! We have reached the top of the mountain at last.
What happens when we arrive?   Bells and whistles?
Breathtaking scenes?   Speakers blaring out Christmas
carols?

To our surprise and maybe disappointment, the top of
the mountain is dark and barren. In the stillness of the
night we see nothing but a poor, humble man and his
young wife. Is this all that awaits us? We remember
what Jesus said about those who went out to see John
the Baptist: "what did you go out to see, a reed shaken
by the wind? People dressed in fine clothes?"

We walk reverently toward the young man and woman,
and as we near them a feeling of deep love and silent
peace begins to overwhelm us.   Coming within
touching distance of the couple we realize they are
huddled over a newborn child. The child is lying in
straw and wrapped in "swaddling clothes". There is
what seems to be a light emanating from the face of the
child that seems to pierce the darkness. Something so
sacred surrounds this young family that we almost
collapse in amazement. God has invaded history but
not in the way we expected. What did we go up the
mountain to see?   A spectacular "God show" or a
"festival of lights?"

Standing near the child we notice in the distance a
group of poor shepherds walking slowly our way.
Some carry lambs, others are trailed by their sheep.
When they come closer we see that they have "stunned"
looks on their faces, as though they had encountered an

angel. Later, we find out they had. Then suddenly there are strange lights dashing above the infant and His parents as though a canopy is being stretched out over them, and we hear a burst of praise coming forth from above and the music surpasses anything we've ever heard on earth. It is as though heaven itself opened up for a moment and angels are singing out over the infant in the same way they sing before the throne of God.

This is not just a cute little nativity scene; this is the real thing. We are seeing Jesus, the Son of God, alive and touchable in our midst. As we fall to the ground in reverent awe, we feel the love that radiates from the Infant coming upon us. We know we unworthy sinners to be this close to God, and yet we open our hearts in expectation to receive His love. Our sins seem to evaporate and a new presence of God's love begins to fill our hearts.

We hear the shepherds explaining to the young woman the encounter they had with an angel; she smiles quietly and seems to store their words in her heart. With excitement the shepherds quickly leave because they want to, *"spread the word concerning what they had been told about the child, and all who heard it were amazed."* (Lk :17).

We remember Isaiah's words (Is 9:6): *"For unto us a Child is born, to us a Son is given, and He will be called Wonderful Counselor, Mighty God, Everlasting Father, Prince of Peace."*

We begin to shout out the words of Psalm 96: *"Sing to the Lord a new song. Sing to the Lord all the earth...Let the heavens rejoice; let the earth be glad...let the sea resound...let the fields be jubilant, and everything in them...let all the trees of the forest sing for joy...for He comes, He comes to judge the earth."*

The time of waiting is over. It is now our time to imitate the shepherds and "spread the word" about what we have seen and heard, and how our lives have been changed. We go forth to tell a world that is steeped in darkness that a Light has come, a divine rescue operation has begun.

Our first stop is our parish church crowded with people to watch the "Christmas show" and listen to the choir sing hymns. The distracted and empty faces we see there make us wonder how many of these people have met Jesus Christ as Lord and Savior. How many of them have been transformed by a "personal Pentecost?" It seems that most are gathering here just because it is the "thing to do" among the many other "things to do" at Christmas time.

We now know why God led us up the Advent mountain and let us witness this encounter of earth with heaven. He needs new shepherds to go forth and proclaim among our own people what God is now doing on the face of the earth.

*"Jesus, we know that Your appearance was not to give us a good feeling of 'Christmas spirit'. It was that we might help awaken the world to what God has in store for **each** person who humbles himself and allows Jesus to take over his life. We surrender to your call and commit ourselves to lay down our lives that others may come to know You as we have."*

88

Family Issues

While the focus of Advent was the coming of Jesus, the Church today broadens the picture and turns our attention to a "threesome"—Jesus, Mary, and Joseph. It is unusual that our Church which creates feast days and names buildings after Jesus, Mary, Angels, and Saints puts a "family" in the same category. Even before Jesus was born, His presence created a family. Three people were drawn together in a unity and love that the world cannot fathom, and as a unit became an instrument of bringing about God's kingdom on earth. For over 90% of His life the presence of Jesus in the world consisted of being part of a simple, Godly family in the remote village of Nazareth.

Most of Jesus' ministry consisted of His care and service to His mother, and to His father (Joseph) even into old age. The passage from Sirach today which calls us to honor, obey, and care for parents especially into their old age (Sir 3:2-14) was modeled by Jesus. This was His ministry for the greater portion of His life. God seems more interested in what goes on in the home than in what goes on in the church. How strange that God would "waste" 30 years of the Messiah's life by having Him live a simple, uneventful family life. What is He trying to tell us?

Jesus' preparation for His public ministry took place in His home within the context of the most ideal family the world has known.

Today's Gospel (Mt 2:13-15, 19-23) gives us a glimpse into the early days of the Holy Family. There are three things I noticed. The First is that the family centers in Jesus and nothing else. Secondly, the forces of evil were trying to destroy them, and their life was one "on the run." Thirdly, they listened to the voice of God (often given through the message of an angel—Joseph's guardian angel?) and did as he told them. Isn't this a wonderful and simple recipe for our lives?

To be like the Holy Family, we focus not on money, family problems, nor personal difficulties—no, we center our lives on Jesus only. And we know that if we are trying to live a life in "fear of the Lord", we will be attacked and satan will want to destroy us any way he can. It is naïve to adopt a "fairy tale" mentality and pretend that this is not true. Remember Peter's admonition to us: *"Be sober; be watchful, for your adversary the devil as a roaring lion goes about seeking someone to devour"* (1 Pt 5:8) Finally we know that the best advice we can get for our lives is to listen to the voice of God and obey it. A good New Year's resolution is to dismantle the "complicatedness" of our lives and follow the simple lead of the Holy Family.

Looking at our real situations today, we probably do not live in "holy families". There is much pain in most of our families. Most of us have families that have, in some way, been broken by such things as divorce, discord, addiction, and tragedy. All of us would like to have a "Jesus, Mary, and Joseph" family.

While this may seem a bleak assessment of things, there is something we can do today to make our families into holy families. We can choose to make Jesus the focus of our own lives. Remember the promises of Psalm 128: *"Blessed are all who fear the Lord...blessings and prosperity will be yours."* The Psalm goes on to explain that this blessing and prosperity will be seen primarily in our families. One of the most wonderful things we can do (and Catholic tradition confirms this) is that we can claim our privilege of being part of the Holy Family of Nazareth. We don't have to try to create the "perfect family" in our homes. Instead we can join the "perfect family" that already exists! Jesus invites us into His home to fellowship with His mother and dad (Joseph) today. Being part of this "perfect family", we get our own needs for family met there and become better empowered to bring this influence into the lives of our spouses, children, brothers and sisters.

"Jesus, Mary, and Joseph, I enter your home today burdened with the pain and concerns I have about my family. Close to you, I will learn love, forbearance, forgiveness, compassion, patience...and thus bring the seed of "holy family" into my own home. Today I ask you to intercede for each member of my family especially those who hurt the most and feel estranged from God."

Another John

Today is the feast of St. John the Apostle. It is interesting that John the Baptist came on the scene to guide us through the "pre Christmas" season, and now another John arrives to discuss with us the "post Christmas" season.

In the Gospel (Jn 20:1-8) we see Peter and John running to the empty tomb. They were the recognized "point men" for Jesus. Mary Magdalene knew to go to them first to share the Good News. Though John reached the tomb first, he waited to allow Peter to enter first. This was in deference to Peter's authority. A priest some years ago at one of our conferences talked about how John represented the "prophetic Church", and Peter represented the "institutional Church." Though John was the first apostle to see the empty tomb, he stood outside and waiting until the slower, Peter, arrived. It was only after Peter went in, that John followed.

Much of the history of the charismatic renewal in the Catholic Church has been a series of "false starts". For some reason God chose lowly lay people, in fact a handful of college kids, to reveal His new work of the Holy Spirit to the Church. Some of us, in our zeal, wanted to "rush into the tomb" and take things over in an effort to move things forward quickly. "No", said the Holy Spirit, "Wait for Peter to get here." And Peter takes his time, knowing that he must follow the Holy Spirit, in His way, as well.

I believe that we are at a moment when Peter has caught up with John and is stooping to enter the empty tomb. In humility, those who have reached the tomb first, stand aside and wait to see what Peter suggests.

I had the privilege this past October of being the third party in a meeting between Archbishop Kurtz and Ralph Martin. Over the years, Ralph has represented the "prophetic Church" as a leader in the charismatic renewal. And Archbishop Kurtz is one emerging leaders in the "institutional Church" in this country. What most amazed me is that, as the conversation evolved, both were speaking the same language, and presenting the same vision. In a concrete way I saw Peter and John meeting at the entrance to the tomb. My interpretation is that we have reached a new turning point in our Church.

After John went into the tomb, *"he saw and believed",* and then went back to his home (Jn 20:1-8).

In today's second reading (1 Jn 1-4) we hear that "false teachers" had infiltrated the early Christian community. John speaks the truth emphatically and talks about the "beginning". He reminds the people of *"that which…we have heard…seen with our eyes…looked at…our hands touched."* He reminded them that he proclaims what he *"has seen…and heard."* There is no mistake about what happened, and what the truth is.

We are in an age that abounds with "false teachers", some of whom have great influence in our own Church. It is time for us to go back to the "beginnings" and talk about what we have "seen and heard" with our own eyes. John warns us not to be misled or to drift away from what we know is the truth. "Something happened, and now I know, He touched me," as we sing at our meetings. Let us be like John and be ready to tell what we have "seen and heard", and thus testify to the truth.

When God plants a new seed of His light and joy, guess who's there to snatch it or stunt its growth. John inspires us to return quickly to "the beginnings."

"Light is shed upon the righteous and joy upon the upright heart." (Ps 97:11). This is the truth that has just happened in our lives. Let us keep focused on it.

"St. John, pray that we exercise wisdom in our use of prophetic awareness. Let us not slip into pride and superiority as many did in the early Church. Help us keep focused on what we have seen and heard and always be ready to testify concerning it."

Rachel Weeps

Today we revisit Matthew's story of the "flight into Egypt" (Mt 2:13-18). Embedded in this story is the report of the massacre of the babies of Bethlehem. Today is the feast of the Holy Innocents. In the afterglow of Christmas joy we hear the voice of Rachel as she weeps and mourns for her children, descendants of her son, Judah. These innocent babies were the first to shed their blood for Jesus; they began a chain of millions, of people who have been martyred for the sake of the kingdom of God.

Herod "was furious" that the Magi had outwitted him. He who had deceived the Magi into thinking he wanted to go worship the newborn king, had the tables turned on him. His prideful heart was exposed and from the deepest cavern of hate he called for the murder of "all the boys" in Bethlehem two years and younger. Imagine a heart so vicious in his hatred for Jesus and so filled with fear of losing his power and position that he would react in this extreme. It would be difficult to find anywhere a more vivid description of the horror of sin.

Remember Jesus' word to His apostles: *"If the world hates you, remember that it hated Me first."* (Jn 15:18) This is a sobering truth to know that because Jesus lives in us, we are hated by the world that refuses to follow Him. Such truth is difficult to accept because, as humans, we so much want to be liked and appreciated by everyone, including those who are not aligned with Jesus.

95

We know that Rachel's weeping did not stop after the days of Herod's massacre, but continues, perhaps more loudly, in our own time. Orders go out even today that the unborn be destroyed so that the gods of lustfulness, greed, irresponsibility, and convenience be served. Subtly we are pushed to bow to the evil forces of our own day. And those who resist and disapprove that innocent babies be the chosen victims of the world's unquenchable appetites are hated as much as Herod hated Jesus.

Praise God that we have been given courage and privilege of being a part of that wonderful army of those who resist and expose the horror of this sin today. Praise God that we have holy bishops and priests who speak out unashamedly against the Herods of our age knowing that, in doing so, they risk their reputations and very lives.

It is coincidental that in today's first reading John also talked about sin. (1 Jn 1:5-2:2). A horrible heresy had invaded the Christian community. Some had claimed that a person could be a Christian and live in sin at the same time. They even denied that their behavior was sinful, and that they had ever been in sin at all. In effect they were saying that salvation was not necessary because their sinful living was acceptable even to God. For them, Jesus' death and resurrection was a waste of time.

Doesn't the situation that John addresses here sound like the prevalent philosophy of our day? The "gospel of the world" says: "Do what you want, whether it conforms to the laws of God or not; there are no consequences, God doesn't care...we'll all go to heaven, if there is a heaven, anyhow. Sin is a myth of outdated religions." And, sadly, all of us have been affected by this way of thinking.

Paul exhorts us to *"...no longer live as the Gentiles do. Having lost all sensitivity they have given themselves over to sensuality so as to indulge in every kind of impurity, with a continual lust for more."* (Eph 4:17-19). *"You were once darkness but now you are light in the Lord. Live as children of the light...have nothing to do with the fruitless deeds of darkness, but rather expose them....be careful then how you live not as unwise but as wise, making the most of every opportunity, because the days are evil."* (Eph 5:8-16)

Has there ever been a time when the call to live holy, pure, and sinless lives has been more important than in the current age? Let us be the "pure of heart" who are able to see the face of God in the midst of a godless world.

"Holy Spirit cleanse my heart from every trace of hatred and sin. Help me to surrender my life so completely to Jesus that I will be a pure vessel of His love and compassion in the midst of a world that needs but ignores Him."

Anna

Is anyone stuck in a "spiritual comfort zone?" Is anyone in a "religion groove" that doesn't seem to be going anywhere except in circles? Is anyone in need of the Holy Spirit to plant a new fire?

In case the answer to any of these questions is "yes", the Church takes us by the hand into the Temple to visit an 84-year old prophetess by the name of Anna. (Today's Gospel is Luke 2:36-40). The Bible says *"she was very old."*

My image of Anna is a tiny, shrunken yet spunky senior citizen that could be mistaken as Mother Teresa's twin sister. What was she doing hanging around the cold Temple when she could be in an assisted living place huddled up in a warm blanket in front of a fireplace with the rest of her peers?

The story of Anna's life begins with a tragedy. She lost her husband after a few short years of marriage, and in her early twenties was left to join the local "widow's club". Her dreams of a large family, creating a home, becoming part of the village scene were destroyed early in life. God had allowed the carpet to be pulled from under Anna's feet. When the women gathered to talk about babies, children, recipes, and who was going to marry whom, Anna felt like an outsider.

Tragedies can turn us against God or toward God. In this case Anna's life circumstances awakened within her a call from God to serve him in prayer and fasting for her whole life. Her mission had been to prepare and wait for the coming of the Messiah. How long did this mission last? Apparently about 60 years.

Anna was not a priest, a deacon, or the member of a religious community, yet she was a "full time" servant of the Lord. Fasting and prayer does not sound like the most exciting or popular way to spend one's life. I'm sure most people looked upon her as a "weird" old lady who didn't seem to fit into the fabric of her society. Luke said that Anna never left the Temple and *"worshipped both night and day."* How do our prayer lives stand in comparison to this model?

As Americans we value our personal comfort even in our spiritual lives. We like to pray as long as it doesn't take up too much of our free time. We don't like to fast and are happy that the Church has relaxed her rules in this regard. Visiting Church now and then is nice, but spending "all day and night" there is out of the question—much less 60 years of our lives. We like being "part time" Christians who do more than the average Catholic, but are careful not to go overboard. Even some priests, deacons, and religious, though by profession are "full timers", can take a "part time" approach to their vocations.

Where are the "Anna-s" of our time? I suggest that you look at the person sitting in the chair reading this message. We are called to be as "radical" as Anna was, no longer living for ourselves, but dedicating our lives, 100%, in service to God. If we fall even 2% short on this, we need to repent and ask God to shake us out of our comfort zones.

How useful was Anna? Her purpose in life arrived after she was 84 years old. Luke said she, *"gave thanks to God and spoke about the child to all who were looking for the redemption of Israel."* I think she was the first evangelist after Mary. She spent her time *"speaking about the child"* to all who needed hope. If any of us is near 84 and believe its time to retire, let Anna wake us up. Our work as evangelists is just beginning. No more excuses like "I'm too old", or "I'm too tired", or "I just don't have the time."

Anna stands before us as a prophet this morning speaking a challenging word from God and stirring us to rise off the couches of our lives to be full-time servants for the Lord. We don't have to spend all day in the Temple to do this.

"Jesus, if I am in a spiritual comfort zone, please shake me loose and set a new fire of the Holy Spirit in my heart. Let me be alert to speak about Jesus to all those I meet who need hope."

Simeon

Today's reading (Lk 2:22-35) tells us that "Joseph and Mary took him [Jesus] to Jerusalem to present him to the Lord. According to the Law, *"every firstborn male is to be consecrated to the Lord."*

While they were presenting Jesus to God, a holy man by the name of Simeon arrived on the scene and began to talk to the couple. We read that Simeon's heart was set on one thing: *"waiting for the consolation of Israel."* We are told that *"the Holy Spirit was upon him"*, and that he had been "moved by the Holy Spirit" to enter into the Temple courts at the precise moment that Jesus appeared there. Sometime earlier in Simeon's life it was *"revealed to him by the Holy Spirit"* that he would not die before he saw the Messiah. His whole life was built on that prophetic word God had given him. Could Simeon be the first to have a devotion to the Holy Spirit?

How was it that Simeon recognized Jesus to be the Messiah? No one else had a clue about the significance of what was taking place. This was just another routine day in the Temple; a poor couple, among other couples, was bringing their first born to go through the consecration ceremony. There was nothing unusual about the couple or the child—so ordinary that they grabbed no one's attention. Who would dream that at that moment the Messiah had entered the Temple for the first time?

It was through the eyes of faith that Simeon recognized Jesus. He was a man accustomed to listening to the Holy Spirit and being led by the Holy Spirit. An inner voice assured him that this poor child was the great Messiah. What faith Simeon had! There were no miracles, no teachings, no casting-out-of-spirits to support his faith. As a "righteous and devout" man he was trained in listening to, and believing in, the voice of the Holy Spirit.

Then Simeon took the Child in his arms and broke out into a prayer of praise. He praised God that His promise was being fulfilled at that moment, and that he was privileged to see the *"light for revelation to the Gentiles"* and, *"the glory of the people of Israel."* Simeon then extended his personal blessing to the holy family while prophesying that Jesus would cause *"the rise and fall of many"*, and that He would *"be a sign that would be spoken against"*. Then he went on to prophesy to Mary that a sword would pierce her heart.

Sometimes we may get weary trying to live a righteous and devout life. We may find it difficult trying to listen daily to the Holy Spirit and keep up the habit of following the promptings of the Holy Spirit. Prophecies have been spoken over us in the past; maybe we've forgotten about them or have dismissed them as unimportant. Simeon visits us today to remind us that our dedication to being "led by the Holy Spirit" will, in time, pay off.

Simeon's whole life was a preparation for that one moment in the Temple. Having seen Jesus, he then told the Lord that he could *"now...dismiss [His] servant in peace."*

There are signs that indicate that our "Simeon moment" has arrived in the charismatic renewal. We live in a day in which old prophecies are being fulfilled and new ones are being spoken. Regardless of how we might feel today, let us join Simeon in praising and glorifying God for the gift He has given us in the "now" appearance of His Son. Maybe Jesus is too big for us to hold in our arms the way Simeon did, but we are not too big for Him to hold us in His. As we experience the embrace of Jesus today, let us rejoice that the great day of salvation has arrived.

"Declare His glory among the nations, His marvelous deeds among all peoples." (Ps 96:3)

"Jesus I repent for growing careless in listening to the Holy Spirit and following His lead. Today, inspired by the example of Simeon, I pray "come Holy Spirit" and resolve again to reverence the presence of the Holy Spirit in my life."

The Truth

We live in an age dominated by the mass media. Great reverence is given to "public opinion." There is an underlying assumption that truth is revealed through opinion, and that the majority can't be wrong. This doesn't sit too well with what Jesus told us: *"broad is the road that leads to destruction and many travel it."* (Mt 7:13)

Truth is not up for grabs; it is not something we have to search for by seeking the opinions of people. Truth is revealed to us simply and clearly by God. And today's Gospel reading (Jn 1:1-18) gives one of the simplest and most profound explanations of the truth that is in the Bible. John reaches back before the book of Genesis and takes us to the start of time.

Before anything existed there was the Word, and through this Word God created all things. *"Without Him was made nothing that has been made."* So now we know exactly how things got started. We also know that the Word was the source of life and gave light to men, and that apart from the Word men stumble around in darkness. Further we know that God so wanted the world to be delivered from darkness that He sent the Word to become flesh and dwell among us. In spite of this we know that the "world did not recognize" the Word made flesh, and God's own people chose not to receive Him. On the other hand some did receive Him, and because of this were elevated to the status of being "children of God." John tells us that *"no one has ever seen God"* but His only Son (the Word made flesh, Jesus), and He has made God known to us. Now Jesus sits at God's side.

There it is in a nutshell. This is revealed truth and not the smartest person in the history of the world could have ever figured this out by thinking hard, experimenting, or assembling public opinions. Nothing in life is more important than knowing this truth and receiving the Word who was sent by God to deliver us from darkness. This is the story of what life is all about; sadly only a few accept it and live their lives according to it.

The benefit of choosing to be part of God's plan is that we receive one blessing after another. God heaps His love, His favor, and His blessings on those who have accepted Jesus thus becoming His sons and daughters. How could anyone want to choose anything else as the solution to their life? And once having made this decision, how could anyone walk away from this path that leads to life?

John's epistle today (1 Jn 18-21) reminds us that it is not easy to stay faithful to the truth. Some do walk away from the right path. Antichrists (opponents of Jesus) who were once part of the Christian community, abandoned the truth and tried to lure others to follow them. This caused great disturbance in the Church. John reminds them that they were anointed by the Holy One and each one now knows the truth in their hearts. *"No one who denies the Son has the Father; whoever acknowledges the Son has the Father also."*

Because of the "truth-is-up-for-grabs" mentality of our culture, it is important that we stay grounded in the Word of God. We listen daily to the truth that is in us, and the truth that God continues to reveal to us by the Holy Spirit.

Many personal versions of "Christianity" are marketed by "antichrists" of today, and some of them seem to make sense. They provide an "easier" way than the way of the Cross. Let us be on our guard and measure all that is said by the truth that God has planted in our hearts—the anointing we have received. Let us be people of the truth.

"Then all the trees of the forest will sing for joy...for He comes, He comes to judge the earth." (Ps 96:12-13)

"Jesus we pray for a love for Your Word and clarity about the truth. We thank You that we are among those who did receive You and share the privilege of being God's sons and daughters. Let us always stay grounded in the truth."

Theotokos

Today we celebrate the feast day of "Mary the Mother of God", in Greek "Theotokos".

A great controversy existed in the 5th century of the Church over the personhood of Jesus. Nestorius, a church leader, claimed that Jesus was two persons, one God and one man, and so Mary could be called "Mother of Jesus", but not "Mother of God". The Council of Ephesus (year 431) was called, apparently at the request of Nestorius, to deal with this issue, and at that Council the teaching Church declared as dogma, that Mary is the Mother of God.

This is not big issue with us today. In fact this dogma is proclaimed at every second of every day throughout the world, when we pray "Holy Mary, <u>Mother of God</u>, pray for us sinners."

While this title may not be a big issue today, motherhood is. When we think of important titles in the Church, we think of priest, deacon, prophet, pastor, evangelist, parish council president, and so on. We don't think of "mother." In the world some have felt timid and maybe even shameful saying "I'm a stay-at-home mom". This doesn't gain kudos from a world that places its highest value on "prestige", "status", and "power."

Yet the Church called a Council to exalt the title "Mother of God" to the level of dogma, and we proclaim this title more than, perhaps, any other dogma that we know.

The "Word Made Flesh" needed an earthly mother to

bear Him in her womb, feed Him, care for His needs, be a model of holiness for Him to follow, and be of support to Him in His direst moments. We know that Jesus was never without a mother. Even at the foot of the cross, she stood there loving Him and suffering with Him. Jesus lost His friends, His honor, and even His own clothes; He never, however, lost His mother.

At the cross Jesus, we recall, gave His mother away to John. In doing this He gave her to each of His disciples, so we would be blessed with His own mother whenever we need her. Mary's charism was "mother of the faithful." We do not know what other charisms she might have had in the early church; we know that being "mother" was her primary charism—and it still is.

As the mother of the Son of God, Mary *"treasured all these things and pondered them in her heart"*. (see today's Gospel, Luke 2:16-21). In a way, her heart was a "living scrapbook" that contained memories of the great works of God in the life of her Son.

St. Paul reminds us that <u>we</u> are sons and daughters of God because, *"God sent the Spirit of his Son into our hearts"*, which allows us to call God "Abba", our personal Dad. Before our salvation we were "slaves"; now we are "sons and daughters." (Gal 4:4-7) If we can call God, "Abba", we can call Mary "Mom", "Mama", or "Mother."

As a New Year's resolution, let me suggest that we schedule "Mary time" into each day. Let us get into the habit of visiting our mother and listening to what she has to tell us. I believe that since our conceptions she has been "storing up memories" of us in her heart, and has a tailor-made scrapbook of each of our lives, ready to share with us. What an exciting thought that we have been given the Mother of God as our own mother, and that God expects us to go to her often. Imagine the treasures she will unfold to us as we spend quiet time in her presence.

"May God be gracious to us and bless us and make his face shine upon us…" (Ps 67:1) Among God's greatest blessings to us is the gift of a new mother-- not just any mother, but the very "Mother of God."

"Holy Mary, Mother of God, pray for us sinners now and at the hour of our death."

Surprise Party

Today we celebrate "Epiphany" which the dictionary defines as a "sudden manifestation." The Gospel passage (Mt 2:1-12) tells of a surprise visit to Jesus by the three magi. Suddenly there was a knock on the door and Mary saw these three strangely dressed men from a Gentile country bearing gifts for the new little king. Matthew tells us that they "bowed down and worshiped" the child. How unusual that Gentile visitors were the first to worship Jesus as though He were a god, while God's own people didn't seem that interested in the poor family from Nazareth.

The three gifts had spiritual significance. Gold was the precious metal that kings possessed. Incense was the sweet smelling substance that priests used in worship. Myrrh was the gum used as a medicine and a perfume. Because of its medicinal value, some see it as a symbol of suffering. Jesus was being honored as a king, a priest, and a prophet by these mysterious heralds who seemed to appear out of nowhere.

Epiphany is the day for giving gifts. By giving gifts on Christmas day we jumped the gun by a week or so. Maybe, now that the flurry of Christmas giving is over, we can focus on the gifts that really matter.

At our baptism and confirmation we have been given, in a way, the same three gifts that Jesus received, though in different forms. We know about the water of baptism and the laying on of hands at confirmation; sometimes we miss that fact that "anointing with oil" is used in both rites. With Jesus, each of us has been anointed as a king, a priest, and a prophet.

Peter tells us that we are a "royal priesthood." (1 Pt 2:9) John tells us that Jesus has made us "to be a kingdom and priests to serve His God and Father." (Rv 1:6). Paul tells us, in effect, that all of us are called to be prophets. (1 Cor 14:1). Luke reminds us that we have been given *"authority...to overcome all the power of the enemy."* (Lk 10:19). Are we aware of this "threefold anointing" that has been given us? Do we take seriously the fact that God expects us to act under this anointing for the sake of His kingdom?

The magi realized that the treasures God had given them were not merely to benefit themselves; they were to be given back to him at appropriate times. Notice that they were laid at the feet of Jesus. Fr. Lauer today exhorts us to "put the gold of your possessions, the frankincense of your prayers, and the myrrh of your suffering at the feet of Jesus for the spread of the Gospel." Our kingly, priestly, and prophetic gifts are not for ourselves but for the Lord and His work. Let us today join the magi in laying all of our gifts at the feet of Jesus. This is the "gift-giving" that most pleases God today.

Today we go from "salvation", a gift for us, to "service" a gift for God.

We live at a significant moment in history. Isaiah's prophecy (Is 60:1-6) is especially true for us today. *"Arise, shine, for your light has come...See darkness has covered the earth but the Lord rises upon you, and his glory appears over you. Nations will come to your light."* While this word was fulfilled in the visit of the magi to Jesus, it is fulfilled in a fresh way today as God does a new work through His people. We ready ourselves, this year, for another "epiphany."

It's time to reawaken to our identity and start using our authority as kings, worshipping in Spirit and truth as priests, and speaking God's word in truth and boldness as prophets. In doing so, God uses us to usher in a new age of grace for the Church of our time.

"All kings will bow down to Him and all nations will serve Him." (Ps 72:11)

"Jesus, today I bring you my possessions and my time, my prayer and my worship, my words and my suffering as gifts for You to be used as You direct. These are not mine to use as I wish; they are Yours to help accomplish the will of the Father on earth."

Something About That Name

Today's Gospel (Mt 4:12-17, 23-25) suddenly takes us from the infant Jesus in Bethlehem to the grown-up Jesus preaching and healing in the land of the Gentiles. A week ago, we encountered the gentle light surrounding the Holy Family on the day of Jesus' birth. Yesterday, the light became brighter as *"nations came to [this] light and kings to the brightness of [this] dawn"* (Is 60:3); the magi followed the bright star to the place where Jesus was living. Today the Church quickly jumps thirty years ahead to when the Light had become so intense that it exploded into powerful preaching and miraculous healing. In Bethlehem there were but a few who came to Jesus; now we learn that "crowds from Galilee, Decapolis, Jerusalem, Judea, and the region across the Jordan followed Him."

No longer did God restrain Himself. It was as though He was launching a full-fledge attack against the imprisoning forces of darkness and the evil grip of sickness and demonic possession. The Church does not linger in talking about the beginnings of the light; almost with a sense of urgency it takes us into the heat of battle with God's power manifested dramatically through Jesus. The hour of deliverance had come and the Church is quick to announce it. And for some reason Jesus was led to reside in Capernaum, and to do his work in the land of Zebulun and Naphtali—"the land of the shadow of death." He chose the unexpected places where the darkness seemed to be most engulfing to launch his ministry.

Recent prophecies lead us to believe that we now live in

a moment when once again there will be an "explosion" of light and power in a world that is steeped in darkness. God is preparing another "full-fledge" attack on the forces of evil that have such a powerful grip on our world. Prophecies charge us to be prepared and ready to be called into action, equipped with the full armor of God. (Eph 6); and if we come up short in this regard, the Holy Spirit tells us to *"repent for the kingdom of God is at hand."*

Today is also the feast of the Holy Name of Jesus. Whenever we feel the need for God's armor and don't know where to start, we can start using the Name of Jesus. In today's epistle reading (1 Jn 3:22-4:6) we are told: *"And this is his command: to believe in the name of His Son Jesus Christ."* One of the songs we sing at our meetings tells us that "in the name of Jesus demons will have to flee."

In the early days of the Church we read that Peter and John were called before the Sanhedrin and asked *"by what power or what name did you do this? [heal the crippled man]"* Peter proclaimed that *"there is no other name under heaven by which a man can be saved."* The religious leaders gave Peter and John just one order—*"not to speak or teach at all in the name of Jesus."* Imagine how the powers of darkness cringe at the mere mention of the Name which is above all names. What a powerful weapon we have at our disposal in uttering the Name of Jesus.

Throughout the history of the Church many found a quick path to holiness and contemplation by reciting over and over again the name of Jesus using the simple prayer: "Lord Jesus Christ, have mercy on me a sinner." Using the Name of Jesus frequently in prayer helps us move quickly into a closer walk with Him. It is a simple prayer form that can help uncomplicate our lives and give us focus in the midst of confusing times.

"Ask of Me and I will make the nations your inheritance, the ends of the earth your possession" (Ps 2:8)

"Come Holy Spirit in our day and let Your wondrous power be seen in our world, that many may repent and come to Jesus. Work new signs and wonders that "crowds" from all over may come to follow Him. We pray this in the Name of Jesus."

Supper Time

Today's Gospel starts off with people chasing Jesus. (Mk 6:34-44). *"So many people were going and coming that they (Jesus and apostles) did not even have a chance to eat."* (v.31). So Jesus and the apostles got into a boat to have a "mental health" break and get away from the people. *"But many saw Him leaving...and ran on foot from all the towns and got there (shore) ahead of them."* By the time Jesus landed there was a large crowd waiting for Him on the shore.

I wonder why the people were "chasing" after Jesus? I wonder why the people of our day are not "chasing" after Jesus? What did Jesus have that the people so desperately wanted?

When Jesus got off the boat, he had every reason to shoo the crowd away and take some time off for Himself. Instead, because of the deep compassion He felt for this people who were like sheep without a shepherd, He stopped and began to teach them "many things." Here we get a glimpse into the heart of God as He looks upon the people of our generation. Beneath the façade of having our acts together, deep inside, we are lost and hurting sheep wandering around looking for a shepherd. Sadly, those of our generation do not know that Jesus is who they are looking for. Meantime they "chase" after every imaginable thing except Him.

What were the apostles thinking as Jesus ministered to the people? Did they also have hearts of compassion as they saw the lost souls gather around Jesus? No. They seemed to be thinking about food. So they took it upon

116

themselves to advise the Son of God what to do: *"Send the people away so they can go...and buy themselves something to eat."* When their stomachs growled loudly enough, they became "lords" and treated Jesus as a "disciple." Of course Jesus never lets His disciples run the show, as we can testify from our own experience.

This is when the surprise begins. *"You give them something to eat,"* replied Jesus. How I wish I had a video clip of the looks on their faces at this moment. Did they say, "sure, Lord, let it happen according to Your will"? No. They began to tell Jesus how unreasonable He was; did He expect them to dig eight months worth of wages out of their treasury and feed this crowd? Could this have been Judas, the treasurer, speaking up? Instead of letting them focus on what they did not have, Jesus asked them what they <u>did</u> have. *"Five (loaves) and two fish,"* they answered. (John's account says the loaves and fish came from a boy in the crowd (see Jn 6:9)) Why did John, who was familiar with the Gospel accounts of the other evangelists, make it a point to mention "the boy?" Does it take childlike faith to believe that the little we have can feed a multitude if we give it to Jesus and let Him bless it?

Then we watch the miracles unfold. Jesus blessed and broke and gave it to His disciples. In a short time *"they all ate and were satisfied",* and there were *"twelve basketfuls of broken pieces left over...."* This is a hint of the abundance of God's blessing to the earth when the *"Word became flesh and dwelt among us."*

We are Jesus' disciples today. When we give up trying to tell Him how to run the Church and the world and

117

start listening, we will hear Him tell us to feed the multitudes. When we complain that all we have is a meager amount of bread and fish, He will tell us to make this available to Him. As we release our meager amount into His hands, we watch Him bless and break it; then we stand in awe to see Jesus pour out His blessings.

The ingredients for this miracle were a group of excuse-making disciples, a small amount of food, and the presence and power of Jesus Christ. Does this give us a hint on how God can use each of us? We listen to Jesus, give Him the little we have, and watch Him go to work.

John's epistle reading today (1 Jn 4:7-11) reminds us that the whole secret of our lives is that God first loved us. If *"he so loved us, we also ought to love one another."* He gives us the loaves of His love, and then instructs us to go distribute this love to the worlds in which we live. Our little, when surrendered to Jesus, can feed thousands.

"In his days the righteous will flourish; prosperity will abound till the moon is no more." (Ps 72:7)

"Jesus, please give me the childlike faith of the young boy who turned his dinner over to You. Deliver me from my selfishness and unbelief. Take all that I have and use if for pouring God's love out to the world."

118

Don't Be Afraid

We continue to celebrate the Christmas season, even though the malls have declared an end to the holidays. For 2000 years God worked with a people to prepare for the greatest move of God in history, the incarnation of His own Son. It is important that we don't shortcut the significance of this event by quickly forgetting it. Today the Church gives us another story to awaken us to the amazing presence of the Son of God in history. Jesus has some kind of "radar-like" vision, He walks on water, and He calms a storm. This is no ordinary human being, holy rabbi, or political leader. Jesus has powers that no human being has ever had before. Truly He is beyond Messiah; He is the very Son of God.

Mark began the story (Mk 6:45-52) by telling us that Jesus needed time with His Father. He dismissed the crowd and the disciples and went up into the mountain to pray. This reminds me that if Jesus needed regular retreat time to be alone with the Father, how much more do I need to carve out time in my schedule to go "into the mountains" to be alone with God. We have three monasteries within an hour and a half from Louisville. God is there waiting for us; do we respond?

We learn that though Jesus was on the land yet, *"He saw the disciples straining at the oars"*, as they tried to fight their way across the raging sea. Some hours later He decided to go out to visit them by taking a shortcut—He walked on the water. He was about to pass them up when they saw Him and were terrified. *"Take courage," Jesus said. "It is I. Don't be afraid."* He then hoisted himself into the boat, and at that moment the wind died down and the sea became calm again. Though the disciples were amazed, Mark tells us that *"their hearts were hardened."* Even the multiplication of the loaves did not change them.

Though Jesus may be "standing on the shore", He sees us clearly and feels compassion for us as we "strain at the oars" of our lives. At the right moment He decides to glide across the water and pay us a surprise visit. Not expecting Him, because we weren't even calling out to Him, we may at first be terrified. Then Jesus tells us in the midst of our personal storms, *"Take courage; It is I. Don't be afraid."* If we let Him into the boat, the winds and the waves of our lives will suddenly cease; peace will again overcome us.

The boat is our current situation in life. It is possible, though, that even after Jesus calms the water, our hearts, like those of the disciples, can remain hardened. We need to take a step beyond letting Jesus in the boat; we need to let Him into our hearts to soften them with His compassion.

What holds us back most in life is <u>fear</u>. We are afraid of things falling apart, afraid of not having enough money, afraid of getting sick, afraid of losing control, afraid of not being perfect, afraid of what God might ask of us, afraid to speak up and witness for Jesus. It is tough for God to use us when our hearts are imprisoned by fear.

So what is the solution? John tells us today (1 Jn 4:11-18) that *"perfect love casts out all fear."* When our hearts are overflowing with God's love, there is no room for fear to hang out with us. John tells us that *"fear has to do with punishment. The one who fears is not made perfect in love."* This may sound like an ideal that is impossible to achieve, yet we have thousands of saints who have gone before us who had become so perfect in love that they even gave up their lives willingly for Jesus. And Paul makes it clear to us that we are all "called to be saints." This is a universal vocation for all Christians.

Poor in spirit, we go before our loving Father with our empty cups and ask Him to fill them to the brim with His love. As this becomes our daily practice, we will find ourselves telling others: "Have courage, Jesus is with us, don't be afraid."

"He will take pity on the weak and the needy, and save the needy from death." (Ps 72:13)

"Jesus fill me with Your love and drive out all of my fears. Come again into my life this day, calm my inner storms, and soften those parts of my heart that have become hardened."

Bombardment of Epiphanies

I learned today that Epiphany is a season of "epiphanies". In the Gospel selections given us by the Church, each day tells of another "epiphany" that accompanied Jesus' entrance into the world. The Church is accenting the unusual manifestations of God seen in the works of Jesus. Yesterday, Jesus walked on the water; the day before, He multiplied bread and fish; today He amazed people in the synagogue. It is as though the Church is "bombarding" us with epiphanies to amaze us about the significance of Jesus coming into the world.

We read today (Lk 4:14-22) that Jesus, *"returned to Galilee in the power of the Spirit."* He had been anointed by God for ministry after being baptized by John the Baptist.

Jesus returned to his hometown and went to the synagogue on Saturday *"as was his custom."* For years Jesus went faithfully to the synagogue and probably took His turn in reading from the Scriptures. This, at first, seemed like just another routine synagogue visit. The attendant handed Jesus the scroll of the prophet Isaiah and asked Jesus to do a reading. Familiar with the text, Jesus unrolled it and found one particular passage (Is 61:1-2) that talked about a day of divine favor when someone would be raised up by God to preach good news to the poor, give sight to the blind, set prisoners free.

There was something so striking about the way Jesus read that Luke tells us, *"the eyes of everyone in the synagogue were fastened on him."* Something had happened to Jesus at the River Jordan. Now when He spoke it was the very voice of God talking directly to the people. They had never heard anything like this before. This was an "epiphany." God had stepped, literally, into the room.

Jesus quietly and deliberately rolled up the scroll and sat down. Then He said, *"Today this scripture is fulfilled in your hearing."* How could it be that, in this small synagogue in the insignificant town of Nazareth, God chose to announce this jubilee of jubilees?

We wonder what the voice of Jesus sounded like as He read the Scriptures. What does the voice of God sound like? Luke offers us a hint by saying the people *"were amazed at the gracious words that came from his [Jesus'] lips."* How wonderful it must have been to hear the gracious voice of God—a voice that overflows with compassion, love, and authority.

Epiphanies continue daily in our time and in our lives. The stories recounted these days by the Church were epiphanies of the "eyes and the ears." People saw bread being multiplied; the disciples saw Jesus walking on top of the turbulent seas; the synagogue attendees heard the gracious voice of God. Most of our encounters with God are "epiphanies" of the heart. Daily we take time to listen to the Holy Spirit speaking graciously in our hearts. Daily we experience Jesus multiplying His love within us. Daily Jesus makes surprise visits to us as though He were walking on the water. The same Holy Spirit that anointed Jesus at the Jordan has anointed us. As a result, we are able, through faith, to live a life of continual epiphanies.

Beyond this, we, like Jesus, have the power to speak the "gracious words" of God to people of our generation. Do we realize this? Are we aware that when led to speak by the Holy Spirit, God speaks directly through us?

We have faithfully attended our parish churches for years. Could it be possible that at a chosen moment, God will use us as He used Jesus to announce a "new springtime" in our churches? This is not about us having a soothing or impressive voice; it is about "timing." At the moment God decides He will manifest Himself in our churches, and it may be through the earthen vessels of ourselves. We make ourselves available to Him.

"May His name endure forever; may It continue as long as the sun." (Ps 72:17)

"Jesus, we are amazed that You continue to bombard us with epiphanies. We pray that You use us to be Your voice, Your hands, Your heart to those in our churches and to the people of our generation."

Leprosy

Try getting up some morning and putting on torn clothes taken from a rag box, not brushing your hair, putting a mask around your mouth, and walking through the mall shouting "unclean! unclean!" I wonder what it would feel like watching others avoid us and look down on us in disgust?

This is what lepers in the Israelite community had to do as a way of keeping people at a distance so they would not catch their infectious disease. The Book of Leviticus tells us that a person who was judged by a priest to have an infectious skin disease *"must wear torn clothes, let his hair be unkempt, cover the lower part of his face, and cry out, 'Unclean! Unclean!'* Furthermore *"he must live alone; he must live outside the camp."* (Lev 13:45-46)

Is there anything worse that could happen to a human being? Is there any thing more shameful and hurtful? Is there a more hopeless condition a human being could be assigned? Lepers, even though inwardly they may have been without sin, were the lowliest of the low.

So with this in mind we can better see why today's Gospel reading qualifies as an "epiphany". (Lk 5:12-15) A man who was "<u>covered</u> with leprosy" fell on his face and begged Jesus for healing. What faith he had, for he said, *"if you are willing, you can make me clean."* Jesus touched the man and said, "Be clean." Immediately the leprosy left him. Notice Jesus' love displayed by "touching" the man, whom everyone was afraid to touch for fear of contracting the disease. Jesus not only healed the man but showed him affectionate love at the same time. Jesus was not afraid of the leper.

Spiritual writers sometimes refer to sin as "spiritual leprosy." When our inner selves are poisoned with the disease of sin, we look on the inside as the leper looked on the outside. In God's eyes sin is more repulsive, and probably just as contagious, as leprosy. We, without God's mercy, deserve to be ostracized to the outside of the camp. Yet when we call out to Jesus for forgiveness, He is not repulsed by our inner condition. Instead He embraces us and says, "You are forgiven." And immediately we are made clean.

Society does not shun us when we bear the leprosy of sin, because it can't see inside us. If we wear fine clothes, comb our hair, fix our faces, and say pleasant things to people, they will have no idea of our inner condition. They will want us to stay inside the camp.

Remember the way Jesus addressed the scribes and Pharisees when He called them *"white-washed sepulchers?"* They were clean on the outside but full of rotten bones on the inside. This is a warning to us! We who won't walk around with a spot on our clothes or one hair out of place can grow comfortable with our inner state of being. We can begin to think that our "small sins" are no big thing. And they aren't-- compared to God's mercy. It is by recognizing and humbly acknowledging our sins that we can go to Jesus and ask for healing. Every time we turn in faith to God and ask His mercy, we see Him as the father of the prodigal son walking toward us and embracing us in love.

Remember how St. Therese of Lisieux rejoiced when she spotted a sin in her life. She did not feel shameful, for she knew that this was another opportunity to run to her Father and receive His embrace of mercy. She lived for those embraces. And how many of our sins arise from our hearts that needed love and didn't get it?

Our sins are blessed invitations to run to Jesus to get another dose of His great love. And we know that it is not our efforts that set us free from sin and habitual faults; it is only the forgiving love of God that has the power to do this. Only by closing ourselves to His mercy do we sentence ourselves to a life of loneliness outside God's camp. Today let's reach out to Jesus in humility and experience a new "epiphany of the heart."

"Extol the Lord, O Jerusalem…for He strengthens the bars of your gates and blesses your children within you." (Ps 147:12-13)

"Lord Jesus Christ, son of God, have mercy on me a sinner. I come to You as I am and expose the condition of my heart to You. If You are willing, You can make me clean."

Salt

Jesus calls us "salt". (Mt 5:13-16…today's Gospel). Is He insulting us or what? If He called us a "filet mignon", "coconut cream pie", or even "broccoli", we might be complimented. But salt?

Googling the uses of salt, I found that there are over 14,000 uses for salt. Besides enhancing the taste of foods, it can be used to deodorize shoes, remove tattoos, relieve bee stings, help with sore throats, remove stains, keep food fresh, clean brass, preserve foods, …and the list goes on. Now we can be proud that Jesus calls us salt. There are thousands of different ways He can use us every day. We are His "multi-purpose" resource.

He can use us to heal, clean, improve the taste of life, make things smell better, preserve the quality of life, and, in short, make this world He created a better place.

The "bad news" is that salt never gets any credit. People brag about the steak, not the salt that brought out its taste. People brag about the shiny bowl, not the salt that helped polish it. As essential and helpful as it is, salt remains unnoticed and unappreciated. It plays a "support" role that brings out the best in more important things.

Are we willing to play a "support" role that helps "magnify" the Lord and improve the zest of lives in others? Or do we insist on being "center stage", using our gifts to draw attention to ourselves? Do we need to be the "filet mignon" that evokes the "oohs and aahs" from the dinner guests, or can we be happy being the salt which helped make the meat taste so good?

Jesus wants us to be the light that shines before men *"that they may see (our) good deeds and give praise to [our] Father in heaven."* Light, like salt, is absolutely necessary to see the beauty in life, yet it is also unnoticed except in its absence. Our good deeds are "salt and light" that enhance and light up the presence of God in the world. When people see our good deeds, they are drawn not to us but to our Father in heaven whom consequently they desire to praise.

What are these "good deeds" we are asked to do that act as salt and light to the world? Isaiah takes over at this point (Is 58:7-10). *"...share your food with the hungry...provide the poor wanderer with shelter...when you see the naked, clothe him...do not turn away from your own flesh and blood."* These good deeds, as Isaiah explained are more pleasing to God than even extreme forms of religious fasting. When we dedicate ourselves to this improved form of fasting, then our *"light will break forth like the dawn and [our] healing will quickly appear."*

Today's Psalm (112) echoes the teaching of Isaiah. *"Even in darkness the light dawns for the upright, for the gracious and compassionate and righteous man"* This man is *"generous and lends freely"*, scatters *"abroad his gifts to the poor"*, *"conducts his affairs with justice."* In turn there are benefits for living this kind of righteous life—*"wealth and riches are in his house...he will have no fear of bad news...his heart is secure and he has no fear."* The reward for being salt

129

and light is not the acclaim of men, but the deep inner blessings of God that cannot be obtained through our own efforts.

Doesn't this remind us of the "fruit of the Holy Spirit?" Remember Paul's exhortation to the Colossians: *"clothe yourselves with compassion, kindness, humility, gentleness, and patience. Bear with one another and forgive whatever grievances you may have against one another...and over all these virtues [fruit] put on love which binds them all together in perfect unity"* (Col 3:12-14)

"Blessed is the man who fears the Lord, who finds great delight in His commands." (Ps 112:1)

"Jesus, I am honored to be the salt and light that helps magnify You and bring glory to the Father in heaven. Give me the courage to let my light shine before men even when I don't feel like it or when others try to put it out."

Friend of the Bridegroom

In today's Gospel reading, (Jn 3:22-30) we may see ourselves in the mirror as we reflect on the attitude of John the Baptist's disciples. John was the most popular religious figure of his time. People flocked to the Jordan to listen to him preach and to come forth for baptism. In this passage John is at a place called "Aenon" which is located near the northern part of the Jordan River. The passage indicates that it is also on the opposite of the river from where Jesus was baptized. So John must have moved from one place to another, drawing people from many places to his ministry. His reputation was widespread. Jesus likened John to the great prophet Elijah, and said he was "more than a prophet." To be associated with John, must have made his disciples feel extremely important.

We are told that John's disciples got into an argument with a certain Jew about ceremonial washing. After that they got upset, probably jealous, that Jesus was baptizing somewhere in Judea and starting to win audiences away from John. It is interesting that John himself did not get into arguments or become jealous about Jesus' rising popularity. It was the disciples who fell into this trap. What was going on with them?

This makes us ask the question. 'why do I follow Jesus?' In the beginning it was surely because I realized I was a sinner and needed His free gift of salvation. As time goes on and I share in His ministry, do I still have the humble attitude I started with? Or am I starting to like the "importance" I feel or maybe the "popularity" that my movement is getting? Am I still in it for Jesus, or am I starting to remain in it for myself?

Notice how John responded to his disciples when they approached him with their problem. "A man can receive only what is given him from heaven." explained John. It is not about John; it is about God and how He chooses to work. John went on to talk about the relationship between the friend of the Bridegroom and the Bridegroom Himself. Who is more important? While people wait for the return of the Bridegroom, the friend is the focus of attention. People gather around him asking information on when he thinks the Groom will return. When the Bridegroom appears on the scene, the friend suddenly becomes a "nobody". All the attention is now directed a new way; the friend sinks into the background. Yet the friend is glad, because he lives not to announce himself, but to announce One greater than himself. The true friend is joyful at the moment he hears the voice of the Bridegroom; his work is complete. *"That joy is mine, and is now complete."* John explains, *"He must become greater; I must become less."*

We all want Jesus to "become greater" in the world. Are we joyful, when at the same time, we "become less"?

Humility is a tricky thing. It is sometimes confused with low self-esteem or a "timid" spirit (which is a form of pride, the opposite of humility). When we choose to "hide our lights" or "bury our talents" so that others will think better of us, we are not acting humbly. Remember John "let out all the stops" when he engaged in his ministry. Humility is using our gifts to the full without fear of what others think of us. Yet we do it so that Jesus will increase, and souls will be saved. At a moment when the attention shifts away from us, or someone else's ministry starts growing more than ours, are we still able to rejoice? Are we content to "let go" and enter into a more "hidden" life, as Fr. Cantalamessa teaches, or do we want to hang onto the "power" and "sense of importance" we used to feel?

It's all about Jesus, the Bridegroom. We are honored to be special "friends of the Bridegroom", and the more attention that is brought to Jesus the more joy we feel. We are honored to be part of preparing ourselves and others for His coming.

"For the Lord takes delight in His people; He crowns the humble with salvation." (Ps 149:4)

"St. John the Baptist, teach me the secret of humility. Pray that I love Jesus so much that I can rejoice when He increases, even if I see myself, at the same time, decreasing."

Merry Christecost

Today is the last day of Christmas, and while it may seem to be a kind of anti-climactic feast day, it is designed to be the highlight of the Christmas season. The nativity was just a beginning; then we had a series of "epiphanies", now the climax is reached in the coming of the Holy Spirit. The grace of Christmas crescendos today!

In a way today is Pentecost Sunday, for we celebrate the unusual coming of the Holy Spirit into the world at the Jordan River. What happened with Jesus that day is a forecast of what would happen to the early Christians a few years later at the Pentecost gathering. Fr. Lauer tells us today: "the purpose of all these days of Christmas is to increase our desire for and openness to the Holy Spirit."

We are told (Mk 1:7-11) that Jesus, just like all the other ordinary people, went forth to be baptized by John. There was nothing unusual about the occasion until Jesus was emerging from the water. Then the heavens were "torn open", and the Holy Spirit came down upon Jesus like a dove. Accompanying this action was the prophetic voice of God which said: *"You are my son, whom I love; with you I am well pleased."* This was Jesus' moment of being baptized in the Holy Spirit. At this point He left his hidden life at Nazareth and was anointed for public ministry.

In a way Jesus underwent a "conversion" at this point. Others brought their sin to the water and left forgiven. Jesus brought his ordinary life to the Jordan, and left as the anointed messiah of the Lord. A sovereign act of God had occurred.

Does this remind you of the time you were baptized in the Holy Spirit? I know for me that this was the most significant turning point of my life. I sat in a chair somewhat confused about what God wanted of me, and I left the chair filled with the Holy Spirit. On this occasion several of the people who prayed with me received prophetic words from God similar to those Jesus received. These words remain in my memory to this day. I knew I was beginning a new and important phase in my walk with God.

It is as though we are having the Pentecost celebration in advance. The Church cannot linger around with the beginnings of Jesus' life. It needs to take us as quickly as possible to the outpouring of the Holy Spirit.

Isaiah foresaw this day when he prophesied: *"Here is my Servant...my chosen One in whom I delight. I will put my Spirit on Him and He will bring justice to the nations."* (Is 42:1*)* *"...new things I declare; before they spring into being I announce them to you."* (Is 42:9) The day of promise had now arrived. *"God anointed Jesus of Nazareth with the Holy Spirit and with power...He went around doing good and healing all who were under the power of the devil..."* (Acts 10:38)

We can expect today that the fullness of Christmas grace is being poured out for us. If we are open to it, the Holy Spirit will descend upon is in a new way, and prophecy will be spoken again to us regarding God's plan for our lives. God seems to be sending us forth to proclaim that the "kingdom of God is at hand", as He did with Jesus after He had been anointed with the Holy Spirit.

We have been exhorted to be still and listen to the voice of God in our hearts. We have been exhorted to have our lamps lit and be dressed for action, so that we can follow the promptings of the Holy Spirit as He calls us forth into a new work for God. Let us not miss the opportunities that lie ahead.

"The voice of the Lord is over the waters; the God of glory thunders. The Lord thunders over the mighty waters." (Ps 29:3)

"Jesus today I walk forth with You into the waters of repentance, and as I walk out with You, I open my heart to receive a new outpouring of the Holy Spirit and to join You in the work of winning souls for the kingdom of God."

Fishing

Pack up because Jesus is inviting us on a fishing expedition this year.

The Christmas season is over and the Church now begins "ordinary time". The word "ordinary" means "numbered", rather than "boring and unexciting". Weeks, instead of having special names, are now numbered; so, for example, this is the "first week of ordinary time."

We start off with something extraordinary. Jesus invites us to leave the humdrum of life and go with Yim on what will prove to be the most exciting adventure of our lives. He asks us to join Him in being *"fishers of men."* (Mk 1:14-20)

Jesus walks onto the scene of our lives and announces "the time has come!" The days of preparation are over; the fish are abundant and ready to be caught. So many people in our world are confused, lost, and looking for an answer to their lives. Even within the Church we see so many *"sheep without a shepherd."* Jesus announces to us that God has come to the rescue; *"repent and believe the good news."* Furthermore, He tells us He needs our help.

Being the Son of God, Jesus could have done the fishing all by Himself. In fact it may have been more efficient without the bumbling presence of Peter and the rest. No, He would not go fishing alone; He wanted to build of team of disciples who would watch Him and learn from Him. Today, we are honored to be called to be part of that fishing team.

I wonder how Peter, Andrew, James, and John felt when they were asked to leave their nets and join Jesus in fishing for men? Did they feel hesitant about leaving the security of their profession, their source of income, their fathers and brothers? Were any of them tempted to pass up the opportunity and stick with what seemed safer and more familiar? I don't know. The more relevant question is, what about us today? Are we ready to leave our nets, our sources of security, even our families' expectations and follow Jesus? What are the "nets" that we must leave if we want to walk a new path with the Lord?

But what if we don't know how to fish? What if we don't know how to evangelize? We have no training or experience. I like Fr. Lauer's comment today when he says "Fishing, as Jesus knew it, was more a matter of repeated effort than of skill. If you keep throwing the net, Jesus will provide the fish." We keep in mind that Jesus is the expert fisherman; all He is asking us to do is follow Him and try. The Holy Spirit will take care of the rest. Every time we are tempted to say "I can't", let's instead say, "Jesus can."

Where do we start? Like Peter, we start by doing what Jesus tells us to do. And how do we know what He is telling us to do, if we don't take time to seriously seek His will in prayer? After we say "yes", the rest is in Jesus' lap. Notice the promise in today's Gospel: *"I will make you fishers of men."* Jesus is the one who makes us into the kind of evangelizers He wants us to be, once we yield to His call.

I'm not sure where this expedition will lead us. Will anyone be called to go out into the streets or the marketplace? Maybe. I think that most of us will be

138

called to go into the "sea of our parishes" and let the Holy Spirit show us how He wants to use us there. And we can never over-estimate the power of intercessory prayer when it comes to the work of evangelization. Jesus said "Pray the Lord of the harvest will send laborers into the harvest."

One additional tip: I believe that the secret "bait" that will draw thousands to Christ today is compassion and love. Our profit-driven society leaves so many empty inside and hungry for God's love. If we put it out there, the fish will quickly "bite."

"The Lord reigns, let the earth be glad; let the distant shores rejoice." (Ps 97:1)

"Jesus, today I let go of the nets of fear, self-centeredness, and personal comfort so I can follow You. I want to be a better instrument in Your hands for gathering souls into your kingdom."

Summer Is Here

Summer is here even though there is a forecast of two inches of snow today. How do we know this? At mass the priest is now wearing "green" vestments, the prescribed color for "ordinary" time. Green means that we've left the winter of darkness, awakened to new life in the spring, and are now living the fullness of this new life in the summer. While nature has to wait another 5 or 6 months for summer, the Church does not. It is now the season to live the life that Jesus bought for us and the Holy Spirit has breathed into us.

Remember that yesterday Jesus called us to join Him in a fishing expedition? Today we watch as He caught His first fish. He was "fishing" in a synagogue at Capernaum (Mk 1:21-28), and we see that He tossed out the "net" of teaching. The fish were immediately attracted, for Mark told us *"the people were amazed at His teaching, because He taught them as one having authority, not as the teachers of the law."* His teaching was beyond the law; it had the power of the Holy Spirit behind it.

And then we see the big catch. Evil cannot tolerate the presence of God's truth, and while Jesus was talking, an evil spirit which possessed one of the men in the synagogue began to taunt Jesus. Not intimidated by the spirit, Jesus addressed it sternly, *"Be quiet! Come out of him!"* The spirit obeyed Jesus and left the synagogue creating a ruckus as it departed. Again, Mark told us that the people were amazed at what they saw. Jesus had fished the imprisoned soul from the dark sea of evil and brought him to the light of freedom. This was something that no one else had been able to do. We can imagine that the possessed man was a constant source of disturbance at the synagogue and continually disrupted the meetings. How relieved the people must have been to see the man set free, and experience God's peace reigning among them.

How impressed we are with Jesus' spiritual authority. Later we read stories in the Acts of the Apostles that the leaders of the early Church exercised the same authority. Furthermore we remember that Jesus told us, that His authority is also for the ordinary members of His body, *"I give you authority to trample on snakes and scorpions and to overcome all the power of the enemy."* (Lk 10:19).

While we have been saved and rescued from the sea of darkness by the saving action of Jesus, there are still areas in our lives that need deliverance. When we are quiet in the presence of Jesus, sometimes we are aware of disturbances in our hearts reflecting attitudes and influences that have not yet been transformed into Christ. With confidence we can exercise authority and with calm sternness tell disturbing spirits to *"be quiet; come out."* We will experience results, not because we ourselves are powerful but because Jesus within us is the Son of God who has been given all authority in heaven and on earth.

We are not talking about exorcism here, but the ordinary use of spiritual gifts that have been given us precisely to keep us at peace in our hearts. The enemy would have us believe that we have no authority and must remain victims to irritating spirits within us. This is, of course, a lie.

141

The reading from Hebrews today (Heb 2:5-12) also speaks about Jesus' authority. *"In putting everything under Him [Jesus], God left nothing that is not subject to Him. But at present we do not see everything subject to Him."* As we look at the world around us, we do not SEE everything subject to Jesus, yet EVERYTHING is under Him whether the world believes this or not. Those who have consciously submitted to the Lordship of Jesus are at the core of God's plan in putting everything under the feet of Jesus. *"Both the one who makes men holy, and those who are made holy are of the same family."* Imagine that, we are "family" with Jesus! We go on to read that *"Jesus is not ashamed to call [us] brothers [and sisters]."* Together with Jesus we are the "reigning family" of the earth. No other ruler or ruling body will succeed unless submitted to the King of kings and Lord of lords . (I encourage you to read this entire passage of Hebrews. Every line is powerful.)

"He remembers His covenant forever, the word He commanded for a thousand generations" (Ps 105:8)

"Jesus, I rejoice that I am a member of the royal family. As I surrender more fully to your Lordship in my life, I believe "my world" will also become more submitted to your reign."

Moving On

Today we see Jesus "on the move." (Mk 1:29-39) He left the synagogue, visited the home of Simon and Andrew, ministered at the front door of their house, got up early in the morning to go off to pray, and then headed to the next village.

This was probably disconcerting for Peter. Remember Peter was a successful businessman who ran his own fishing business; he was a "take charge" guy who jumped on an opportunity when he saw it. Why did Jesus go to Simon's home after the synagogue meeting instead of James' home or the synagogue leader's? Do you think that Simon Peter grabbed Jesus by the arm and said "come to my house and pray for my mother-in-law?" Then we read: *"the whole town gathered at the door (Simon's house)."* Imagine how important that must have made Simon feel.

Simon had big plans for Jesus. Here was an amazing rabbi who was a captivating teacher, a healer, and had authority over demons. Simon and his fishing buddies could set up a ministry right here in Capernaum and make a name for Jesus and themselves. The next morning when Jesus had disappeared, Simon was upset. When he found Jesus praying in a "solitary place", he exclaimed *"Everyone is looking for you."* It was as though Peter was telling Jesus, "come on, do you realize how popular you are? There's a golden opportunity at my doorstep. Let's start building on what you started yesterday."

Peter didn't know that the Father was in charge of

Jesus' life, and that He was led by the Holy Spirit not by the ambitions of men. *"Let us go somewhere else,"* Jesus replied, *"so I can preach there also."* Jesus was not called to settle in at Capernaum and to establish a local ministry in that town.

I wonder how confused Simon and the others must have felt?

Jesus is "on the move" in our lives as well. We like to grab onto something, get settled in, and lock into a comfort zone. We like to think about "my ministry." When we experience certain charismatic gifts we start thinking, "I'm a prophet. Or I'm a healer, a teacher, or a preacher." We can start using our gifts to help establish our identities, forgetting that our identities are tied into one thing only-- being sons and daughters of God. And when we start thinking "my ministry", we've already dropped the ball and headed off course. What we do is "Jesus' ministry" not ours. We are the earthen vessels He has chosen to help carry His love and His power to the world. There is nothing "my" about it.

Several years ago one of our teachers pointed out how within the Catholic renewal, charisms are not locked into individual people. Many healings, deliverances, and teachings flow from a community of people gathered in prayer. We are not sure who said the prayer that brought healing or who spoke a word that changed our lives. All we really know is that it came from the Holy Spirit. Isn't this wonderful?

It is difficult at times to let go of a ministry that has

brought us attention or satisfaction. It is difficult to move on with Jesus to a new "village" in our lives. We have many examples in the lives of the saints of those who gave up fame or position to take a more humbling ministry for God. Look at John the Baptist giving up his preaching ministry to take a place in prison to begin a suffering ministry. It is "not about me"; it is about Jesus and where He wants to travel next in my life.

I was impressed with a line in today's reading from Hebrews (2:14-18). *"Because he himself suffered when He was tempted, He is able to help those who are being tempted."* We sometimes forget that Jesus was tempted during His life. And we have a hard time believing that temptation caused Him suffering. We think that because He was the Son of God, He was exempt from this kind of thing. So why are we surprised if we are tempted, suffer, have to let go of our own importance, let go of having our way, and experience the inner pain that is a normal part of the Christian life? How can we help suffering people if God exempts us from difficulties and sufferings? If we want an easy, pain-free life, we chose the wrong person to follow.

"Look to the Lord and his strength; seek his face always." (Ps 105:4)

"'I have decided to follow Jesus, no turning back, no turning back'. Holy Spirit help me to let go of yesterday and its treasures, so I can move forward with Jesus today."

145

Jesus, Healer or Lord?

Today we are given an important lesson about listening to the voice of God and obeying it. We read about the miraculous healing of a leper (Mk 1:40-45). Jesus gave him a "strong warning" (not a casual suggestion) not to tell this to "anyone", but to go show himself to the priest and fulfill the requirements of the Mosaic Law. Though Jesus was the Son of God and would set people free from the Covenant of the Law, he insisted that people remain in submission to God's directions as revealed through Moses.

The healed leper ignored the warning of Jesus, and *"Instead he went out and began talking freely, spreading the news."* He accepted Jesus as "healer" but did not accept him as "Lord". Preferring to do things his own way, the leper through a wrench into Jesus' ministry. After that *"Jesus could no longer go into a town openly but stayed outside in lonely places."* If Jesus had not been able to go into a town openly, He would have never met the leper in the first place. Had Jesus been a "popular" figure, the crowds would swarm Him when He walked into a town, and the lepers, by law, would have been forced to keep their distance. How selfish was the leper to think only of himself and no one else. Who knows, maybe he had ADHD and couldn't keep his mouth shut. Nonetheless his indiscretion did more harm than good. He didn't realize that Jesus as Lord saw a much bigger picture than would fit into his tiny mind.

Jesus avoided popularity. He knew that fads draw crowds but do not win disciples. And all fads eventually give way to a newer fad. Those who were attracted to the "popular" Jesus were not around when the unpopular Jesus hung naked and nailed to a cross. Those who fastened on "fads" were part of the unthinking crowd that screamed out *"crucify him, crucify him"* on that lonely Good Friday morning (where Jesus was again confined to a "lonely place").

Let's not be too hard on the excited leper. If honest, we can all admit to doing the same kind of thing at one time or another. We are eager to see our "movement" become popular in the Church, so sometimes we speak or act indiscreetly. Not seeing God's whole picture we accept Jesus as "popular leader", and ignore Him as "Lord". How many times have we been told to "talk with the priest", do what the Church advises? And how many times have we ignored God's wisdom and done what we thought was a better idea?

Today's reading from Hebrews (3:7-14) backs up the Gospel message. *"Today, if you hear His voice, harden not your hearts."* During the days in the desert, the people were constantly "testing and trying" God. *"Their hearts were always going astray."* We would think that after the miracles of the Red Sea, the pillar of fire, the manna, the Sinai experience, and so on, the Israelites would have been obediently tuned in to the will of God. Sadly they angered God, and as a result He pronounced that *"they shall never enter My rest."*

The author of Hebrews includes this exhortation as a warning to us. *"See to it, brothers, that none of you has a sinful, unbelieving heart that turns away from the living God."* These words were written to born-again, baptized, Bible-believing, Spirit-filled, charismatic church people. So they are appropriate for us as well.

What can we do to keep from falling into the trap of "going astray?" The answer to this is "encourage one another daily...so that none of you may be hardened" to God's voice.

If I am "daily" encouraging my brothers and sisters to remain faithful to their call, this weakens the chance that I will, myself, drift into unfaithfulness.

"Come let us bow down in worship, let us kneel before the Lord our Maker; for He is our God and we are the people of His pasture, the flock under His care." (Ps 95:6-7)

"Jesus, I accept You again as Lord of my life. I repent of the times I sought my own will rather than Yours. I ask the grace to follow You wherever You go, even if it be to the lonely place of 'unpopularity'".

Forgiveness

Today Jesus is getting down to business, making clear His purpose for coming to earth. In the story (Mk 2:1-12) Jesus was teaching a crowd of people that seemed to be swarming around Him like flies. His house was packed, the area outside His house was packed, and there was no hope for a paralyzed man to find his way up to Jesus.

The four friends of the man must have had my fifth grade teacher in class because they knew that "where there's a will, there's a way." If we want something bad enough, we'll travel all over town till we find it. We are touched also by the motivation behind this extraordinary determination—they loved their paralyzed friend. So through the roof they went!

Jesus was moved by their faith in Him, and went straight to the point saying, *"Son your sins are forgiven."* Notice the endearing term *"son"* that He used to address the paralyzed man. Is there a more endearing expressing of love than to say, "I feel toward you the same compassion a father does toward a hurting son"? Jesus was now working out of the heart of His ministry. Yes, the healing, teaching, and expelling of demons was important, but Jesus' deepest purpose was reaching into the paralyzed hearts of people and setting them free. Beyond being healer and teacher, He was now acting as Savior.

The teachers of the law were well aware of the "audacity" of Jesus' words. They knew, and they were correct, that only God has the power to forgive sins. They knew the prescriptions of the law, and the extremes that had to be taken to have God forgive various sins. How could this man, Jesus, have the boldness to claim power to forgive without going through the complicated rituals prescribed by Moses? While the teachers of the law were usually wearing "black hats" in the Gospel stories, in this case we can sympathize with them.

We can't see if sins are forgiven or not. Only the paralyzed man knew for sure that he was forgiven because he felt a deep inner burden being immediately lifted when Jesus spoke to him. The onlookers saw no evidence that Jesus had really done anything for the man. Then, to demonstrate that a spiritual miracle had taken place, Jesus commanded the man to take up his mat and walk. And, we know, the man did just that. The physical healing testified to the real miracle that had taken place that day.

Most of us are good Catholics, prayerful charismatics, readers of God's word, and overall good people. We probably are not paralyzed and maybe have no serious debilitating physical illness; we may feel that we don't need Jesus as healer in our lives. Let's go deeper, do we need forgiveness? At mass every day we "confess to Almighty God" and to our brothers and sisters that "we have sinned in thought, word, and deed." Yes, as Catholics, we admit daily that we need the forgiveness of God.

Our society, in general, thinks it can solve its own problems. It acts as though man has the power to forgive himself, by rationalizing his behavior. Rationalizing is a form of denial; it is not real forgiveness. When a whole society is caught up in "political correctness", it rationalizes away any "sin" that is politically correct. In effect we get into the dangerous game of thinking society has the power to judge and to forgive sin.

Now we need to mention a disclaimer. Many Catholics have the problem of dealing with "false guilt", where they think everything is a sin, and that God is the heavenly policeman keeping track of their mistakes. This is an illness from which God wants to deliver us. A tired and frustrated mom may burst out in anger when a child has gotten on her "last nerve". Then she feels overwhelmed with remorse, thinking she has sinned deeply. I doubt it. On the other hand she can look down upon the neighbor next door who skips church and curses like a trooper, thinking how righteous she is in comparison to the neighbor. She might even feel good about herself for thinking this way. Here is a deeper sin, in my opinion. We need to be aware of misguided guilt. God does not want us weighed down with guilt, ever. He wants to forgive and set us free. He wants to immerse us always in His mercy.

How easy it is for Jesus to say to us "Daughter, your sins are forgiven," and, voila, it's done. We are free to take up our mats and go on with life. Let us seek the wonder of His forgiveness as eagerly as the four friends sought healing for their paralyzed buddy.

"Then they would they would put their trust in God and would not forget his deeds." (Ps 78:7)

"Lord Jesus Christ, Son of the living God, have mercy on me a sinner. Set me free from my sins and from any false guilt that has crept into my life."

Help

I went to a men's spirituality conference some years ago, and the speaker began his talk with the question: "what is the thing that men are most afraid of?" The answer came spontaneously from the group: "asking for help".

What is it about us that we want to figure things out ourselves and not ask help from others, even God? Is it pride? Are we afraid to admit we are powerless in many life situations, and keep trying to work out of our own self-sufficiency and personal power?

Today we read about the call of Levi the tax collector. (Mk 2:13-17). Jesus was criticized for eating with tax collectors and sinners. He reminded His critics that *"It is not the healthy who need a doctor, but the sick. I have not come to call the righteous, but sinners."* The righteous do not need Jesus because they do not believe they need help. They **tell** people what to do; they don't humble themselves to **ask** for assistance.

Levi needed Jesus' help. He was chained to a job and a position in society that caused the people to look down upon him. As a tax collector he was seen as a sinner, outside the camp, condemned by God. Levi had no way out of his predicament until Jesus walked by his booth. *"Follow me"*, is all Jesus said. This word set Levi, the captive, free. In an instant he left his job, left his reputation, and received a new identity—a disciple of Jesus. What if Levi would have been too proud to admit his need for Jesus? He could have said "no, I'm doing fine; I have enough money coming in here to take care of my needs."

How often during the day do we call out to God for help? What does it take for us to realize that there is a part of us that is constant need of Jesus? Do we need a "wake up" call in our lives to catch our attention, or are we able to walk in humility and turn our daily needs to God, asking for His help?

Sometimes we are blind to our own needs and work under the illusion that we've got everything under control. In this case we may need to go to the doctor for a "check-up". The reading from Hebrews today (4:12-16) talks about the equipment we will find in Dr. Jesus' office. We read about the Word of God which is sharper than a two-edged sword. It is able to penetrate so deep that it is even able to divide soul and spirit. Moreover, *"it judges the thoughts and attitudes of the heart."* In Jesus' office, *"everything is uncovered and laid bare before the eyes of him to whom we must give an account."* There we see ourselves through God's eyes and realize how we need his help in our lives today. He will show us the exact nature of our "heart condition."

Then Jesus offers us a simple remedy for our problems. He tells us to approach the *"throne of grace with confidence, so that we may receive mercy and find grace to help us in our time of need."*

Our "time of need" then is a gift, for it reminds us to approach God's throne of grace, knowing that He is always ready to pour out his mercy on us and give us whatever help we need. He is a loving Father who delights in coming to the aid of His children; He tells us to "ask" and we will receive. If we are bound by a righteous attitude, we do not reach out to God and "ask", thus we find ourselves unable to approach the throne of His grace. There is a part in each of us that prefers at times to stay behind our "booths" of self-sufficiency, instead of jumping up, as Matthew did, accepting Jesus' help, and following Him.

"The precepts of the Lord are right, giving joy to the heart." (Ps 19:8)

"Jesus, today when You call I will let go of the chains of righteousness and say "yes" to whatever You ask of me. May the captive in me be set free."

What is My Mission?

Our Sunday readings today depict three of the greatest men in history—the prophet Isaiah, the baptizer John, and the apostle Paul. Each of these men played significant roles in God's plan for bringing salvation to the world.

I am impressed how each of these men had a clear focus on his call, and how the mission assigned them was the driving force of their lives. Isaiah (Is 49-3-6) reflected aloud on his mission from God: *"He who formed me in the womb to be His servant, to bring Jacob back to Him and gather Israel to Himself."* He went on to say that he had been, *"honored in the eyes of the Lord"* when entrusted with such a monumental call. Then Paul addressed the Corinthians (1 Cor 1:1-3) by identifying himself immediately as *"called to be an apostle of Christ Jesus, by the will of God."* And John the Baptist let his disciples know exactly why he was sent (Jn 1:29-34): *"...the reason I came baptizing with water is that He might be made known to Israel."*

Notice the boldness of all three of these men. They were not timid in claiming who they were. Isaiah reported that God chose him for this great mission even before he was born. Paul said his status was that of "apostle", the same level as Peter and the other leaders of the Church. He was chosen to lead and form new Christian communities around the world. John knew that he was privileged to introduce to the world the Messiah, the very Son of God. What more important position could anyone have held?

We know from Paul's teachings (see 1 Cor 12) that every member of the Body of Christ is vitally important and has a specific mission to accomplish while on earth. Our missions may not be as impressive as that of Isaiah, Paul, and John, yet they are just as important. Think of Pope John Paul (whose canonization process has been advancing, now already to "blessed"); what was his mother's mission in the Church? Did she realize that by being a devoted mother and holy woman of God, she was going to set the stage for her son to literally change the entire course of history?

I believe that God wants each of us to have a well-defined vision of our own mission from Him. It is easier to prioritize our lives and to invest 100% of our talents into a work, when we know specifically what is expected of us. Knowing we are disciples of Jesus Christ in the 21st century, and that He has assigned us a definite purpose allows us to be confident and energetic as we go about doing His work.

Sometimes low self-esteem issues block our minds from realizing what God has called us to do. Sometimes we don't want to believe our importance in the Body of Christ. If this is true, we need to seek God's healing. Isaiah, Paul, and John were not ashamed of who they were, because they knew it was about God's plan, not about their own reputations.

Isaiah honestly admitted his feelings of being a failure: *"I have labored to no purpose; I have spent my strength in vain and for nothing."* Paul made frequent reference to his own weakness and sinfulness...saying Jesus came to save sinners of which He was the worst. John knew that his fame would soon fade, and that he would spend the last days of his life in Herod's prison. Their weaknesses, however, did not keep them from being all that God had intended them to be.

What about Jesus? John the Baptist made it clear that while his purpose was to baptize in water, the purpose of Jesus was to "baptize with the Holy Spirit." What we have experienced as charismatics is the fulfillment of Jesus' mission on earth. And, we notice that this mission was not completed until after Jesus ascended to heaven and sent the Holy Spirit to His disciples. It is not for us to judge when our mission is completed.

"Here I am, I have come—I desire to Your will O my God; Your law is within my heart." (Ps 40:7-8)

"Jesus, I ask for a clear vision of my mission and the confidence to work at it with all of my heart."

Focus on the Bridegroom

Jesus and His followers did not fit the "model" that was expected of a religious leader and His disciples. Some people approached Him (Mk 2 :18-22) and challenged Him with the question, *"How is it that John's disciples and the disciples of the Pharisees are fasting, but yours are not"?* When a new rabbi emerged, there were certain standards and expectations that they followed, one of which was to have a plan of "fasting" built into their system, John the Baptist and the Pharisees being examples of this.

Jesus shifted from talking about the "system" into talking about a wedding. The focus on the wedding is the bridegroom and the bride, not on religious discipline. In a way "Jesus was the system." He was the fulfillment of God's plan for the salvation of people; all other religious systems find their meaning in relationship to this one truth. The way of life Jesus prescribed was that of being His disciple, closely connected with Him and drawing life from Him. Jesus is the Bridegroom and all that counts is our connection to Him.

The examples Jesus used were about patching garments and storing wine. People knew that to patch an old garment with new cloth would not work. They knew that to pour fresh wine into an old wineskin would end up in a loss of the wine. To try to pour Jesus into an old system would not work. This was an age of new wine, and in time new wineskins would be grown to bear this new wine of God's power and grace.

As charismatics we have always struggled with the

tension between "spontaneity" and "structure". Following the Holy Spirit was falling in love with the Bridegroom and seeing the insignificance of everything else. The spontaneity of "young love" became a way of life. And, sometimes, "spontaneity" became a "system" in itself, and the Bridegroom was lost sight of. Sometimes we tried to create our own wineskins to hold the new wine of the Holy Spirit, and in time, these old wineskins burst on us. We sometimes wanted wine but rejected all wineskins. This did not work out.

Some ran away from the Church for fear of the structure which they felt might stifle the free flowing life of the Holy Spirit. Ironically most of those who ran off, quickly found "new wineskins" which also cramped their style.

All life needs structure to support it. All wine needs wineskins to hold it. When the structure becomes more important than the life it contains, there is a problem. The answer is not necessarily to throw away the structure, but to restore the life within it. In the context of our lives as Christians, it means to return to our first love for Jesus, rather than wasting our efforts in shopping for new wineskins.

As Catholics we have a Church which is a "living wineskin"; it is alive and adapts from age to age. It is strong enough and flexible enough to hold the new wine that God pours out to every generation. The God who generates the new wine for the wedding feast, is the same God who generates new wineskins that are appropriate for containing the wine.

For me, this Gospel is a reminder to keep my eyes on the Bridegroom, Jesus. And if I have bought into a system, even one that is "charismatic" in style, which I am holding on to more tightly than to Jesus, I am in spiritual trouble. It is a matter of time before my "wineskin" bursts, or my supply of "new wine" runs out.

God helps us develop structure to stabilize our spiritual lives. Without these frameworks, we will soon give way to anxiety or luke-warmness. We are blessed with a Church led by the Holy Spirit, which provides the stability, guidance and authority to help us keep Jesus in focus, and to find a place to both receive new wine and let it overflow to others.

"Arrayed in holy majesty, from the womb of the dawn, you will receive the dew of your youth." (Ps 110:3)

"Jesus, if I am holding on too tightly to the religious systems or ideas that I depend on, please set me free. May I return to the 'dew of my youth', and fall in love again with You, the Bridegroom of my soul."

Sabbath

Who remembers the commandment of the Church: *"remember to keep holy the Lord's Day"*? How seriously do we take the "Sabbath" today? Sunday has become a "business as usual" day for the world and even for Catholics.

The *Catechism of the Catholic Church* reminds us of the importance of keeping the Lord's Day holy. Referring back to the beginnings of this observance the Church says: *"God entrusted the Sabbath to Israel to keep as a sign of the irrevocable covenant. The Sabbath is for the Lord, holy and set apart for the praise of God, His work of creation, and His saving action on behalf of Israel."* (CCC # 2171) We who have entered into a sacred covenant with the Lord show our allegiance to this covenant by setting aside one-seventh of our week just for Him. Further we read: *"The Sabbath brings every day work to a halt and provides a respite. It is a day of protest against the servitude of work and the worship of money."* (CCR #2172). In the Book of Exodus God explains that the purpose of the Sabbath is to remind Israel that they were once slaves in Egypt, and now children of the living God. They are no longer to act as slaves but as children. In setting aside the Sabbath, they renewed the covenant and reminded themselves who they were.

How important was Sabbath observance in the Old Testament? We read *"Whoever does any work on the Sabbath must be put to death."* (Ex 31:15). In the Book of Numbers we read about a man who was found gathering wood on the Sabbath; *"the assembly took him outside the camp and stoned him to death, as the Lord commanded Moses."* We read in Jeremiah that the Lord commanded the people to quit carrying loads into Jerusalem on the Sabbath day. God meant business when he said this. *"...if you do not obey me...then I will kindle an unquenchable fire in the gates of Jerusalem that will consume her fortresses."*(Jer 17:27). These readings let us know how serious Sabbath observance was in the eyes of God. It was as serious as life and death.

So when Jesus and His disciples were picking heads of grain on the Sabbath (Mk 2:23-28), it is not surprising that the Pharisees were upset. Surely a holy man would go to extremes in Sabbath observance and would not cut corners like this. Jesus reminded them of how David and his men overstepped the law and ate "consecrated bread" from the Temple when they were hungry. Jesus took the Sabbath very seriously as every devout Jew would do. He reminded the Pharisees, however, that the Sabbath was a means to a higher end—union with God. *"The Sabbath was made for man, not man for the Sabbath."* Jesus was the fulfillment of the Sabbath; to be connected with Him was to be living in the Sabbath rest. Jesus was not a lawgiver who lived to support the Law; no, the Law existed to point to and support Jesus.

So walking with Jesus on the Sabbath day picking grains (which is not the same as spending the day on the farm harvesting bundles of grain—again the Pharisees were looking at gnats instead of camels) was the highest possible level of Sabbath observance because it represented the ultimate union with God. It celebrated the fullness of freedom from slavery and membership in God's family.

Do we take union with Jesus, the Lord of the Sabbath, as seriously as the Israelites took the commandment to *"keep the Sabbath holy."*?

"The fear of the Lord is the beginning of wisdom; prudent are all who live by it." (Ps 111:10)

"Jesus I repent of disregarding the holiness of the Lord's Day, and also for putting more attention on rules than on union with You. Help me again to keep my focus on the Lord of the Sabbath."

Dealing with Opposition

"Some of them were looking for a reason to accuse Jesus, so they watched him closely to see if he would heal on the Sabbath." (today's reading is Mark 3:1-6) The story begins with Jesus going to the synagogue where there was a man with a shriveled hand. Imagine all the trouble the Pharisees went to trying to find Jesus making a mistake. What was going on with them that they were so motivated to undermine Jesus? What was going on with them that they would collude with their hated enemies, the Herodians, to find a way of killing Jesus?

Jesus was bringing in a new order as was manifested by the power of God He displayed. In time He would bring in even a New Covenant between God and His people that would bring an end to the Old Covenant once made with Abraham. As Jesus broke through the boundaries of the Law, His enemies realized that their reign was coming to an end. The control they had over the people would no longer mean anything. Their world, in which they were seen as the "top dogs" was quickly collapsing. Fear led to anger which led to hate. Nothing would stop them in their determination to do away with Jesus. It is ironical that the very ones who accused Jesus of breaking the Sabbath by bringing freedom to a lame man, gathered on the same Sabbath with the "unclean" Herodians to plan to murder the Son of God.

One choice they had that day was to let go, accept the new order Jesus was bringing in, and praise God for the miracle that had taken place in their midst. Instead their hearts froze in hate as they rejected this moment of grace that was within their very reach.

Is there an "old order" within us that we are hanging on to for dear life? And when Jesus approaches us to set us free, do we let go and say "yes" without regard for the consequences? Someone said that God loves us just the way we are, and He loves us so much that He won't let us stay just the way we are. God is constantly calling us to take new steps, to leave what is behind and move forward with Jesus. As humans we all face the temptation of wanting to stick with the "old order" of our lives.

We notice Jesus today and how He acted in face of the intimidating presence of His opponents. He could have adjusted His plan in a way that would have better pleased them. Instead of healing the lame man, Jesus could have said "let us keep our lame brother in our prayers", or "I suggest we take up a collection today and give it to our lame brother to help him cover grocery expenses." This would have been the safe way, and would have protected Him from the "evidence-gathering" Pharisees. Jesus would not bend one millimeter in their direction. He challenged them with a question: *"Which is lawful on the Sabbath, to do good or to do evil; to save life or to kill?"* They maintained an embarrassed silence. Then Jesus, instead of quietly healing the man, became very dramatic and had the man stand up in front of the assembly. *"Stretch out your hand"*, Jesus commanded. The man did and his hand was totally healed. How much bolder could Jesus have been? His action screamed in the faces of His opponents that God was at work bringing in a new order of mercy and love. Was He afraid they might get angry? No, in fact He did all He could to provoke their anger. This was a matter of life or death as far as the man with the shriveled hand was concerned. Had the Pharisees thought of this?

This made me wonder if we allow ourselves to be intimidated by the enemies of Jesus. Do we hold back from letting our lights shine for fear of what prominent people might think of us? Do we have the boldness to stand up for Jesus in a dramatic way even if our opponents are present?

We can learn something from the Pharisees. First of all they, *"showed up"* to see Jesus. Secondly they *"watched him closely"*. Do we go to as much trouble of "showing up" because we love Him as they did because they hated Him? And when we do show up do we *"watch Jesus [as] closely"* to detect His word for us as they did to detect Him violating a Sabbath law? When our eyes are glued on Jesus, we are so set on pleasing Him that we are no longer intimidated by His enemies.

"The Lord said to my Lord 'sit at my right hand until I make your enemies a footstool for your feet." (Ps 110:1)

"Jesus, I let go of the old order and embrace the new order You offer me today. Though I will be hated and opposed as You were, I will remain bold and confident in standing with You, knowing the enemy is being put under Your feet as a footstool."

Charismatic Priest

In the early days of the charismatic renewal I remember people musing, "if only we had a charismatic priest in our parish..." Dreams of charismatic priests in parishes leading prayer meetings and charismatic masses seemed to capture imaginations. And when most priests were reserved in their response to the charismatic renewal, many became discouraged, for they believed that a "super priest" was the answer to all of our problems.

Well, guess what? We do have a "super, charismatic priest" in our parish. Today's first reading from Hebrews (7:25-8:6) tells us *"We do have such a high priest, who sits at the right hand of the throne of the Majesty in heaven."* This priest is *"holy, blameless, pure, set apart from sinners, exalted above the heavens."* In the Old Covenant, *"the law appointed as high priests men who are weak"*. In the New Covenant God appointed as High Priest *"the Son, who has been made perfect forever."*

Therefore, no more complaining about our parish priests, and no more wishful thinking about a "super priest" riding into our church on a white horse! None can surpass the Great High Priest, Himself, Jesus Christ the Son of God. So if things aren't happening well in our parishes, it is not because of the priest.

Then where is the problem?

We now turn to the Gospel reading for today (Mk 3:7-12). The word was out about Jesus. People came from all parts of Palestine for, *"they heard all He was doing."*

167

People *"were pushing forward to touch"* Jesus, and to escape the pressure, He had to get into a small boat and distance Himself from the eager crowd. When *"evil spirits saw Him, they fell down before Him."* See what happens when the Great High Priest of God emerges into the world!

What motivated people to want to come to Jesus and touch Him? They wanted His help; they wanted to be touched by His power. Some, perhaps, just wanted to make contact with a great person the way kids do when they swarm into a rock concert.

Are people pushing and shoving in our parishes to be able to touch Jesus and come near this great "charismatic" Priest who is a permanent resident in our church? We know that everyday, Jesus is present not just to be touched, but to touch people in the most intimate way possible by feeding them with His very body and blood. We also know that we don't have to travel across the countryside or even down the street to have a personal encounter with this great high priest. He is there by our "prayer chair" waiting for us to spend an hour with Him, so He can minister His love to us in a personal way and prepare us for our ministries. Fr. Mike Scanlon once reminded us of the absolute need to make a daily "appointment with God" just as we make our business appointments.

So why aren't we swarming to get in touch with Jesus? Maybe our motivation is still about "what we can get out of Him", the way the needy people in the Gospel needed His healing power. If we truly loved Jesus with all of our hearts, that love would drive us to seek Him daily with all of our hearts. Love is more powerful than need. And love would prompt us to go humbly in prayer before Jesus and ask "what can I do for You Jesus?" rather than "what can You do for me."

The problem in our parishes is not a "priest problem"; it is a "heart problem." Lukewarm hearts are not motivated enough to seek out deeper union with the beloved or to serve Him in a more passionate way. Let us pray that we will have the kind of heart David had when he sang: *"I desire to do Your will, O my God; Your law is within my heart."* (Ps 40:8)

"Jesus, I repent of having a lukewarm heart. May the Holy Spirit kindle new fire in my heart so that the driving force of my life is to love You and to serve You."

Do You Know Your Name?

Today we read of a turning point in Jesus' ministry. Up to this point He did everything Himself. There came a point that He was to share His charismatic power with others, and so He appointed the twelve apostles to extend His preaching and deliverance ministries. (Mk 3:13-19) What a risk that the Son of God would share His ministry with untrained, blundering men.

This was not a casual decision on Jesus' part. The decision was made during His time of prayer on the mountainside; these men were carefully selected by God. And Jesus was not content to use these men as they were; He gave them new identities signified by "renaming" them—giving them a "kingdom" name. Now their old names, signifying their old lives, died out, and their new names, signifying their role in Jesus' kingdom, came to birth.

Simon, the impetuous. loud-mouth, became "Peter", a quiet solid rock on whom Jesus would build His church. James and John, who once were background sons of the fisherman Zebedee were now, contrary to their natures, "sons of thunder." When Jesus names someone He readjusts their identity and points them in a new direction. Their "old story" comes to an end and their "Jesus story" begins.

So when we yield our lives to Jesus and allow Him to rename us, we can expect to see changes within ourselves. The quiet, timid young girl may be seen now standing on the corner outside the abortion clinic praying boldly for the rights of the unborn. The impetuous, ego-centered man may be seen now in chapel spending many hours in quiet, humble prayer before Jesus.

Each of us has been carefully hand-picked by God to follow Jesus. Our call was not of our own doing. If we listen to His voice, Jesus gives each of us a new name to help identify how He sees us and how we are to serve in His kingdom. And we too, though not apostles, share some way in the preaching and deliverance ministries of Jesus.

We have an enemy who wants to convince us that all of this is not true. Working on our tendencies to low self esteem, he tells us that we were not "hand-picked", that our old name is who we really are, and that we are powerless over the darkness of which he is the prince. These are lies that need to be exposed and vigorously renounced. If God could use the likes of Peter, James, and John, He can certainly use the likes of us. Only our weak faith can limit the amazing ways that God can use us when we embrace our new names and step out boldly in the name of Jesus Christ, His Son.

This weekend thousands of our sisters and brothers are inconveniencing themselves by traveling to Washington to pray and speak up for unborn children. Our politically correct society is trying to keep the screams of the unborn hidden from the public scene, and lull pro-life Christians into an attitude of discouragement and even apathy about their cause. "Don't make such a big deal about abortion," they say. "This is just one of *many* important political issues." Hopefully we are not falling for this lie. Our country does not realize that as long as it tolerates the shedding of its children's blood, there is little hope that it will ever get healthy again.

What is my new name? How is God asking me to share in Jesus' preaching ministry today? What message am I preaching to others by the way I live my life? How is God asking me to expel demons today? Do I believe that I have authority over the demons that govern our society, including the demon of abortion? Am I allowing myself to be intimidated by the enemy even if Jesus has named me "son of thunder?" These are great questions to take to God in prayer today.

"I will listen to what the Lord God will say; He promises peace to His people, His saints—but let them not return to folly." (Ps 85:8)

"Speak Lord. Your servant is listening to Your voice. I embrace my new name; in faith I take up the ministries You give me; in love I walk wherever You lead me."

Who's in Charge?

What was going on with Jesus' family while He was out proclaiming the kingdom of God? We don't hear much about Jesus' family in the Gospels; today, however, they make their presence felt. (Mk 3:20-21)

While Jesus was dealing with the crowds and was so busy He was "not able to eat", His family got together to talk about Him. The consensus was that Jesus was *"out of his mind"*, and that it was time for them to intervene and take charge. Why were they wasting time discussing what was wrong with Jesus and how they could control Him? Did they have any idea of who Jesus really was?

It is a dangerous thing to become too familiar in our attitude toward Jesus. When we try to put Him at our level or even "under us", we harbor the illusion that we have some kind of power over Him. In doing this we risk the welfare of our own souls!

Even Mary, His mother, learned early in life that she was not in charge of Jesus. Remember when Jesus was twelve and the Father called Him to teach in the Temple? Mary learned that Jesus was called to do *"His Father's business"*, not the family's business. Too bad the rest of His family wasn't there that day to learn more about who Jesus really was.

Contrast the attitude of Jesus' family with what is said about Jesus in today's word from the Book of Hebrews (9:2-3, 11-14). *"When Christ came as high priest...He went through a greater and more perfect tabernacle that is not man-made...not a part of this creation."* He was worthy to enter the "Most Holy Place", and the offering of His blood was so powerful that it was able to, *"cleanse our consciences from acts that lead to death, so that we may serve the living God."* Remember, only the high priest was allowed to enter the Holy of Holies, and then only once a year. Jesus was entering a tabernacle that far exceeds, in importance, the Holy of Holies. He is beyond the greatest of the greatest!

Were the members of Jesus' family who decided to step into His business even faintly aware of who it was they were trying to take charge of? They were trying to manipulate the Son of God, the great High Priest, the Lamb that was slain for our sins. They were trying to direct the very course of God's plan for the history of the world. What pride! What presumption!

When we receive Jesus as Lord and Savior and become members of His family on earth, and even share in His ministry to the Church, we are humbled and honored that such a great gift is bestowed upon us. In time, though, we run the risk of becoming so comfortable in our relationship with Jesus that we think we can take charge of Him, maybe by trying to take charge of the Church. There is a danger of being overtaken by a "spirit of superiority", to the point that we think we stand above the Church and even above Jesus.

As a matter of fact, when we give our lives to Jesus, we become His *servants* and no longer have charge even of our own lives, much less His. I hear stories of some priests and Church employees who confidently assert opinions that are contrary to the teachings of the Church. They forget that the more important we are in the Church, the heavier is our responsibility to submit to Jesus as Lord and the Church as extension of His ministry.

Let us not become prey to the temptation to take charge of Jesus. Had His family been busy seeking the kingdom of God and repenting at the announcement of the Good News, they wouldn't have had time to plot a plan to take over Jesus' life.

"God reigns over the nations; God is seated on His holy throne." (Ps 47:8)

"Jesus, I honor You as my Lord and rejoice that I am Your chosen servant. Remind me daily that You are in charge and I am not. Not my will but Yours be done."

Zebulun and Naphtali

Whoever heard of Zebulun and Naphtali? These are two sons of Jacob whom we know little about. They inherited a forsaken land in the northern part of Palestine about as far away from Jerusalem as you could get. They seem to be the "nobodies" of Israel. They are described by Isaiah as *"people walking in darkness"* and as *"those living in the land of the shadow of death."* (see today's reading Is 8:23-9:3).

This was not an advisable place for a new rabbi to begin his ministry; yet this is exactly where Jesus first camped out. *"Leaving Nazareth, He [Jesus] went and lived in Capernaum, which was by the lake in the area of Zebulun and Naphtali"* (see Mt 4:12-23 for the rest of today's Gospel reading). Why did the Holy Spirit lead Jesus to establish His ministry in this place of darkness instead of an area closer to Jerusalem?

Jesus is The Light of the world. *"The Light shines in the darkness, and the darkness cannot put It out."* (Jn 1:5) Where better to plant a powerful light than in a place of deepest darkness? People who believe they are already living in light do not need the *"light of the world."* The unlikely choice of the forsaken "land of darkness", tells us from the beginning that the salvation God brings through Jesus is for the entire world. **No one,** no matter how deep their darkness, is excluded from God's free gift. In Jesus everyone has hope; and the gift He gives is always available.

This is the Good News that we have been entrusted with. Jesus says to us *"You are the light of the world."*

(Mt 5:14).   With Jesus alive in our hearts we too have the power within us to overcome all darkness. And we were given this light not just for ourselves but to light up the darkest regions of our world. Jesus reminded us of the common sense truth that no one lights a lamp and puts it under a bowl. Rather he lights the lamp and puts it on a lampstand so everyone in the house can see. Did God light us up with the Holy Spirit so we can hide inside our houses for fear that those in darkness would see the light?

We like to hang out where there is already plenty of light. We feel safer there. Yet God wants to send His light to places that need it—to *"people walking in darkness."*

In the verses prior to the ones we read today from Isaiah, we get a more detailed account of what it was like with those who walked in the land of darkness. *"Distressed and hungry, they will roam through the land; when they are famished they will become enraged, and looking upward they will curse their king and their God. Then they will look to the earth and see only distress and darkness and fearful gloom, and they will be thrust into utter darkness."* (Is 8:21-22)   In attempting to fight their own way out of darkness, the people consulted fortune tellers and mediums. (Is 8:19) The more they sought an answer in the wrong places, the more miserable they became.

Does this land of Zebulun and Naphtali sound anything like our world today, a world that has been described as living in a "culture of death."? We are in a prideful world that thinks it can find its own solution to its darkness. When other solutions fail, maybe people will

177

turn to the only "light" there is—Jesus Christ the Son of God!

We praise and thank God that we have found the solution to life and have allowed the Holy Spirit to come into our hearts. Now we bring hope to those who are engulfed in the darkness of life's problems. God will send us to many people who have lost their way and are desperately looking for a way out of their darkness. When we share the light of Jesus with them, they will at last experience the hope they need.

"The Lord is my light and my salvation, whom need I fear." (Ps 27:1)

"Jesus, I ask for the courage to bring Your light even into the 'land of he shadow of death'. Let me be a beacon of hope to those who are caught up in the whirlwind of despair."

Sin Against the Holy Spirit

Enter again those pesky "teachers of the Law". They came all the way from Jerusalem to Capernaum to "straighten things out." They tried to discredit Jesus by explaining to the people that *"He is possessed by Beelzebub. By the prince of demons he is driving out demons."* (Gospel today is from Mark 3:12-30). Jesus quickly refuted their empty claim and went on to warn them that if they chose to blaspheme the Holy Spirit there was no hope for them for they would be *"guilty of an eternal sin."*

What terrible thing did Jesus do to motivate the religious leaders (my guess they were overweight and out-of-shape, not likely to want to go to the trouble to walk all the way to Galilee) to take such extremes measures to shut Jesus down? Was it the fact that He was a prayerful man who never sinned? Was it that He taught with authority and attracted great crowds? Was it the fact that He was filled with compassion and healed people? Was it that demons cowered in His presence and ran at His command? What law did Jesus break?

Were you ever sound asleep in a dark room when someone burst into the room and flipped on the lights? This happened to me several times while I was in the hospital; an energetic nurse burst into the room, flipped on the overhead lights, and stuck a thermometer in my mouth. You can imagine how angry I felt, and I let the nurse know it, too. I would have done anything to turn off that switch.

Jesus flipped on a bright light in the midst of the darkness of his times. Not only did he flip on the light, He was the light that came to shatter the darkness. John in his Gospel explains it this way: *"Light has come into the world, but men loved darkness instead of the light because their deeds were evil. Everyone who does evil hates the light, and will not come into the light for fear that his deeds will be exposed."* Those who believed that the dead Law had the power to save, and made their living teaching and defending this law, were living in darkness. They were careful to keep their own sins hidden from the people, and led others to believe they were on the edge of perfection. Then along came the "Light" who exposed the true contents of their hearts and threatened their very existence. No wonder they were mad enough to walk all the way to Capernaum to try to turn off the light.

Of course when the "light" is God's own Son they were wasting their time trying to turn it off. Jesus was here to stay until the end of time. His light has continued to shine through every age of the church, and the powers of darkness always came out losers when they resisted Him.

The good news is that thousands who were trapped in the dungeon of darkness, did welcome the light being flipped on. They were happy to be healed, enlightened, set free of demons, and giving hope about their future and the future of Israel. It was the poor, the sick, and the outcasts who were able to welcome Jesus with joy.

Jesus proclaimed the Good News that the "kingdom of God" had come. What is this "kingdom of God" that we hear so much talk about at Church. Is it the ideal world where everyone loves each other—the world envisioned by the hippies of the 60's? Is it the Catholic

Church? Is it the United States of America as described in the promotional speeches of ambitious politicians? Is it perfect self-fulfillment?

I believe the "kingdom of God" was the presence of the Holy Spirit in Jesus. The kingdom of God was "at hand" when Jesus appeared on the earth. This kingdom became available to humans after the death, resurrection, and ascension of Jesus when the Holy Spirit was breathed into the hearts of believers. "The kingdom of God is within you," Jesus taught.

If people believe that the Holy Spirit, present in Jesus, is in reality Beelzebub, they commit the "eternal sin." To believe that the Holy Spirit is in fact an evil spirit is a sin that, *"will never be forgiven."*

The key issue today continues to be "Pentecost" for this is when ordinary believers receive the Holy Spirit into their hearts and are released from the kingdom of darkness. There will always be opponents of those who despise this light. This is reality; Jesus promised that we, His servants, would be treated the same way He was treated. In this we rejoice because, *"the Spirit of glory rests on you."* (1 Pt 4:12-14)

"He has remembered His love and His faithfulness to the house of Israel; all the ends of the earth will see the salvation of our God." (Ps 98:3)

"Jesus, I pray today for the gift of discernment to be able always to recognize what is of the Holy Spirit and what is of an alien Spirit."

181

Is the Bible True

Is the Bible true? Does God mean what He says in His Word? There is a popular belief that the parts of the Bible that we feel comfortable with are true, and those that disturb us are not. Some find it hard, for example, to believe that Jesus really meant it when He said, *"this is my body, this is my blood."* It just seems too far out for some, so they adjust the Word to fit what their minds can grasp, and say "well Jesus was just talking symbolically here."   We remember (John 6:53-66) when Jesus told his disciples *"my flesh is real food and my blood is real drink"*, and, *"unless you eat the flesh of the Son of Man and drink His blood, you have no life in you."* This was so hard to take that many of His disciples turned back and no longer followed Him.

In today's Gospel reading (Mk 16:15-18) we read an "either-or" statement that few, in our age, believe is true. Jesus tells his apostles to, *"go forth and preach the good news to all creation. Whoever believes and is baptized will be saved, but whoever does not believe will be condemned."* Does Jesus really mean that there are just two options: salvation or condemnation?   Is believing in the Gospel and receiving Jesus into our hearts that necessary? Would a gracious, merciful God really condemn anyone to hell for all eternity? This is hard to believe.

Consider this story.   Molly visits the doctor and is diagnosed with cancer. The doctor who is kind, loving, and merciful says "Molly you have cancer, but we've caught it in time. I have a program that will send it into remission and perhaps cure you permanently. Meet me at the hospital tomorrow and we will start chemotherapy treatments. Molly is feeling good and has a full schedule for tomorrow. In fact she has so many other important things in her life that she doesn't want to "convert" and readjust her life according to the doctor's wishes. So she ignores the doctor's advice and warnings and goes her merry way. A year later, Molly dies. She condemned herself to death when she refused the doctor's prescription. Do we blame this on the doctor? Was he really a mean, vicious person inside? No, the doctor probably grieved over Molly's bad choice; he remained a loving, kind, and merciful physician. He offered her a choice; she refused to go along with it and so reaped the consequences.

Isn't that the issue with salvation? We know that God is such a loving Father that He sent His only Son to die on a cross that we may be saved. We know from Scripture that He desires that all be saved (1 Tim 2:4). We also know that our part in salvation is absolutely necessary. *"Whoever believes"* means that it is our free choice to say "yes" or "no" to God's plan for us. Jesus is the way back to the Father; there is no other way. He told Nicodemus that unless a man is born again of water and the Holy Spirit, he cannot enter the kingdom of God. This sounds rather "narrow" of God, doesn't it? Yet it is the truth. We know that unless we plug the vacuum into the wall, it will not work. That doesn't mean the vacuum manufacturer was "narrow"; it's just the way the machine was designed.

Today we celebrate the feast of St. Paul's conversion. Here we have a dramatic testimony of what it means to "believe in the good news", and what a significant decision it is to follow Jesus. Paul said "yes" to God's invitation and his life went from murderer to evangelist. So much did he believe the reality of the good news— and the salvation/condemnation option—that his heart was ablaze convincing people of this truth.

Is this "bottom line Gospel talk" relevant to us, who already believe in the good news and have made a decision for Jesus? Yes it is for two reasons. First it helps us maintain the same healthy fear Paul had when he wrote that he treated his body hard so that after calling others to the contest, he, himself would not be disqualified. (1 Cor 9:27) Secondly, when the truth of the Gospel burns in our hearts, we become impassioned to bring God's truth to "the world" that God so loves that He allowed His only son to be crucified that it might be saved.

"For how great is His love toward us." (Ps 117:2)

"St. Paul, intercede for us that we have the same passion for saving souls as you did. Pray that we will not redefine God's word to fit our fancies, but that we let it be the two-edged sword that awakens the true contents of our hearts."

Seed and Soil

Please read today's Gospel parable (Mk 4:1-20) and decide which of the four categories below best fits most of the people you know, and which fits you. And which fits the way you would like to be? The scattered seed falls in four places:

1. The path the surrounds the field
2. The rocky places
3. Among the thorns
4. The good soil

Each of us fits one of these categories, and it is important to know into which we fit.

Never in history has the seed of God's Word been spread so prolifically. Christian churches exist in most neighborhoods (there are at least 4 within walking distance of my house). God's word is given out over the radio, on TV, in books for sale in the supermarket, through the witness of the many Christians we live with or work with. Is there anyone who hasn't had some of this seed scattered on the ground of his/her mind?

I think most of the world falls into category number one. People hear the word and for a moment wonder if it might be true. Then a little bird comes by, grabs the thought and flies off with it. Before we have allowed the seed to be tossed around in our minds, we are off to the next urgent matter of our lives. And even for those who give longer consideration to the Word, there are larger birds, like those who belittle Christianity on TV, that are ready to pull it out of our minds before it has time to root.

The category I am most concerned about is number three—the thorns. We live in a "hyper busy" world that generates distractions by the millions. Notice the three "species" of thorns that we have to cope with:

1) Worries of life
2) Deceitfulness of wealth, and
3) Desires for other things (other than the inner life of the Holy Spirit).

Can any of us say that we can go through a day "worry free"? - And what about money issues? How much time do we spend earning, saving, spending, and worrying about money—either ours or our children's? And think about the category of "desiring other things". What are some of the desires that drive us? - New products for our homes, recreational needs, the latest product that will eliminate all of our pains. Are any of these thorns present in the gardens of our heart, slowly choking out the vibrant life of the Holy Spirit in us? If so, we need to take immediate action, just the way a farmer would do when he sees his crop being choked out by intruding thorns. Let's ask "is my spiritual life slumping?"

I will now be a "mind reader" and guess which of the categories you would like to describe yourself at this moment in your life. Is it category "#4"? Good soil is not just an accident of nature. A farmer spends many hours tilling the soil, removing rocks and thorns, fertilizing the soil, and seeing that it gets sufficient water. Applied to our own hearts this means we take necessary means to nurture the life of the Holy Spirit within us. Do we expose our inner life to the sunshine of prayer and the nourishment of the Eucharist and God's Word? Do we deal with sin and imbalance in our lives by talking it over with others, repenting, and using the sacrament of Reconciliation regularly? Do we seek out healthy fellowship and develop Christian relationships that support us, nourish us, and help correct us as we seek to keep the ground of our hearts at quality level?

A careless farmer soon finds that weeds have taken over parts of his field, and some of his crops are wilting for lack of care. Jesus and us are a team tending to the soil of our hearts helping it to be a place where His Word can flourish and produce an abundant crop— maybe even "100 times" what was sown. In the midst of the demands of life, let us not neglect to keep enriching the soil of our hearts."

We also remember that God has empowered us with the Holy Spirit so we can partner with him in making sure His Word is scattered to every nook and cranny of the world. We are "sowers" of the seed as well as the ground that absorbs it.

"Sing to the Lord, praise his name; proclaim his salvation day after day." (Ps 96:2)

"Sts. Timothy and Titus, who gave your lives in maintaining good soil in the early church, intercede for us that we remain fertile ground that will produce fruit *100-fold to enrich the life of God's kingdom in our day."*

Stinginess

The message for me in today's Gospel reading (Mk 4:21-25) is "don't be stingy with what God gave you."

Today I watched "salt trucks" go up and down the streets to combat the ice and snow that has accumulated there. Imagine "Joe the salter" being stingy with the salt, because he wants to save most of the salt for his own needs and maybe those of his family. Salt was given to bring protection and help to the city. It was not meant to be saved for Joe's personal purposes. Joe is being stingy and dishonest at the same time.

Jesus talks about lighting lamps. If someone gives me a beautiful lamp for my house, and I store it under my bed, thinking maybe some day I can sell it for a profit, I not only do myself and my family a disservice, but also insult my friend who gave me the gift. A lamp is meant to be used to add light for all those who are in the house.

Jesus also talks to us about being generous in giving. *"With the measure you use, it will be measured to you—and even more."* If we are generous in sharing the gifts God has given us, He will be even more generous in filling our needs. On the other hand if we are stingy, we close ourselves to much of what God wants to give us.

Today is the feast day of St. Angela Merici, the founder of the Ursuline Sisters. If she was stingy with her gifts and her time, those of us who had the services of the Ursuline sisters would be less blessed than we are. And if the Ursuline Sisters had not given their lives in God's service, I for one, would have missed out on one of the greatest experiences of my life.

Hebrews exhorts us today (Heb 10: 19-25) *"Let us not give up meeting together as some are in the habit of doing, but let us encourage one another..."* Stinginess with our time sometimes keeps us from going to Church and prayer meetings. We hear: "I have outgrown prayer meetings; I get nothing out of them any more; I find them boring; besides I want to watch the Cards on TV this evening." I...I...I... Has Jesus been pushed aside in my life and the god named "I" taken His place? We go to our meetings to share our gifts, not to be entertained. If I stay home to watch the Cards, someone misses out on the gift that I have to share for building up the Body of Christ. Are my decisions dictated by the Holy Spirit or by a "spirit of stinginess?"

Now for a disclaimer. Some have a problem of "indiscriminate giving". This appears as generosity but is actually generated by false guilt and maybe by personal insecurity regarding one's salvation. "Christian giving" is guided by the Holy Spirit and is driven by love of God, not guilt or fear.

The second disclaimer is this. There is a psychological illness called "codependency." In this case a person centers his/her life on filling the needs of someone else, and at the same time neglects his/her own needs. Sometimes a low self-esteem problem has the person thinking that they are not important and the other person is. We do someone a disservice when we rob them of the opportunity to take responsibility for their own lives. And we do ourselves a grave disservice when we fail to love ourselves enough to take sufficient care of our own needs. We are to love ourselves as well as others just as Jesus loves us. (John 15:12)

Neither "indiscriminate giving" nor "codependency" glorifies God. These are indications that we probably need to seek "inner healing".

The reading from Hebrews also reminds us of the magnificent love God has shown us in Jesus. He has opened for us a way to enter the Most Holy Place, by the blood of Jesus. He has sprinkled our hearts, *"to cleanse us from a guilty conscience"* and our bodies he has, *"washed with pure water."* Through the gift of the Holy Spirit we have received a hope that few others have. After being so blessed by God, how can we be stingy with these gifts he has given us?

"Make the Lord your only delight and He will give you the desires of your heart." (Ps 37:4)

"Holy Spirit, help us to 'spur one another toward love and good deeds...and to encourage one another—all the more as we see the Day approaching.' "

Smaller Is Better

Seeds do not impress us. First of all they are so small we can barely see them. Secondly they take too long to become something worthwhile.

Yet, when searching for a way to describe the kingdom of God, Jesus used the analogy of seeds. (Mk 4:26-34). In the first parable of today's Gospel, Jesus spoke about the mystery of a seed. It starts off small and never stops growing. It doesn't take off at 4:30 and wait until 8:00 the next day to continue doing its thing. *"Night and day"* whether the farmer is sleeping or not, the seed keeps sprouting, growing, and reaching toward maturity. Jesus reminds us that even the farmer *"does not know how"* this happens. At a given moment after the seed has produced stalk, head, and kernel (stages of growth), it reaches maturity and is harvested.

Jesus said that this is how the kingdom of God happens in us. In the beginning we say "yes" and allow God to plant the seed of the Holy Spirit within our hearts. We may notice some initial change in our lives, but we may not see any spectacular growth taking place. Being Americans who like to see "instant everythings", we may lose our patience with the little, take-your-time, seed and abandon it for something that gives us quicker results. Many have become discouraged with the slow progress of their Christian life and abandoned it for some alternative the world offered them. And, just as there are stages in the development of the seed, so there are stages in our life with the Lord. We may fall in love with the "stalk" stage and be upset when it starts to die off to allow the head to begin to grow. And then we may not want to wait for the kernel to emerge, forgetting that without kernels there is no point to harvesting.

God plants small seeds within us and among us as we grow in union with him through Jesus. A "bigger is better" mentality may cause us to miss the significance of a tiny new seed that God is planting. Looking for the "spectacular", we may cause us to ignore the mustard seed that God has put into our lives.

God never stops planting seeds. We stay open each day to the new seeds He plants and nourish them with our faith, knowing that whether or not we see progress, the seed of His life and His plan is growing steadily both during the day and during the night. We never know the end results of the seeds God has planted in us and in our prayer groups. Who knows, the little sprout of today may become as large as a mustard tree 10 years from now, where thousands of birds can find a safe place to live. Faith and one mustard seed can change the world. Look at Mary's faith walk to confirm this truth.

Hebrews today (Heb 10:32-39) complements Jesus' teaching very well. Trying to sustain ourselves as the seed of God's life grows slowly within us, is not easy. The enemy is quick to sow seeds of discouragement in our minds when we see little progress, or when we see ourselves coming up short in our Christian walk. We read: *"...do not throw away your confidence; it will be richly rewarded. You need to persevere so when you have done the will of God, you will receive what He has promised."* And further, *"Remember those earlier days after you had received the light, when you stood your ground in a great contest in the face of suffering."* We don't want the enemy to steal what we've invested so many years in building, and have, at times, suffered for severely. Having run the race this far, are we going to let feelings of discouragement cause us to give up?

The Life of the Holy Spirit is growing within us even when we are not aware of it and when it is not maturing as quickly as we wish it would.

"If the Lord delights in a man's way, He makes his steps firm. Though he stumble, he will not fall, for the Lord upholds him with His hand." (Ps 37:23-24)

"St.Thomas Aquinas, you who labored so steadily for years to provide a 'tree' that would harbor many in the church for centuries after your death, pray that we work steadily for the Lord and trust that He will bring fruit through the holiness of our lives."

Jesus Takes a Nap

Today's Gospel (Mk 4:35-41) tells us about Jesus taking a nap. I find it interesting that the Gospels tell us about Jesus sleeping, washing feet, and weeping at the death of a friend. When someone writes stories about great religious leaders, do they include these kind of "human" details? Jesus was shockingly human.

The story began with Jesus and His disciples getting into a boat to cross over the Sea of Galilee. Mark said that Jesus got into the boat *"just as He was."* I take this to mean that He didn't put on any protective gear that the others probably donned. This sea was noted for its sudden, unannounced storms. Fishermen probably wore the equivalent of rain coats, rain hats, maybe even life preservers for protection. They knew how difficult some of the storms could be. Yet Jesus came *"just as He was." The* fishermen assigned the inexperienced Jesus to the back of the boat; they really didn't need His services at the front to help lead the way. So Jesus took a nap.

Sure enough a "squall" suddenly came upon the Sea and tossed the boat so violently that the boat starting drinking in water to the point of starting to swamp. These tough, take-charge fishermen realized that they were in danger of drowning. As they worked desperately to bail out water and keep the boat on course, they noticed Jesus snoring away in the back of the boat. The rest all pitched in to save their lives, and Jesus hadn't been helping with the work. So they woke Jesus and they got on His case saying, *"Teacher, don't you care if we drown?"* At the point when their own efforts were powerless, they decided to wake Jesus.

Did Jesus grab a bucket and start bailing water? No, instead He spoke to the wind saying *"Quiet, be still!"* Instantly the wind died down and the sea became *"completely calm."* Jesus, *"just as He was"*, could do what the combined efforts of these strong, experienced seamen could not. Instead of trying to save the boat, He spoke to the source of the problem—the wind and the sea, and they obeyed Him.

Does this story remind us of ourselves? We equip ourselves with many tools to help deal with the difficulties of our lives. We believe we can handle our inner "squalls" using our own efforts and our own tools. Then suddenly a life circumstance arises that is beyond our abilities to cope; our fears and anxieties start getting the best of us. And all the time Jesus is sleeping in the back of our boats as though He doesn't care if we are drowning or not. He lets us go ahead and try to save ourselves.

Then, exasperated and maybe angry with what seems Jesus' "I don't care" attitude, we scream at Him to wake up. We realize we are up against a storm much bigger than all of our resources put together. At last, we invite Jesus into our circumstances. With a look on His face that says "I thought you'd never ask", Jesus says, "Quiet. Be still!" Then, miraculously, a peace comes upon us that, *"surpasses all understanding"*, and we are amazed how easy it was for Jesus to save us. We then wonder why we didn't turn to Him in the first place. We wonder why we assigned Him a position in the back of our boat.

Jesus then turns to us, as He did with the disciples, and admonishes us with, ***"Why are you so afraid? Do you still have no faith?"*** And so we stand before Him humbled and convicted. In spite of our claims to faith, when the chips are down, we do not trust in His promises or power.

It is interesting that the Hebrews reading today (Heb 11:1-19) also speaks about faith. It is the "assurance" of what we hope for, and the "certainty" of what we do not see. It rests on the inner conviction that we are aliens and strangers on earth and we are longing for a better country—a heavenly one. So, we are no longer afraid of losing our grip on what is now, because we know that we really have nothing to lose. Today and its problems are just one step in our journey home.

"He has raised up a horn of salvation...to rescue us from the hand of our enemies, and to enable us to serve him without fear." (Lk 1: 69,74)

"Jesus, forgive me for my lack of faith. Please come to the front of the boat of my life and take over the helm. I let go and stay awake to your presence."

New Springtime

This Saturday we experienced a surprise springtime in the middle of winter, and this happened in more than one way. A small group from our prayer group finished a Life in the Spirit Seminar and several new people were baptized in the Holy Spirit and experienced the gift of tongues. It was as though a new springtime were happening in the renewal and in the Church. Then the added surprise was when we left Flaget Center in the early afternoon: the sun was out, a spring breeze was blowing, and the temperature had jumped to what seemed like about 60 degrees. God was breathing the wind of the Holy Spirit upon us in a new way. Praise Him!

The sense we had is that "more is yet to come." Keep praying and expecting.

It is fitting that today's Gospel was about the eight beatitudes. (Mt 5:1-12). As He sat on the mountainside, Jesus began to talk about a whole new collection of gifts that God was about to give. What are the gifts that God wants to give the world?

What about membership in the kingdom of heaven? Here Jesus is not talking about the after-life. He is talking about what is available now. The kingdom of heaven is the "kingdom within" that Jesus talked about; it is the "life of the Holy Spirit" that fills the hearts of the faithful and kindles in them the fire of His love.

What about owning the entire earth as an inheritance? What about total inner satisfaction so that our deepest thirsts are totally quenched? What about a full dose of the mercy of God that wipes out all sin and all guilt from our hearts? What about the gift of "spiritual vision" so that we can see God even before we die? What about a new identity that will entitle us to be, literally, *"sons and daughters of God"* with all that entails?

Can we think of any set of gifts that will come close to matching these blessings that God is longing to give to the world? Who would not want to receive these treasures? They are real; they are free; they are available at this very moment to us. These treasures are the secrets for bringing peace and happiness into the world.

Is there a catch here? Yes there is. Not everyone qualifies for this bundle of unsurpassed blessings from God. Here is the list of qualifications that Jesus presents on the mountain.

"Poverty of spirit." If the cups of our hearts are filled with earthly desires and worldly treasures, there is no room for them to be filled with the new wine of the Holy Spirit. "Mourning." If we are not uncomfortable with our sins and those of the world, and see no real need for repentance, of seeking God's forgiveness, then we lose out on what God wants to give us. "Meekness". This is not popular in a world where "powerfulness" is most admired and valued. What about having a "forgiving and merciful" attitude toward others, even those who have offended us? What about "purity of heart", in the midst of a lustful and greedy world? What about being "hungry and thirsty" for union with

God, and not being content with anything less than this? What about being a "peacemaker" instead of insisting on having our own way? And what about accepting "persecution" as a price to pay in yielding our lives to Jesus?

Do we qualify for God's greatest blessings? Are we willing to surrender to God's vision for our lives, and let the world's vision pass us up? If we're not where we want to be, we know the steps to take—repentance and prayer. Is there any other treasure in life that compares to what Jesus is offering us as we read His Sermon on the Mount?

Not everyone is aware of the new springtime that God is sending into the world. Sadly, most don't even care. We, however, have been touched by the Holy Spirit and know that this is a moment of grace that we do not want to let pass us up. We, also, want to do all we can so that others can be part of the blessings Jesus is offering.

"Blessed is he whose help is the God of Jacob, whose hope is in the Lord his God." (Ps 146:5)

"Come Holy Spirit. Stir within me a desire to want the treasures that God is offering me, and settle for nothing less."

Dealing with Evil Spirits

Jesus went across the lake away from His home base, Capernaum, to a land of spiritual darkness, the land of the Gerasenes. (Mk 5:1-20). An extraordinary event occurred that was different from anything Jesus had done before.

The evil of the land seemed to be focused in a chained up demoniac who was forced to live outside the city in the tombs. We are told that the people did all they could to contain the forces inside this man, but *"no one was strong enough to subdue him."* Later in the story we are told that he was inhabited by a band of evil spirits that were named "legion", which in the Roman army was a company of 6000 soldiers. No wonder they could not restrain him by their natural powers!

When Jesus landed on the shore, the possessed man ran to Jesus and fell on his knees before Him. Prompted probably by the evil spirits within him he began to shout out to Jesus like he was used to doing as a way of disturbing the people of the town. Jesus, with a voice of authority, commanded, "Come out of this man, you evil spirit", and the evil spirits let go of their grip. We get a glimpse into the divine authority of Jesus. All the strong men of the town equipped with chains and shackles could not contain this man, and yet one short sentence from the mouth of Jesus solved the problem. Later we read that Jesus "gave permission" to the evil spirits to enter the herd of swine. Imagine, these fallen angels under the dominion of Satan, groveling before the feet of Jesus begging permission to live among pigs. The works of darkness can do nothing without explicit permission from Jesus. They can't even hang around the unclean pigs without His say so. This gives us a faith perspective on how safe we are when it comes to the influence of Satan and his buddies.

It is interesting to note that the man ran toward Jesus and fell on his knees. Surely the evil spirits would have preferred to run away from the Son of God who was so much more powerful than they. And the last thing an evil spirit wants to do is bow down before the Word made flesh. Was it the Holy Spirit, the man's guardian angel, the prayers of his family? What was it that gave the man the power to come to Jesus? Even in the case of this possessed man, the forces of evil had limited power.

Now the story gets more puzzling. The people of the town came out to the tombs to see what happened. The pig herders ran to town and told the people that years worth of food had drown themselves in the lake. When the people came out to see what happened, they saw this scene of great peace and calm (like the boat after Jesus calmed the seas). Jesus was sitting there, and next to Him was the former demoniac, *"dressed and in his right mind."* What a "happily ever after ending." At this point we would expect the people to jump up and down praising God and thanking Him for setting the town free of this disturbing maniac. Then we would expect them to beg Jesus to stay with them a few days to help others who were possessed, heal their sick, and teach them about the goodness of God. Sad to say, it didn't happen this way. Mark tells us that *"they were afraid"*, and *"they began to plead with Jesus to leave their region."* Jesus complied with their request. Did they realize that Jesus could have allowed this "legion" of spirits to inhabit their town instead of their pigs?

John tells us that, *"light has come into the world, but men loved darkness instead of light, because their deeds were evil Everyone who does evil hates the light and will not come into the light for fear that his deeds will be exposed."* (Jn 3:19-20)

It seems that the town people were more possessed than the "tomb man". He fell on his knees before Jesus; they tried to drive Jesus out of town maybe because he upset their economy, who knows?

The demons begged Jesus to send them into the pigs; the people begged Jesus to leave town. He said "yes" to both requests. Then we hear that the cured man begged Jesus to let him be a disciple, and Jesus said, "No". Instead Jesus told him to continue to live among the Gerasenes, and there be a light to his family and others who dwelled in this land of darkness. Is there a lesson here for us?

"Love the Lord all his saints! The Lord preserves the faithful but the proud He pays back in full." (Ps 31:23)

"St. John Bosco,, you were a light who brought Jesus to the young men of the streets. Pray that we be as bold and compassionate as you were in bringing Jesus to those who live in the darkness of our age—especially our youth."

Jesus and Women

Jesus, the Light of the world, continued to surprise His contemporaries with the direction of His ministry. In today's Gospel (Mk 5:21-43) Jesus healed two females. Considering the subordinate role that women had in that society, the fact that men were not to have contact with women in public, that children were next to insignificant, and that a "bleeding" woman was ritually unclean, it is shocking what Jesus chose to do. He healed a woman who had been bleeding for 12 years, and He raised from death a girl who was just 12 years old. Was Jesus making a deliberate effort to upset the religious people of His day, or was He showing the inclusiveness of God's infinite compassion?

Let's review what the law said about "bleeding" women. *"She must not touch anything sacred or go into the sanctuary until the days of her purification are over. If she gives birth to a daughter, for two weeks she will be unclean, as during her period. Then she must wait 66 days to be purified from her bleeding."* (note, that if she gave birth to a son, it was only 33 days—a glimpse into the way women were viewed as "less than" in that society.) Next she was required to bring to the priest at the *"entrance to the Tent of Meeting"* a year-old lamb and a young pigeon or dove as a sin offering. The priest offered them before the Lord *"to make atonement for her and then she will be ceremonially clean from her flow of blood."* (Read Leviticus 12:4-7)

Imagine the shame connected with childbirth and the subsequent bleeding. It was tied in with sin and required "atonement". The woman was declared unclean and needed to be "purified" by a formal religious ceremony, out in the open, led by the priest. Can you imagine the shame and embarrassment this must have caused women?

Jesus came to set the captives free and release people from the prison of dark shame that was instigated by the Jewish law. Now let's return to the Gospel scene. The sick woman had the audacity to "touch" the garment of Jesus. She knew what the law said; she was not permitted to touch anything sacred. And we know, by faith, that the garment of Jesus was more sacred than even the curtain that hid the "Holy of Holies". No wonder she was terrified when Jesus stopped and called her to come forward. She had clearly broken the law, and may have ((I don't know) qualified for stoning. Now the greatest surprise of the story. Having healed her and called her out into the open, Jesus said, *"Daughter, your faith has healed you. Go in peace and be freed from your suffering."* Imagine, that He would call her by the intimate, affectionate title of "daughter"? Imagine, that instead of rebuking her for violating the law, He praised her for her "faith"? Imagine, instead of telling her to go get a lamb and atone for her sins, He says "go in peace."

Notice the divine power that resided in Jesus' garment. And notice that this power went into the woman apart from a conscious decision by Jesus. The decision to heal this unclean woman was a sovereign act of God that seemed to surprise even Jesus.

The bystanders must have been turned upside-down

when they witnessed not only the miracle, but the way Jesus spoke to this shamed woman. He wanted to free her not just from her physical suffering but from her inner shame. What kind of God was Jesus representing who had such compassion even toward the greatest outcasts of society? What kind of God would send His Son into the world so that the shaming restrictions of the His law could be bypassed?

Then Jesus continued to Jairus' house. Because of the delay, perhaps caused by the hemorrhaging woman, Jesus was too late. The daughter had already died and the dramatic mourning had begun. Some men came and told Jairus the news. They advised him not to bother this busy teacher any more. Jesus, *"ignoring what they said...told the synagogue ruler, 'Don't be afraid, just believe'."* Yes, the female child was worth interrupting His mission and any inconvenience this might have involved. Jesus raised the little girl from the dead. This is the first recorded "raising from the dead" in Jesus' ministry, and it was a female child, at that.

"...all those who go down to the dust will kneel before Him—those who cannot keep themselves alive." (Ps 22:29)

"Praise you God for Your expansive love. Forgive me for my sins of prejudice and all the times I have looked down upon anyone whom I considered less than myself."

Parish Renewal

When I have discussions with Catholic charismatics, the topic of "spiritual renewal in our parishes" often comes up. When I talk with priests the same topic frequently comes up. We all hunger for new spiritual life in our parishes. Some people think naively that the pastor holds the "switch" that can turn spiritual renewal on or off in his parish. We know, of course, that neither we nor our pastors have this kind of magical power.

Today is the feast of the Presentation of Jesus in the Temple. Hidden in the Scriptures today is a recipe for "parish renewal". Let's see if we can find it.

The Church starts off with a Word from the prophet Malachi. *"See, I will send my messenger who will prepare the way before me. Then suddenly the Lord you are seeking will come into His Temple"*. (Mal 3:1-4). Suppose we replace "Temple" with "parish church." What do we envision the fulfillment of this prophecy to be? Do we see a giant, angel-like creature, - call him "Lightning Man", who bursts into the door of our Church, stuns people with his thunderous voice, fires a few lightning bolts around the Church, and commands everyone to drop to their knees? In the case of the Jews, did they see "Lightning Man" suddenly coming to the Temple to declare the reign of God, then swiftly defeat all the Roman soldiers and leaders?

God surprises us today (Lk 2:22-40). "Suddenly" the Lord did come into the Temple, not as "Lightning Man" but as a 33-day old baby boy. He was accompanied by His poor, unimpressive parents who could not afford to provide the lamb offering and so offered "two doves or pigeons" instead. This was what the poor people brought (see Lev 12:8). No one seemed to notice them except for two holy old people who came up to them and prophesied to them about who this child was. So Jesus was not "Lightning Man"; in fact He was the very opposite—a powerless baby whom no one seemed to even know was there except His parents and the two old people. Are we willing to be like Mary and Joseph, poor and unimpressive, or do we insist on being in the limelight?

Notice how many times in this passage Luke lets us know that Mary and Joseph remained carefully under the Law of Moses. *"When the time of purification according to the Law of Moses had been completed..."* they offered a sacrifice *"in keeping with what is said in the Law";* *"When Mary and Joseph had done everything required by the Law...."* Though they were parents of the Messiah who was, in fact, beyond the constraints of the Law, they did "everything required by the Law." And Jesus did the same even in His public ministry, to the point of paying the Temple tax though He was exempt. They were "religious people" who remained faithful to the Law.

In our eagerness and sometimes impatience to see the Holy Spirit catch fire in our churches, we sometimes exempt ourselves from the rules. We want to try the "short cut" way by taking matters into our own hands or giving directions to the pastor on how he needs to change things. Because we have special charisms we sometimes start "feeling our oats" and trying to take our churches by storm. Some of us in our impatience have become negative and critical about the Church. Others have left the Church altogether or gone "shopping" to find more satisfying places of worship. The key is that we go where God wants us and where our gifts are needed rather than to place that "feels good" to us. If my ear didn't like the looks of my body and wanted to leave, and maybe become Brad Pitt's ear, it would be sorely disappointed when it found out that Brad already has two good ears and doesn't want a third one—especially one as old as mine. A long time ago in the renewal we were told to "bloom where you are planted", rather than uproot ourselves and crowd someone else's garden.

In the second reading today (Heb 2:14-18) we read that Jesus "had to be made like His brothers in every way in order that He might become a merciful and faithful high priest." Imagine how lowly Jesus had to become in submitting to the limitations of humanity. This makes our "submission" to our parish status look like nothing in comparison. Humility and patience are fruit of the Holy Spirit. How ripe is our fruit in this regard? Being like our brothers and sisters we learn to grow in mercy and faithfulness as Jesus did. How to renew our parishes. Keep growing the fruit of the Holy Spirit. As we get healthier, so do our parishes.

Then Simeon and Anna give us a few practical tips. Simeon proclaimed, *"my eyes have seen Your salvation."* In the baby, Simeon saw the beginning of a promise fulfilled. He rejoiced not because "Lightning Man" had invaded the Temple, but because he saw "in the flesh" the seed of promise even though he knew he would not see the day when this promise became ripe. He knew in faith by the power of the Holy Spirit that this child would cause, *"the falling and the rising of many in Israel."* These two holy people kept their eyes on Jesus and rejoiced in the stage of promise in which they lived. We do not see them getting impatient because Jesus hadn't grown up yet, or because He didn't fit the description that Malachi seemed to be talking about. They rejoiced because they lived to see the beginning of God's promise to redeem Israel. Did they take this experience and run to the high priest and the rulers to instruct them how to run their business? I don't think so. They did the part assigned them; that was enough.

I have already gone far beyond my quota of words. The desire for a renewal in the Holy Spirit to take place in our parishes consumes us. And that is good. In humility we stay where God wants us and let Him do things through us His way rather than our way. He will unfold his vision in our hearts and be quite specific about the roles we are to play in our current parish situation. At this moment we can rejoice because our eyes have seen the "seed of promise" already burst forth in our own hearts. The fruit of joy for what God has done will broadcast to others the fact that God has returned to the Temple; a negative, critical, or even bitter spirit will give the devil the satisfaction of knowing he has quenched our joy. We don't want to let this happen.

"Lift up your head, O you gates; be lifted up O ancient doors, that the King of glory may come in." (Ps 24:7)

"Come Holy Spirit, continue to enkindle in our hearts the fire of your love. Let us always rejoice in Your consolation. Help us to grow in wisdom, gratitude, humility, and patience as we watch Your plan of renewal unfold in Your church."

Who's My Shepherd?

We are all sheep who need a shepherd of some sort, even if we don't want to admit it. Some find their shepherd in a group of friends who determine what they wear, what they believe, and whom they gossip about. Others find their shepherd in an over-powering friend who controls their life. Still others find their shepherd in a bottle of whiskey or container of pills that they run to whenever they have a problem too big for them to solve.

Today's readings get us thinking about shepherds. The Gospel story is a gruesome one that reminds us of what will happen if we choose the wrong shepherd. (Mk 6:14-29). Herod, who admired John the Baptist and even liked to listen to him, had John *"bound and put in prison. He did this because of Herodias, his brother Philip's wife whom he had married."* Herod, the king, had selected an adultress as his shepherd. We read on to find that she, in her resentment, directed Herod to decapitate John the Baptist, the holy precursor of the Messiah. Herod had a backup shepherd—his drinking buddies who were there when he boasted that he would give the daughter of Herodias anything she wanted. When she asked for the head of John the Baptist, Herod, though "greatly distressed", complied out of fear of what his dinner guests would think of him if he backed out of his oath.

When we see where Herod's shepherds led him, we are able to check these two candidates off our personal "shepherd list."

In the reading from Hebrews, (13:15-17, 20-21) we are told to, *"Obey your leaders and submit to their authority. They keep watch over you as men who must give an account. Obey them so that their work will be a joy and not a burden...."*

When a church was established, the apostle ordained leaders to shepherd the flock. These leaders were under the hand of God and acted in His behalf. Jesus would not create a flock and then leave them on their own to shepherd themselves. We know that "false shepherds", probably visiting preachers, (commentary in the Bible I read) invaded the Christian flocks. Attracted by the more appealing "charisma" of these shepherds, some early believers ignored their appointed shepherds and followed the more attractive ones. Earlier in this passage (Heb 13:9) the people are warned: *"Do not be carried away by all kinds of **strange** teachings...."*

Now we can check "false teachers" off our list of candidates for a personal shepherd—in spite of the "pizzaz" these people might possess. When we obey the appointed leaders that represent the true authority of Jesus, we are safe.

The Book of Hebrews closes with a recognition that God, by bringing Jesus back from the dead, has given us, *"that great Shepherd of the sheep"*, who is actively leading His flock so that none may be lost.

We know, then, that there is only one, *"Good Shepherd"*, and that our focus needs to be on His leading, alone, not that of any other "wannabe" shepherd.

Today's psalm is Psalm 23, where we read about the wonderful benefits of having Jesus as our Shepherd. *"He makes us lie in green pastures, He leads us beside still waters."* There He renews us and *"restores our soul[s]."* He *"guides us in the path of righteousness"* and protects us even when we walk, *"through the valley of the shadow of death".* So safe are we with our Shepherd that, we *"fear no evil",* knowing He is with us.

Yes, we have found the Good Shepherd; rather He has found us! Now, there is nothing that we lack. Let us not become careless in following Him, nor be misled by the "wannabes" who try to lure us in a dangerous direction.

"The Lord is my Shepherd, I shall not be in want." (Ps 23:1)

"God our Father, thank you for giving us Jesus as our Good Shepherd. We know that through Him you provide for all our needs. Thank you for appointing shepherds in Your Church to lead us and keep us spiritually safe. Help us, through our obedience, to make their work a joy and not a burden."

Heavenly Jerusalem

Today's first reading, from Hebrews (12:18-19, 12-24), speaks of the "spectacular" It says to see it *"... you have come to Mt. Zion, the heavenly Jerusalem, the city of the Living God."*

This Mt. Zion reminds us of the great Mt. Sinai where God appeared to Moses and addressed the people of the Exodus. That Old Testament mountain was described as "burning with fire", a place of darkness, gloom and storm. A voice spoke words that so frightened the people they, *"begged that no further word be spoken to them."* It was such holy ground that even if an animal touched the mountain that animal was to be stoned. Even Moses was terrified by the experience that took place on this mountain, for He said, *"I am trembling with fear."* Such was the effect of a moment when God allowed a ray of His glory to shine directly on earth.

If this manifestation of God's glory to Moses was so spectacular, imagine what is it like to experience the new Mt. Sinai and the new Moses. If Moses trembled with fear, what will happen when the new Moses, Jesus Christ, takes us up Mt. Zion to experience the heavenly Jerusalem? Can the presence of God surpass what Moses experienced?

We listen to the author of Hebrews describe what happens when we enter into the *"city of the Living God."* Keep in mind that this is not a prophecy about what heaven will be like; it is an "on site" description of what is available for Christians to experience now, whether they realize it or not. This is an exhortation

213

written for a living Christian community who were struggling to persevere in their walk with Jesus.

What do we see on this new Mt. Zion? *"Thousands upon thousands of angels in joyful assembly, the church of the first-born whose names are written in heaven."* Does this mean that when we gather to worship there are millions of angels gathered in the congregation exulting with praise before God? Yes! Does this mean that the church of Jesus Christ exists on this mountain, and that its members have their names written, not in a ledger at some parish office, but in heaven itself? Yes! Imagine having our names written on a scroll in heaven! Do we realize how spectacular this honor is?

What else do we see? *"You have come to God, the judge of all men."* Yes, we are now in the direct presence of the living God; no longer is there distance between us and Him as it was in the days of Moses. Also, we have come into contact with *"the spirits of the righteous men made perfect."* This gives us a Biblical insight into the "communion of saints"—the fact that we are in direct contact with the saints who have been purified and taken into heaven (made perfect). Hold on, there's even more. We come *"to Jesus, the mediator of a new covenant, and to the sprinkled blood that speaks a better word than the blood of Abel."* Imagine that we are meeting one greater than Moses, and coming in touch with a "blood" that surpasses the blood at that first Biblical sacrifice, offered by Abel.

As we come to this *"heavenly Jerusalem"*, do we tremble with fear at its magnificence or do we get

214

overwhelmed with a divine peace, and have the deepest part of our hearts "burn within us"?*   We are encountering here a spiritual experience that is hundreds of times more sensational than the physical experience the Israelites had at the base of Mt. Sinai!

Where do we find this experience of the "city of God" on earth? Where do we find this direct contact with the inhabitants of heaven as they worship before God's throne?   What is the author of Hebrews trying to describe to us? It is my opinion that he is talking about the Eucharistic celebration. This is a direct contact with heaven! We have heavenly food (the new manna—the resurrected Jesus present in the form of bread). We have the blood of the New Covenant to drink into our bodies. When we sing "Holy, Holy, Holy", we are joining the Seraphim as they gather around this altar singing praises to God.   In the Eucharistic prayers we call on some of the "righteous made perfect" by name—including Mary and Joseph. Seen through the eyes of faith, we know that this glorious Mt. Zion appears every time we go to Mass. If we kept this truth before us, nothing could keep us from Church in the morning.

The most humbling part of this passage is that we are entitled to enter the city of God by virtue of our baptism and membership in the Body of Christ.   The angels check it out, and see that our names are written in the county clerk's office of heaven. When we realize this truth, we are overwhelmed and may even join Moses in "trembling with fear."

"Great is the Lord and most worthy of praise, in the city of our God, the holy mountain. It is beautiful in its loftiness, the joy of the whole earth." (Ps 48 1, 2)

"Jesus, deepen our love for the Eucharist, and give us the spiritual vision to see what is really happening every time we come to your table to eat your flesh and drink your blood."

* Ref: Luke 24:32 "Were not our hearts burning within us as He talked with us on the road and explained the Scriptures to us?"

Get Some Rest

We live in a society that is addicted to "doing". Many companies are asking employees to work longer hours than in the past because of downsizing decisions. Coaches are demanding more time of players than they did years ago. Some sports are no longer seasonal but last year round. For some people, Sunday is no longer a day off; it is just another workday. And if employers do not require Sunday work, we find ourselves finding "things to do" or "to catch up on" around the house. Students are being pushed to do more homework than in years past and to add service hours and music practice to their already over-crowded schedules.

So we wonder why our society is so tired, so stressed, so susceptible to illness, so anxious, so depressed.

There seems to be no time to rest. And then when we do have "free time", we use it to watch TV, play on the computer, snack, or find other ways to "keep busy." We don't even know how to rest; it is a lost art. Even our so-called vacations are dedicated to doing, doing, doing.

Where does Jesus fit into all this? Is He pushing us to do more work at Church or drive ourselves to do more ministry? What is the voice of the Shepherd saying to us these days? After all, that's all that really counts.

"Come with me by yourselves to a quiet place and get some rest." (from today's Gospel, Mk 6:30-34) Jesus tells the apostles. They had just returned from a mission and were reporting to Jesus all that they had

217

done and taught. People were, *"coming and going, and they did not even have a chance to eat."* They were probably caught up in the excitement and elated with the attention they were getting from people. Anyone who has been involved in a successful ministry knows about the feelings of excitement that can accompany God's work. How does Jesus see all this? Does He say "great job, keep up the good work, let's expand this ministry and make it worldwide" ? No, He is focused on the human needs of the apostles. He cared about this little flock that was committed to following Him. "You guys look exhausted," Jesus seems to be saying, "lets have a retreat so you can get some rest."

Could Jesus be saying to us, "come apart with me, to renew your health, to get focused on a new vision, and deepen your relationship with Me?"

Notice that Jesus told the apostles to, *"come with Me"*. He didn't tell them to go off someplace by themselves and enjoy life for awhile. Apart from Jesus we can do nothing, even rest well. In Psalm 62 we pray, *"my soul finds rest in God alone."* Sometimes we can make, even prayer, a chore—a duty to be accomplished. We can exhaust ourselves getting our spiritual "to do" list accomplished during the course of a day. Prayer at its best is resting in and enjoying the company of God. Remember St. Therese rejoiced when she fell asleep during prayers knowing that, *"He gives to His beloved in sleep."* (Ps 127:2)

Our Christian life is primarily a love affair with God. It is not a matter of "doing" many things for Him. A rich, fulfilling relationship with our beloved is what God desires for all of us. And this is impossible if we don't come with Him, *"to a quiet place and get some rest"* from time to time. One spiritual writer said "more is accomplished in one hour of work preceded by 100 hours of prayer, than 100 hours of work preceded by one hour of prayer." Remember the 3000 souls won over in one day after the disciples had prayed for days in the Upper Room?

Jesus, our tender shepherd, is more interested in our well-being than He is on how much wool we produce during the course of the year.

"For in the day of trouble He will keep me safe in His dwelling." (Ps 27:5)

"Jesus, my Shepherd, today I will find a quiet place and spend time with You alone, and learn what true rest really is."

Living Water

Next to the air we breathe, water is our most precious commodity. When Haiti was besieged with earthquakes, and ordinary water supplies were interrupted, people became desperate for water. When relief planes landed, the first thing that was tossed from the cargo compartments were bottles of water. People came by the hundreds seeking to receive the precious water that was now available to them.

Jesus, filled with the Holy Spirit, became a fountain of *"living water"* in the midst of a spiritually parched land. He came among a people who had been without spiritual water for centuries, and who were hungry and thirsty for a new visitation from God. So when the water of the Holy Spirit began to flow abundantly from Jesus, people came by the droves to drink of this fountain of life.

Today's Gospel tells us about how Jesus' presence affected people (Mk 6:53-56). When word got out that Jesus was in the area, people *"ran throughout that whole region and carried the sick on mats to wherever they heard He was."* How thirsty they were for the healing, saving power of God. And when they came near to Jesus, *"they begged Him to let them touch even the edge of His cloak."* Even if they could get just a "sip" of the water that flowed from Him, they would be happy. Mark tells us: *"all who touched Him were healed."* By merely touching the garment of Jesus, people were transformed by the power that flowed out from Him.

From a spiritual point of view our world is a vast desert of spiritual dryness. People are desperately looking for the same "living water" that Jesus offered the woman He met at the well (Jn 4). Trouble is they do not even realize it. Seeking a solution to their spiritual thirst, people desperately try all sorts of alternatives to the only water that satisfies. In time they are not only disillusioned, they are thirstier than they ever had been before.

God is not stingy in providing people with His living water. In fact He so much wants everyone to drink of it that He sent his only Son on earth to die so that this water would be available for everyone. Jesus' primary mission, as John the Baptist proclaimed, is to *"baptize people in the Holy Spirit."*—that is to wash people and fill them with the living water, which we know is the Holy Spirit.

If God is making His "water stations" available, why does the thirst issue persist? That is a good question. For one thing, God does not force His gifts upon us. He cannot pour water into a container that has a lid screwed tightly down on itself. He cannot pour water into a jar that is filled with something else.

Besides the fact that some are not seeking God's "living water", the people who are suppose to be dispensing it may not be doing a very good job. It is as though someone was assigned to fly a plane of water bottles to Haiti and just didn't feel up to it that day. Jesus dispensed living water wherever He went, and crowds gather. We are Jesus in the world today. Are we dispensing the living water as generously and eagerly as

Jesus did? Why did God baptize us in the Holy Spirit? Was it not so that we could be fountains of living water to the world? Have we let the fountain rising up within us dry up? Have we capped it so that others would not crowd around us seeking a drink? What is our part in keeping the living water of the Holy Spirit flowing out to the crowds of our time? Are we measuring up to what God expects of us?

Today we begin an excursion through the Book of Genesis. (Today's reading is Gn 1:1-19). Notice the theme of water in this reading and its role in the beginning of creation. In reading today's Psalm (104) we see how God is depicted pouring an abundance of water upon all creation. The waters, *"fled down the mountains into the valleys"*, *"springs pour* water into the ravines", water quenches the thirst of *"wild donkeys"*, *"the birds of the air nest by the waters"*, *"He waters the mountains"*, *"the trees are well watered."* If God is so eager to pour water on all His creation, imagine how much more He wants to pour "living water" upon us today.

"At Your rebuke the waters fled; at the sound of Your thunder they took to flight." (Ps 104:7)

"Holy Spirit, fill us anew with an overflow of living water, so that we may help dispense this greatest of all gifts to a world dying of thirst."

Cleanliness

There has probably never been a more "cleanliness conscious" society than ours. People carry "hand sanitizers" in their purses; some churches even have hand-sanitizer dispensers near the communion rail so ministers of the Eucharist can clean their hands. Employees at restaurants put on latex gloves as they put our food on plates. When we spill some spaghetti sauce on our shirts, we jump up from the table instantly and seek to remove it. And what about our cars? How much money and time is being spent this winter in washing the salt stains off the sides of our cars? "Cleanliness" is a value near the top of the list in our society today; would that it were a fruit of the Holy Spirit.

Jesus addresses the issue of cleanliness in today's Gospel reading (Mk 7:1-13). It seems the Pharisees were the "Mr. Cleans" of Jesus' era. They would not eat without *"ceremonial washings"*. They observed the traditions of their elders which required special washing of *"cups, pitchers, and kettles."* And not only did they go to extremes in keeping themselves clean, they took it upon themselves to be the "cleanliness policemen" of their day. They were quick to criticize Jesus and disciples for eating with "unclean" hands.

Would that the Pharisees had been as conscientious about "inner cleanliness" as they were about "outer cleanliness". Would that they would have held, as earnestly, to the important traditions of their elders like loving the Lord with their whole hearts and fighting for the rights of the poor and the outcasts.

223

Jesus turns our attention to what really matters. *"These people honor Me with their lips, but their hearts are far from Me. They worship Me in vain."* Lip service and lip worship disgust God even though they might impress the people at church. It is what actors do on the stage when they perform. They do not really mean what they say as they play their parts for the audience; they are just trying to impress their listeners. Jesus goes on to say that, *"their teachings are but rules taught by men. You have let go of the commands of God, and are holding on to the traditions of men."* The hypocrites are quick to catch someone violating an insignificant man-made rule, and think nothing of violating such basic commands of God like, *"honor your father and your mother"*.

Is there a lesson for us here? Are we as intent to keep our hearts clean as we are to keep our hand, clothes, and cars clean? When we become aware, for example, of a resentment in our lives, do we quickly repent and expose it to the cleansing power of God or do we brush it off with a rationalization like "no one is perfect", or after all "I'm no Mother Teresa." When we become as eager to deal with our sins as we are to deal with the spaghetti sauce on our shirts, we will move rapidly into a deeper level of holiness.

Let's make it clear. It is not about "keeping our souls clean", as much as it is "keeping our hearts exposed to the mercy of God." There is a spiritual disorder called "scrupulosity" in which a person sees God as the "heavenly policeman" waiting, as the Pharisees did, to catch us make a mistake or commit a sin. The scrupulous person is obsessed with his own faults and feel he has to run almost daily to confession. God does not want us to live in fear and be on edge about our relationship with Him. When we recognize a sin against love—like holding a grudge, being jealous, harboring resentment, even judging another—we quickly bring it into the open and turn to the loving face of God in repentance, and allow Him to wash us in the healing water of His mercy. And the more we are turned to the loving face of God, the less often do we find ourselves sinning against Him or our neighbors. We know that God does not want us burdened by the fear of "getting dirty."

Let our passion for "cleanliness" be turned into passion for the real fruit of the Holy Spirit. (listed in Galatians 5:22)

"What is man that you are mindful of him, the son of man that you care for him?" (Psalm 8:4)

"Create in me a clean heart, O God, and a steadfast spirit renew within me."

Stomachs or Hearts?

Once, while living in New York City, I hopped a subway train to visit Chinatown. When I got off the subway, I wasn't sure which way to turn so I asked a pizza vendor for directions. Realizing we were not going to buy pizza he pointed us in the exact opposite direction from where we wanted to go. Naively we trusted him and started walking the wrong way. It took some time before we realized we had been misled. A more trustworthy person helped get us back on track.

Jesus is trying to "get us back on track" today. The Gospel reading (Mk 7:14-23) is a follow-up to Jesus' encounter with the Pharisees. Jesus continued to talk about what really is important and what is not. He spoke in language that kindergarten children can clearly understand. Religious leaders were putting great emphasis on cleanliness and the eating of proper foods. People were misled into thinking that by adhering religiously to these regulations, they would please God and find eternal happiness. Jesus explains that what goes into the mouth, food, ends up in the stomach not in the heart. What goes out of the mouth is what really counts, because what comes from within us reveals the contents of our hearts. If we want to head the right direction in our lives, then we need to focus on matters of the heart, not matters of the stomach.

Though we do not live in a society dominated by legalistic religious leaders, we do live in a world whose focus is on "externals" not "internals." Keeping up good appearances, developing good eating habits, and taking care to stay within the boundaries of "political correctness" are some of the values that are drummed into us by the secular society in which we live. Little is said about the contents of our hearts. Absorbing the beliefs of our society, we sometimes begin to think that "externals" are what it's all about. Yet we look around us and see that those who keep the rules of secularism are not happy at all; in fact the more money and materialistic things that preoccupy a person's life, the more unhappy they seem to become.

"Seek ye first the kingdom of God and his righteousness," Jesus teaches, *"and all these things will be given you besides."* (Mt 6:33). God's kingdom is a kingdom in hearts, not a material kingdom. Jesus tells us to, *"store up for yourselves treasures in heaven, where moth and rust do not destroy, and where thieves do not break in and steal."* (Mt 6:20) And further, *"do not worry about your life, what you will eat and drink."* God sent His only Son, not to fix up the externals of the world, but to point the right direction to inner happiness. While this teaching seems simple, we are so engulfed in "wrong directional" messages that it is hard to keep on the *"path that leads to life."* (Mt 8:13-14)

How do we know the contents of our hearts? Jesus points out the fruit that comes from a sick heart: *"evil thoughts, sexual immorality, theft, murder, adultery, greed, malice, deceit, lewdness, envy, slander, arrogance, and folly."* Ironically the religious leaders who were so meticulous about clean stomachs, bore spiritual garbage in their own hearts. How many of this "bad fruit" was evident in their lives? Evil thoughts, greed, arrogance, deceit, and even murder (they arranged the murder of God's own son.)

227

We know that when we received the gift of salvation and the outpouring of the Holy Spirit, a fundamental change took place in our hearts. God planted His own life within us, so that now what comes from us are *"good fruit"*, the fruit of the Holy Spirit. Contrast the *"good fruit"* with the list of "rotten fruit" that Jesus lists in this passage. It is not always easy to manifest the good fruit of our hearts. It is easier to go the path of least resistance and act as the world prefers we would act. Still we know that the fruit we bear brings life and healing to the world, and points the world in the only direction that leads to life. Let us persevere in the direction that Jesus has pointed to no matter the price we may have to pay.

"When you send your Spirit (we) are created and You renew the face of the earth." (Ps 104: 30)

"Jesus, guard my heart that nothing may enter it except what honors You, and guard my lips that all that comes forth from within me brings glory to Your Name."

Jesus is Outfoxed

We read so many stories in which the teachers of the Law tried to corner Jesus or trap Him into making a mistake. In spite of the conniving of these leaders, Jesus foiled them every time, usually turning their issue back on them. Divine wisdom always outsmarts even the highest levels of human thinking.

Today, though, we read a story of Jesus being "outfoxed" by a Gentile woman (Mk 7:24-30).

"Jesus left that place and went to the vicinity of Tyre." Tyre was a coastal town in Lebanon and was about 30 miles northwest of Capernaum. Today it is a center for tourism, and it may have been a popular vacation spot in Jesus' day. Mark tells us that Jesus *"entered a house and did not want anyone to know it."* It seems He had no intentions of doing any ministry while in Tyre; maybe He went there as a "mental health" break. God, apparently, had other ideas for His Son.

Somehow word leaked out that the acclaimed rabbi who had power over demons, was visiting the town. And a "pushy" Gentile woman, driven by her love for her daughter, found a way of making contact with Jesus. Let us remember that Jewish men were not allowed to speak to a woman in public, and above all, not a Gentile woman. Jesus again breaks through the religious traditions in response to a higher Law. First He did the "unthinkable" and talked to this Gentile woman (a Syro-Phoenician) in public. Though His response seemed to be rude, Jesus was engaging in scandalous behavior—and He was supposed to be a distinguished man of God! To make things worse, we learn that the woman was a Greek. Of all the Gentiles, the Greeks were probably the worst as far as the Jews were concerned. Remember that the Greeks were the ones who several centuries before, took over Jerusalem, desecrated the Temple, and tried to force Greek religion and Greek ways upon the Jews. Rome, at least, allowed the Jewish people to continue their religious traditions and culture. The Greeks tried to snuff out all traces of Judaism by force. So if God was going to choose a woman, even a Gentile woman, for Jesus to minister to, surely He would never decide upon a Greek.

When the woman takes a beggars position before Jesus, seeking His intervention with her demon-possessed daughter, Jesus responds to her. His response, however, seems extremely rude and uncompassionate. *"...it is not right to take the children's bread and toss it to their dogs."* Was Jesus just irritated because the woman messed up His vacation? No, He took the stance that any reputable rabbi would have taken. God's chosen people were blessed with His presence and were a notch above all others. In comparison, the Gentiles were seen as "dogs". The pesky woman wouldn't give up, and reminded Jesus that *"even the dogs under the table eat of the children's crumbs"*. What child does not drop some of its food on the floor—and sometimes deliberately. In effect, she said even children have compassion on their pets; do you not have, at least, the compassion of a child.

Jesus was "outfoxed". Moved by the woman's persistent faith, He expelled the demon from her daughter. *"She went home and found her child lying on the bed, and the demon gone."*

Is Jesus being too "uppity" here? The Jews knew they were a "sacred" people, and that in history whenever they compromised with Gentiles, their faith was weakened and they suffered great setbacks. It made sense that they would strictly adhere to the "avoid-Gentiles-at-all-cost" practice. A parallel is in the way we treat the chalice used at Mass. If someone went into the sacristy for a drink of water and grabbed the chalice to use as a cup, this would be a sacrilege. A chalice is set aside for a sacred purpose and actually holds the blood of Jesus. How irreverent to use it as an ordinary drinking glass. So, likewise, the Jews knew they had come in personal contact with the living God. They had no business mixing with people who were not part of the "chosen" race.

The new Law emanates from the heart of God who lets *"His rain pour on the just and unjust alike"*. There is no exclusivity with God; even Gentile Greeks are capable of being saved and set apart as holy vessels in His kingdom. Jesus, once again, reveals the unlimited scope of the New Covenant, and the expansiveness of God.

"Thus is the man blessed who fears the Lord." (Ps 128:4)

"Jesus, let me be guided by the Law of Love, and keep my heart open to all others as You've kept Your heart open to me."

Is Jesus Reluctant to Heal?

Today we read that Jesus returned from Tyre into the Sea of Galilee area, and people were after Him again. This time they brought to Him a man who was deaf and partially dumb, and *"begged"* Jesus to lay hands on him, the way He had been doing with people in the past. It seems that Jesus was reluctant to work a "quick miracle" for them. (Mk 7:31-37)

Why did people have to "beg" Jesus for help? It seems that if He wanted to build His popularity, He would be looking for new jobs. Jesus seems to be playing "hard to get". Jesus takes the man away from the crowd; He was not interested in "sensationalizing" His work so as to amaze the onlookers. In a private setting Jesus did what a physician would do—the ordinary gesture of putting His hands in the man's ears and using spittle as medicine (the commentary I read says that use of spittle was a common medicinal practice of that time—the healthy cells one person would get into the body of the sick person). He then *"sighed"* and spoke a word of command *"Ephphatha."* The man was cured.

It seems Jesus was transferring His work from the "spectacular" to the "ordinary". Jesus had a mission that went much deeper than being a "heavenly physician" who came to put doctors out of business. He gave the group His familiar command *"not to tell anyone"*, and, as usual, the more He told them to keep the matter quiet, *"the more they kept talking about it."*

By moving His healing ministry in a different direction, is Jesus indicating that He was getting "burnt out" in healing people? Or was He keeping His focus on the reason He was sent by the Father, to restore, not just ears and tongues, but the hearts of people. His ultimate goal was to open the door for the Holy Spirit to come so that fallen human beings could once again be restored to union with the Father in love. If people kept getting hung up with what they could get out of Jesus in order to "make their world a better place", they would miss the whole point of His coming to earth.

It is interesting that the Genesis reading this morning (3:1-8) is the story of the fall of Adam and Eve. Though they enjoyed friendship and union with God, there was a seed of "dissatisfaction" in them. The serpent played on this and engaged Eve in a friendly conversation. We know the rest of the story. It was only after they broke from God that our first parents felt the "shame" of being naked. "Shame" is the fundamental feeling of being "disconnected", and it is most intense when the "disconnection" is from the primordial union with God.

At the cross Jesus took all shame upon Himself, and re-established the possibility of "connection" or union with Father again. This is God's vision for humanity, and it was fulfilled on Pentecost when the Holy Spirit took up residence in the hearts of a few faithful disciples. Jesus' healing ministry was just a step along the way to full redemption.

Sometimes we still look for what we can "get out of Jesus" to make our world "a better place". We are content to go part of the way with Him, but not all the way into deep union with the Father. We sometimes hold on so tightly to one gift that Jesus has given us along the way that we are unable to yield to the next step in His plan for our lives. Getting healed can leave us still "in control"; full surrender to God's will frees us to be totally under His control.

Today, coincidentally, also happens to be the feast of Our Lady of Lourdes. God used Bernadette to release a stream of healing waters that, in time, would draw people from across the world to bathe in it. Ironically, Bernadette herself, did not receive healing from her tuberculosis (I think that was her disease) when she touched the water. Instead she received the gift of "union of heart" with her Father, and in time died at a young age.

What perspective is Jesus trying to give me today, regarding my walk with Him?

"Then I acknowledged my sin to you...and you forgave the guilt of my sin." (Ps 32:5)

"St. Bernadette, intercede for us that we might possess the purity of heart that allowed you to experience the gift of 'seeing God' even before you died."

About Being Perfect

How perfect does God expect us to be? When is enough, enough? Jesus teaches us today (Mt 5:17-37) that, *"unless your righteousness surpasses that of the Pharisees and the teachers of the law, you will certainly not enter the kingdom of heaven."* If I were one of Jesus' disciples, I think I would given up at this point and walked away. Remember the Pharisees and the teachers of the law were the most "near perfect' people in the community. They probably had most all the Bible verses memorized. They never missed synagogue and Temple services. They tithed even the spices they grew. They "out-washed" everyone before they sat down to eat. Surpassing the Pharisees was like telling an ambitious young basketball player, "unless your skills are better than those of LeBron James, you can't play on the team."

Now we know that Jesus came as a "new Moses", and seemed to bypass provisions of the Law in His actions. He, for example, broke the Sabbath rules in healing a man and allowing His disciples to pick grain from the field on the Sabbath day. Jesus had conversations with women, even Gentile women in public. He had the audacity to dine and mingle with prostitutes and tax collectors. It seemed He was "letting up" a little from the Old Law. Now He's told people to "out-do" the Pharisees. What was going on here?

"Do not think I have come to abolish the Law or the Prophets; I have not come to abolish them but to fulfill them." He brought the purpose of the Law to completion by letting it "ripen" into "kingdom law".

235

People noted that Jesus was "near perfect"; they observed that *"He has done everything well."* (Mk 7:37). None could find sin in Him.

Listen to how high His standards are. *"...anyone who is angry with his brother will be subject to judgment...anyone who says 'you fool' will be in danger of hell fire."* His law went far beyond Moses's injunction *"Thou shalt not kill."* He goes on to say: *"he who looks at a woman lustfully has committed adultery in his heart."* Jesus extends sin beyond breaking commandments into attitudes of the mind and heart. In "kingdom law", He toughens the standards of divorce and is much stricter on the policy of oaths.

Jesus seems to be asking his disciples to be "more perfect than perfect."

Only a person filled with the Holy Spirit, as Jesus was, could measure up to these standards. And that is exactly what Jesus is talking about, being filled with the Holy Spirit. We know that when we are baptized, we are elevated to a "kingdom level" of existence. Now, Jesus lives in us through the Holy Spirit. It is possible now to be guided by the Spirit and not by the flesh. The flesh can keep laws but cannot create a clean heart. Yes, the Pharisees had "perfect" control (so they pretended) as far as the outside is concerned. Inside, however, they were *"filled with dead mens' bones."* So once we yield our hearts to the inpouring of the Holy Spirit, we pass up all those who were living a life that relied totally on keeping the externals of the Law.

This is good news! Now we can make Jesus' team.

The kingdom is reachable if we let God reach into us and fill us with the Holy Spirit.

The action of God throughout Old Testament history was like a tree He had planted on the earth. Through the Law and Prophets it grew giving hope as far as the future was concerned. When Jesus came, the tree had finally produced the fruit for which it was intended. In Jesus the Law and Prophets were "fulfilled"—that is their purpose had finally come to pass. Jesus preaches a kingdom which does not focus on keeping rules as much as letting the divine life of the Trinity take residence in human hearts.

Perfection, then for us, is allowing ourselves to be filled more and more with the life of the Holy Spirit, thus letting God take total charge of our lives.

"Do good to your servant and I will live; I will obey your word." (Ps 119:17)

"Jesus, thank you for planting Your kingdom in my heart. Help me treasure this above all else in my life, and try to obey the inner voice of the Holy Spirit in all I do."

It Was a Sign

We watched a rerun of "Sleepless in Seattle" last night. Throughout the movie Annie and Sam were interpreting various unusual events as "signs" that they were going to meet, and of course, live "happily ever after." The closing scene is on top of the Empire State Building where the two finally connect. At this point, as we know, the movie ends.

Once they met, the "signs" discontinued, because they had found what they were looking for. When we travel, we are careful to follow the road signs that lead us to our destination. Once we reach that destination, we don't need the signs any more.

In today's Gospel, (Mk 8:11-13) the Pharisees come to bother Jesus again. They challenge Him to give them *"a sign from heaven."* Their purpose was "to test him." Who do they think they are "testing" the Son of God? Whoever heard of a student giving a test to the teacher? The one in charge is the one who gives the tests, not the subordinates. The Pharisees were under the illusion that they were the ones in charge; they thought they were God's "policemen."

Jesus *"sighed deeply,"* and asked *"why does this generation ask for a miraculous sign?"* It seems that Jesus had "had it" with the lack of faith of the people who were supposed to be welcoming Him with open arms. He solemnly assures them that, *"no sign will be given"* to them. God will not play by man's rules.

The destination of the Old Covenant was reached; the

reality of *"God enfleshed among men"* was present. Signs were no longer needed; their purpose of pointing the way had been fulfilled. And yet the Pharisees want more signs—they demanded miracles if they were going to believe. If they had not been touched by the works Jesus had already performed and His loving presence among them, what good would another miracle accomplish? It seems to me that Jesus' "sighing" is His way of saying "it's hopeless with these people." Hardened hearts cannot be moved even by a sensational act of God.

What about us? Do we still look for the "unusual" to prove that Jesus is real and available to us? We have found the treasure in the field; signs are no longer needed. Jesus is in the "ordinary" events of each day, showing His love for us and leading us closer to Him. The rising of the sun, the air we breathe, the *"daily bread"* of life He gives us are enough to remind us that He has come and that He lives within us. Elijah taught us long ago that if we want evidence that God is with us, we need to be still and listen to the, *"small still voice,"* of the Holy Spirit in our hearts. He is speaking His word of love to us at every moment; are we listening? Do we still expect him to give us a "sign" to grab our attention? Are we still expecting to find Him in the ferocious wind or the mighty earthquake.

We all have a tendency to be like the Pharisees and *"never be satisfied"* with what God has done for us and is doing for us. We have been told in recent prophecy that He is asking "more" of each of us. Hopefully we have matured past the stage when we keep looking for "more" from Him. Hasn't He already given us more than enough? It is now time to do what the Pharisees were too proud to do—let Him ask us questions; let Him ask us for a sign of our love for Him. Are we ready to take the test? Are we going to take time today to listen to the, *"small, still voice"* of Jesus in our hearts?

"The Mighty One, God, the Lord speaks and summons the earth from the rising of the sun to the place it sets." (Ps 50:1)

"Holy Spirit, help me to cultivate the habit of listening often to the small still voice within me. That is sign enough for me."

Biblical Arithmetic

We have been seeing Jesus as teacher, healer, deliverer, and preacher. Today, for the first time, we see Jesus as a "Biblical Math Teacher." Have we ever thought of Him that way before? (Mk 8:14-21) We hear him talk about the numbers: "5", "5000", "12", "4000", "7", and even "1". What is He doing, giving a math quiz?

We know that numbers had special meaning and significance in the Hebrew and other ancient cultures. They were not just tossed around blithely the way we do. "3" and "4", were considered sacred numbers—"3" the three levels of the universe, "4" the four compass directions. When these numbers were added, "7" is reached, the <u>most sacred</u> of all numbers (maybe the days of creation, the Sabbath day, the jubilee year connections). When these numbers were multiplied we get yet another sacred number, "12" (tribes of Israel, lunar calendar). It was not accidental that in the "multiplication" stories, "12" and then "7" baskets of bread remained. God was pointing to the fact that <u>the</u> most sacred moment in history had arrived. This was the "full" day, the "fulfillment" of all days.

And, as usual, the disciples didn't catch on. When Jesus mentioned "leaven", they thought of bread and how hungry they were. Matthew mentions that they forgot to bring bread with them (if Jesus had included "wives" in the band of apostles, there would have been bread). Mark, building on the detailed recollections of Peter (who was in the food business), adds the note to Matthew's account that there was "one loaf". Who knows, maybe Peter had it hidden away in his pocket so that even his buddies didn't know about it, including Matthew. Maybe Peter was including a "personal confession" in the account he gave to Mark?

Jesus was giving a warning to His followers. They knew the hidden power of leaven. Mysteriously it releases gases that cause a heavy, unchewable piece of dough to rise and become appealing to people. A little bit took over the entire batch of dough. And we know that people kept "yeast cultures" which they fed on a regular basis so that the yeast would continue to be available for future generations. Leaven, though seemingly small and insignificant, is alive and can last for generations.

Jesus is talking about the "hidden power" that drove Herod and the Pharisees. Herod was in some ways a hero for he authorized the restoration of the Jerusalem Temple. Was he trying to give honor to God, or was he wise enough to know that his luxurious lifestyle depended on the "Temple economy"? What was the "leaven" that empowered Herod and helped bring about the restoration of the Temple? The Pharisees were religious "supermen", as we know. Their actions proved that they were the most God-centered people on the planet, and they made sure everyone knew this. Yet what was their empowering leaven? What was the "gas" that filled them and kept them going "in the name of God?" It was selfish ambition and the need to maintain the illusion of status among the people.

Jesus knew that if His disciples fell into the trap of mixing a tiny bit of "Herod leaven" or "Pharisee leaven" into their spirits, it could destroy them and contaminate generations of their followers. We see this actually happening in the early church when the leaven of various false teachings misled and divided the Christian flocks.

The true leaven is the "yeast of the Holy Spirit" in our hearts. This is the "gas" that inflates us with the love of God and empowers us to become Temples and to "fill" the Law with God's power. It makes us appealing and "chewable" to those who are spiritually hungry. Our world is generating "bad leaven" by the tons, and we are exposed to it every day. We can "hide out" in fear so that this "worldly leaven" doesn't contaminate our spirits, or we can take a proactive approach, and drink in daily doses of "Holy Spirit leaven." When we pray, read God's Word, fellowship with one another, participate in the Eucharist our "leaven culture" is strengthened and renewed. Then the dough of our lives will have no room for "alien yeasts."

"Numbers don't lie". The "12" and the "7" remind us that the most sacred of ages has arrived, and we are invited to be part of it. The "new leaven" of the Holy Spirit has been planted in the Church and in our hearts. We take warning not to let the leaven of Herod, the Pharisees, or any other similar kinds take root within us and contaminate the Temples of our hearts. Let's continue to study our arithmetic.

"The voice of the Lord twists the oaks and strips the forests bare. And in his Temple, all cry 'glory'" (Ps 29:9)

"Father, as Your voice goes out to our age, twisting oaks and stripping forests, let the Temples of our hearts be so filled with the leaven of the Holy Spirit that we continue to cry out 'glory'. "

243

"Don't Go into the Village"

In the late 1960's I enrolled in a Master's Degree program at a Catholic institution in Chicago. The program brought us in touch with a great outpouring of new life that followed in the wake of the second Vatican Council. There I was exposed to some dynamic theologians who were well versed in the message the Holy Spirit was giving through the Council. I was also exposed to, what I now see as, "false teaching" that had erupted at the same time—weeds had been planted in the field of wheat. During this time of "new beginnings" in the Church, some began to question everything, from the existence of God, to the reality of Jesus, to the existence of the Church.

I remember watching a gifted religious sister literally lose her faith in the process. She began to develop a religion built on the constructs of her own creative ideas and abandoned her Christian faith. This frightened me.

One night as I was going to sleep I felt a force come upon me that seemed to be trying to steal my faith. At that time I knew nothing about the reality of "spiritual warfare", and a new trend in theology was denying the existence of Satan. I was frightened and knew I was coming up against something stronger than I was. Instinctively I began to recite the Creed over and over again, and, as I recall, began to pray "Hail Marys". After a time of struggle, the "battle" ceased and I felt peace come back over me. In retrospect I realized that for days my mind was being "set up", and at a certain moment the "robber" tried to break into my spiritual house. Except for the grace of God,, I would have likely followed the path of "unbelief" that I saw taking place in the religious sister.

When I didn't know what to do, I turned to the Church. At that moment I realized what a gift it is to be able to find refuge in the teachings, practices, and beliefs of the Catholic Church. It was as though the Church were an "ark" where I could be protected from the ravages of the spiritual flooding that was taking place at that time.

The Church's readings now are from the Book of Genesis, and specifically we are listening to the story of Noah, the lone survivor of the great flood. He found favor with God, and was given a secret plan for making it through the flood. How fitting we have this story now. There is a flood of opinions that fill the "air waves" and "video waves" of our day, and we can bet that Satan is masterminding a plan to steal the faith of believers. John tells us that Satan is a thief who comes to "steal, kill, and destroy." Praise God we know where the ark is and that we have committed ourselves to joining the "new Noah" who is leading us safely to dry land.

Jesus, in today's reading, heals a blind man in a strange sort of way, and then tells him, *"Don't go into the village."* In an earlier story a man was told to go back home and tell his family. Why the inconsistency? Jesus spent time with this blind man. He took him outside the village and went through a lengthy process of healing him. We know that Jesus could have done this more "efficiently" by just saying a word. Instead Jesus chose to spend time with the man, no doubt to help awaken spiritual sight in him as well as physical sight. Jesus was establishing a relationship of faith with the man. If the man returned to the village, chances are he would keep his eyesight but lose his "soul-sight".

Jesus knows the situation in the world today, and He knows the tactics of the "thief". He knows that if we wander "naively" back into *"the village"*, we run the risk of losing what He gave us. All of our strength is in Him and apart from Him *"we can do nothing"*. If Jesus is warning us to stay away from certain villages of our past, even if it makes no sense to us, it is wise to obey His voice. It is also wise to embrace, always, the safety of the Church.

"Let this be written for a future generation, that a people not yet born may praise the Lord." (Ps 102:18)

"Jesus, I pray that you will abide in me and that I will abide in You all the days of my life. And I pray that this blessing extend to my children, grandchildren, and generations to come."

Heads or Hearts

As if Jesus hadn't shocked His disciples enough, He led them northeast, above Galilee, to a city called Caesarea Philippi. In some ways this was "Satan's den". It had been the center of Baal worship and now was a city of gods, the foremost being Pan. It is told that a beautiful temple was erected there dedicated to the godhead, Caesar. Caves set in the cliffs that bordered the city emitted waters in springtime and became the occasion of grotesque fertility rites. People believed that the gods dwelled in the darkness of these caves, and they became known as the "gates of hell." What is a holy rabbi doing walking right up to the "gates of hell?"

It was in this setting that Jesus chose to ask what was probably the most important questions ever asked? *"Who do people say I am?"* *"Who do you say I am?"* (Mk 8:27-33). The disciples responded to this "group quiz" by sharing grapevine news—Jesus was John the Baptist raised from the dead, or maybe Elijah, or maybe the famous prophet (Jeremiah?). There was no doubt that Jesus was the greatest man who ever lived, and the greatest man they had ever known up to now was John the Baptist. Another common opinion was that His miracles and fiery preaching made Him seem like Elijah. His great wisdom and prophetic teaching seemed to mirror the depths of Jeremiah. Public opinion, however, did not even suggest He was "the Christ", the "Messiah." Jesus did not seem to have the "kingly anointing" that characterized a "Messiah." Also, it was public knowledge that He was from Galilee not Bethlehem of Judea.

Now to the second question, *"Who do you say that I am?"* One of the disciples, Peter, who seemed to have been emerging as the "spokesman" for the disciples, had a ready answer: *"You are the Christ."* Though Jesus didn't fit the expectations of Messiah, Peter had enough faith to believe that in time He would "pull it off." His <u>head</u> knew the right answer. Peter passed the quiz with glowing colors. Here in "Satan's den" Jesus was proclaimed, for the first time, as "the Christ", the anointed One promised by God. His power and reign would be so great that even the "gates of hell", the underground regions of the gods, would come under His authority.

I find it amazingly creative that God chose the Caesarea-Philippi backdrop to as the place to proclaim the true identity of His Son.

Jesus was at a turning point now. From healer, preacher, deliverer, and prophet, He was now ready to act like "the Messiah." This must have been good news for the disciples who were beginning to taste the ambition of getting into the world of power. This was a moment when Jesus seemed to be clearly shifting directions in His work. He spoke to His disciples about the next phase—the new directions. Suffering, rejection, and even death awaited Him in Jerusalem. "Hey!" Peter seemed to be saying, "What's going on here? At this moment of breakthrough you are talking about losing everything." Though Peter got 100% on the first quiz, he flunked this one big time. *"Get behind me, Satan,"* Jesus replied.

Peter's head knew Jesus was "the Christ"; his heart

could not accept where Jesus was headed. What was in Peter's heart? Fear, ambition, pride, self-seeking, disappointment, false dreams? The contents of his heart did not match the contents of his "theological brain." Can we identify with this in our own lives? When our hearts match our brains we say "Yes, Lord…Amen." When our hearts don't like the "new direction" of Jesus in our lives, we say "whoa, wait a minute, let me think about it." As long as Jesus is giving us spiritual "goodies", we are ready to keep following Him. When He offers us the *"will of the Father"*, we start to balk.

The Holy Spirit fills us with love, life, and power and wants to use us in ministry. We rejoice. Then the Holy Spirit says, "I want you to start losing weight and get in control of your eating habits." We ignore this message because it doesn't "fit" our definition of the Messiah of our dreams. "Who does he think he is, trying to be Lord of my personal life, and challenging me in the area of self discipline?"

I'm glad Peter was the first Pope, because we can so identify with him.

"For the Lord will rebuild Zion, and appear in His glory." (Ps 102:16)

"Jesus, you are the Christ, there is no other. Again today I turn my will and my life over to You, and choose to follow You, even if it does mean going to Jerusalem with You."

249

An Unpopular Message

Jesus is not going to win a popularity contest with His message today. (Mk 8:34-9:1). He had crowds gather around Him wherever He went. He was such a celebrity that some thought He was John the Baptist, Elijah, or a famous Old Testament prophet. The word was out that He could do just about anything— heal the sick, drive out demons, multiply bread, and even out-argue the religious authorities. Jesus was on a sure path to success—a path that was leading to His becoming "the Christ" of Israel. Now He seems to pull the carpet out from under Himself.

After He gathered the crowd and His disciples, Jesus told them that if they wanted to follow Him, they would have to deny themselves, take up their cross, lose their lives, and give up all that the world holds dear. I wonder how many "new recruits" He got after this message?

Would this message "go over" today, even in Christian Churches? We Americans do not like any *"deny yourself"* talk. We find it hard to pass up that extra piece of cake or that bowl of potato chips on the table. "Taking up the cross" meant joining those who were sentenced to death by crucifixion, the most torturous form of execution. Who, today, is willing to join criminals on death row for the sake of Jesus? And who is willing to step forward for Jesus when it means losing one's popularity and reputation with the world?

We are getting down to "bottom line" thinking and the reality of what Jesus came to offer us. The divine life of the Holy Spirit that he gives does not come cheap. It costs us everything we have, even our own lives. And we can't have our "cake and eat it", as many, today, believe is possible. Yet when we look at what the world has to offer and imagine having all of it, are we willing to exchange that for our own souls? Is this of more value that having our hearts connected in love to God?

Though Jesus is posing a tough, nearly impossible challenge, He balances His message of the cross with a reminder of the treasure the are gaining. Also, we need to keep in mind that Mark was writing to a church that was in persecution. They had already chosen to be disciples of Jesus and were facing the "price" that this choice entailed. Nero was throwing Christians to the lions in the Coliseum, and using Christians as human torches at his garden parties. *"Taking up the cross"* was a "normal" part of life for the Christians in Rome. No one knew which of their Christian friends might be hauled off by Nero's soldiers tomorrow. Mark was reminding them that what they were giving up was not worthy to be compared with the salvation they were gaining.

How strong is our faith? Are we ready to lose our lives so as to save them? Do we still think that it is possible to be a disciple and at the same time compromise with the values of the world? When our reputations are at stake, are we ashamed to be identified with Jesus?

Is our age an, *"adulterous and sinful generation"*, the words Jesus used to describe those of His generation? Are people so caught up with adulterous living that they are exchanging their souls for the pleasures and promises of the world? Are people even aware that they are living an "adulterous" life, or do they even know the ultimate consequences of their choices?

When we hide our lights in shame, we deprive a confused world of knowing where they are headed, and where "real life" can be found. Though testifying to Jesus may incur some persecution, it will also help others to find their way to life. Yes, the price that Jesus proposes today is worth it, considering the gift He offers us in return!

"...the plans of the Lord stand firm forever, the purposes of His heart through all generations." (Psalm 33:11)

"Christian martyrs of the Church, keep reminding me that 'losing my life for the sake of Jesus', is no big deal compared with the eternal union with Him that I will gain."

Save Your Family

When the new outpouring of the Holy Spirit in the late 1960's touched our personal lives, the first thing we wanted to do was to get our families involved. Some family members began to come to prayer meetings, others gave us guarded support, and still others kept a safe distance from our newfound enthusiasm. From the moment of our "conversion" we had a deep desire that our families would follow in our footsteps. As I see it, percentage wise, few did.

A line from today's reading from the Book of Hebrews (11:1-7) says that, *"...Noah, when warned about things not yet seen, in holy fear built an ark to save his family."* Noah believed that God's word was true even though there was no sign of impending rain. Alone, probably with little support, he undertook the project that God assigned him. Being a dad, who from time to time came up with "crazy ideas", I can imagine Noah won more jeers than applauds from members of his family. Nonetheless his response in faith to God's call eventually won the salvation of his family. And his was the only family that survived the great flood. No other boats, rafts, or flotation devices were strong enough to endure the raging waters of his day.

Each of us is involved in building an ark of some kind. Our efforts may not be understood or appreciated by family members. Still we journey on in faith knowing that only God can see what lies ahead. Our faithfulness is built on, *"being sure of what we hope for and certain of what we do not see."* Each day through prayer and obedience we put a few more planks in the ark that will in time save our families.

Lest we have too narrow a view of what our family members have to do to be saved, we take to heart Paul's words to the Corinthians. *"For the unbelieving husband has been sanctified through his wife, and the unbelieving wife has been sanctified through her believing husband. Otherwise your children would be unclean, but as it is, they are holy."* (1 Cor 7:14). Whether or not our spouses or our children imitate our style of belief, they are holy by virtue of our belief and our holiness of life.

Let's now move to the Gospel reading for today. (Mk 9:2-23). Jesus invited a select group of three apostles to join him in climbing Mt. Tabor. Why did He limit this moment to just three? Why did He limit His "flood preparation" team to just one, Noah? Why did He seem to limit His call within our families to just one or two? Questions to ponder.

When the three apostles saw the three heavenly figures in front of them, Peter, the compulsive talker, *"did not know what to say."* (v.6) So, instead of just keeping his mouth shut and listening, he blurted out: *"Let us put up three shelters."* If they could just set up a small shrine here, Peter thought, then all their family members and friends could come up and see this vision of heaven as they did. Then, they would all believe, and Peter's wife would quit complaining about him never being home for supper (this is not in the Bible, incidentally). This would be a good way for Peter, like Noah, to save his family.

God was not sidetracked by Peter's nervous chatter.

254

Instead after a time of silence, the Father spoke perhaps the most important words ever given to humans: *"This is my Son, whom I love. Listen to him!"* If that is the only piece of the Gospels we've ever heard, it is enough. Here in a 3-second "sound byte" is the secret to life! Instead of encouraging the "three" to run down and tell the other apostles and members of their families what they saw, Jesus *"gave them orders not to tell anyone"* until after the resurrection. They did, however, keep discussing this among themselves. Only God knew what was really going on.

Do we, like Peter, have schemes on what we can do to save our families? Do we even try to manipulate them into believing or scare them into accepting Jesus? Are we willing to trust, endure the silence, and wait to hear the voice of God? Are we willing to walk by faith, like Noah did, and keep handing the planks of our daily faithfulness to God, to let Him build an ark that will save us, our family members, and others from this *"adulterous and sinful"* generation?

"All You have made will praise You, O Lord; Your saints will extol You. They will tell of the glory of Your kingdom and speak of Your might." (Ps 145: 10-11)

"Jesus, we have witnessed Your transfiguration within our hearts. May Your presence within us shine so brightly that many, including our family members, will be drawn into a deep relationship with You."

Do Not Resist an Evil Person. Really?

The Church puts before us today one of the most disturbing of Jesus' teachings. (Mt 5:38-48). Jesus said *"do not resist an evil person"*, *"turn the other cheek"*, if someone wants your tunic, *"let him have your cloak as well"*, *" if someone forces you to go one mile with him, go with him two miles"*, *"do not turn away from someone who wants to borrow from you."*

Did Jesus mean what He said here? Or is this a poetic exaggeration on Jesus' part? Is Jesus calling Christians to be wimps who let people walk all over them?

Certainly Jesus wasn't a wimp and He did not let people walk all over Him. Ask the pesky Pharisees if you don't believe this. Or ask the guys who were exchanging money in the Temple the day that Jesus flipped over their tables. Yet Jesus literally followed His own exhortations at the sacred moment when He was called to freely become a victim for our sins. He did not resist the evil Judas who led others to arrest Jesus; He turned His other cheek to the soldiers who slapped Him; He gave up all of his clothes at the foot of the cross; He walked the extra mile to Calvary carrying His own cross; He gave up everything He had including His own life for the salvation of souls; He felt compassion even for His executioners and prayed for them as He was dying. This passage is not to be "theologized" away, but to be taken literally.

If this is so then, how does the teaching reconcile with the Leviticus passage today (chapter 19, 1-2, 17-18) where the Holy Spirit said: *"rebuke your neighbor frankly, so you will not share in his guilt."*? There are moments in which we are to rebuke our neighbor; there are other moments in which we are to give him our cloak. Is Jesus' advice about dealing with mistreatment meant to be used at every time and in every circumstance—including the case when someone is a being a victim of spouse abuse? Did Jesus flip tables over every time He entered the Temple area? I don't think so.

Let's go back to the start of the Sermon on the Mount. When Jesus sat down to teach, His disciples came to Him; His class was the group of disciples not the crowd. (Mt 5:1). This teaching then, is not for the world, or the crowds, but for His chosen disciples who said "yes' to His call. These are the ones who had already left everything to follow Jesus.

Who are these disciples? These are the ones who take seriously the injunction of Leviticus, *"Be holy, because I the Lord your God, am holy"* (Lv 19:1). These are the ones who are literally, *"temples of the Holy Spirit"* and who are so sacred that if anyone destroys them, *"God will destroy him",* [that is, the perpetrator]. (1 Cor 3:16-17). These are the ones to whom the Holy Spirit said *"all things are yours...whether the world or life or death or the present or the future...and you are of Christ, and Christ is of God."* (1 Cor 3:21-23). These are the people who are so filled with the gift of the Holy Spirit that they have become identified with Christ—they are becoming Jesus in a literal way.

So transformed into Christ are His disciples, that they will be given the extraordinary power to follow in His footsteps even to the sacred moment of Calvary. Not every disciple has matured into that "sacred moment" when he is called to be one with the crucified Jesus. Not every situation is this "sacred moment"; that has to be discerned as we respond to the wisdom of the Holy Spirit. Jesus is not telling us to let ourselves be abused, bullied, and degraded indiscriminately. If we submit to abuse because of our low self-esteem or because we have had our self-confidence undermined, then this is a "sacred moment" in which we need to stand up for ourselves and reach out for support from others.

There are Christians who are being called to "crucifixion" today, so to speak. I read of a contemporary Chinese missionary who has been imprisoned and abused more times than he can count. I read, this year, of a Pakistani Catholic woman who has been unjustly hauled off to jail for being a Christian. By now she may have been executed by the government. I have a Catholic friend (in our community) who has been taken to court, threatened with imprisonment, and treated unjustly on the basis of the false testimony of family members. The era of persecution did not end 1900 years ago.

How is Jesus calling us, His 21st century disciples, to respond to this difficult teaching today? We can pray for our enemies, and if our hearts are too hurt to do this, we can pray that God will heal and transform our hearts until they become one with the Heart of Jesus. We can be "inclusive" in extending our love to others, instead of just picking and choosing whom we want to love. Jesus said that even the pagans do the latter. The Father does not pick and choose whom He will let the sun shine on, or the rain fall upon. We are to imitate our heavenly Father: *"Be perfect, as your heavenly Father is perfect."* I have been taught that "perfect" does not mean "free from sin or from making mistakes". Rather it means being "all inclusive in love", the way God is toward all His creatures, including the enemies of Jesus.

For those who choose to persecute the disciples of Jesus, there is the promise of "pay back". Revenge will be given, but at God's hand not ours. (Rom 12:19, Lev 19:18)

"He does not treat us as our sins deserve or repay us according to our iniquities." (Ps 103: 10)

"Jesus, I believe that day by day the Holy Spirit is so transforming my heart that I am beginning to look more and more like You. May I grow daily in love even to the point of loving my enemies and praying for those who persecute me."

Spellbound -
To Fear or not to Fear

When I was a senior in high school, I went to 4th and Broadway to watch the celebrities emerge from the Brown Hotel after the premier showing of the movie *Raintree County.*   As I stood against the ropes that were used to fence off the crowd, a news reporter asked me if I would carry his camera equipment. Accepting the job, I was allowed to go on the other side of the ropes and follow the reporter into the Hotel. To my amazement I came within a few feet of some of the most famous movie stars of the day. I remember the moment I stood across from Elizabeth Taylor. It is hard to describe the "spellbound" feeling I had as I gazed upon the most beautiful human being I had ever seen. Everything else in the Brown Hotel lobby seemed to sink into the background for me at that moment. This sense of being captivated and silenced by the presence of a famous and beautiful person can be labeled as "fear" in the positive sense of the word.   Had Ms. Taylor spoken to me, I think I would have collapsed.

When we read about *"fear of the Lord"* in Scripture, we are talking about an experience similar to my "fear of Elizabeth Taylor". It is the sense of wonder that we may feel when we are captivated by the presence of the Lord.

"Fear of the Lord is glory and splendor, gladness and a festive crown. Fear of the Lord warms the heart, giving gladness and joy, and length of days." (Sir 1:9-10) Imagine what it's like to be caught up in the glory of God's presence and feel we have a crown of happiness

on our heads. Imagine that special inner warmth in our hearts, a joyful spirit, and knowing that this experience will help us live a longer life. And, this is just the introduction to what Sirach has to say about having *"fear of the Lord."* Read the rest of chapter 1 to get a further description. If I take the "fear of Elizabeth Taylor" and multiply it by 1000, I might have an inkling of how Sirach experienced the fear of the Lord.

Isn't this enough to make us long and pray for the gift of fearing the Lord? The fact is we already have it by virtue of our Confirmation. Read Isaiah 11:2 to learn of the gifts of the Holy Spirit that rested on the Messiah, and by virtue of our Confirmation now rest within us. If we never experience the *"fear of the Lord"* gift, we are missing out on something wonderful God has provided for us. Maybe our Confirmation is still a phone card that we haven't yet activated.

The Gospel story today (Mk 9:14-29) describes a *"fear of the Lord"* scene. When the crowd saw Jesus, coming down from the mountain, *"they were overwhelmed with wonder and ran to greet Him."* Caught up in the confusion of listening to the incompetent disciples of Jesus trying to out-argue the teachers of the law, they were elated to see "the answer" appear at a distance. Jesus' very presence was a light that brought them peace and hope amidst their predicament. What does it feel like to be "overwhelmed with wonder", as we experience Jesus emerge on the scene? What does it feel like to be so happy that Jesus has arrived that we drop everything and run to greet Him?

Let us activate the gift of *"fear of the Lord"* today. We

261

don't have to wait for Jesus to come back down a mountain; He is with us now. Sometimes we are like the two disciples on the way to Emmaus who were walking side-by-side with Jesus yet did not recognized Him. Tangled in the confusion of our problems and the chaos of our world, we must stop and "turn our eyes upon Jesus." Let us take time out to experience the *"fear of the Lord"*.

At the end of today's reading we hear about another kind of fear. Having heard Jesus talk about His impending death, the disciples, *"did not understand what He meant, and were afraid to ask Him about it."* Were they afraid to face the answer He might give them? Can we identify with the fear of not wanting to know too much? Because Jesus walked in the *"fear of the Lord"*, He was not afraid to talk to the Father and accept the events that lay ahead.

"The Lord reigns, He is robed in majesty...and is armed with strength." (Ps 93:1)

"Come Holy Spirit, help us to let go of our distractions and once again be captivated by the glorious, heart-warming presence of God."

Chair of Peter

Today is the feast day of Peter's Chair, commemorating St. Peter as the, *"rock"* on whom Jesus builds His Church. In honoring the "chair" (there really is a chair, in St. Peter's Basilica), we are honoring the "office" of Peter more than Peter himself. Today's Gospel is Matthew's version of the Caesarea-Philippi story in which Jesus tells Peter, *"...you are Peter and on this rock I will build My church, and the gates of hell shall not prevail against it. I will give you the keys of the kingdom of heaven..."* (Mt 16:13-19) What a moment this was that the Son of God would entrust to a man the authority and leadership of his Church! And we know that through "Apostolic succession" this position has been passed down through the centuries even to our present Pope, Benedict XVI.

Remember when Jesus got off the boat and saw a large crowd, and his heart was touched with deep compassion because they, *"were like sheep without a shepherd"* (Mk 6:34). A little sheep without a shepherd is like a lost child wandering around the mall looking for his parents. Jesus would make sure that His sheep would always have a visible shepherd to look after them. Thus, the gift of the papacy and the authority structure in the Church.

It is interesting that "shepherd" is the primary image we are to have of the pope. He is not depicted as ruler, teacher, monarch, or any traditional view we have of authority figures. When we see the pope, it is a shepherd's staff that he carries. In today's reading from Peter (1 Pt 5: 1-4), Peter spoke to the leaders of the

263

Church in his day and tells them they are to be shepherds, not lording it over their flocks but leading primarily by example. The Church chooses Psalm23 today, the Good Shepherd psalm.

The word "pope" means "papa", or the term of endearment a young child uses in talking to his father (from the encyclopedia). I believe Jesus wants us to love the pope as a child loves his father or a sheep loves its shepherd. Sadly, our secular press often depicts the pope as a heartless ruler trying to rob people of their freedom. And some Catholics in a spirit of rebellion have picked up on this. Let us remember that the first 17 popes were martyred for the faith; they were as sheep led to the slaughter not powerful monarchs.

Isn't Jesus our Shepherd? Isn't the Father our "papa"? Of course. We know, however, that the Church is the Body of Christ serving one another and the world through our charisms. Jesus continues His ministry on earth in a concrete way by working through His Body, not just in a purely "spiritual" way. We all have the power of the Holy Spirit to be Jesus to one another. Our shepherds have the power of the Holy Spirit to lead us and shepherd us according the mind of Jesus.

I always find it interesting that God chose *"Simon son of Jonah"* as the leader of the Church. The way the Gospel reads, God revealed to Simon who Jesus was, and this was the signal for Jesus to appoint him as rock and holder of the keys. Peter did not figure this out himself. Why Peter? He wasn't the smartest of the group (I think Matthew was); he wasn't the holiest (denied Christ), he wasn't the fastest (John beat him to the tomb), he wasn't the most self-controlled (couldn't keep his mouth shut), he wasn't the wisest (advised Jesus against going to Jerusalem). What did Peter have going for him? Maybe his weakness, his humility, and his sinfulness. In doing this God lets us know that it is not the ingenuity of Peter that guides the Church, it is Jesus Himself guiding the Church through such earthen vessels as Peter. We don't have to worry about how smart or holy the pope is (praise God we have had intelligent and holy popes in recent times), because it is about the Great Shepherd empowering and leading humble men to stand in as shepherds to His flock.

We are as important to the Church as Pope Benedict. Remember Paul's teaching about how the Body of Christ works? (1 Cor 12)—*"the weaker are indispensable"*. Our leaders depend on us to do our parts, as much as we depend on them to be good and wise shepherds. When we hold back, it makes their burden much heavier. Also each of us shares in the "shepherd" ministry, because there are people in our lives who look to us as their shepherds and try to imitate our example. When we are careless in our walk with the Lord, it affects those "sheep" who depend on us for inspiration, care, and leadership.

"Even though I should walk through the valley of the shadow of death, I will fear no evil for You are with me; Your rod and Your staff comfort me." (Ps 23:4)

"Good Shepherd Jesus, thank You for each of the shepherds you have given us. Help us to be a support and not a burden to them."

Jesus' Policemen

Many years ago I was waiting at a stop light in lower Manhattan (N.Y.) and I noticed a policeman approaching an elderly homeless man. Expecting the policeman to chide the man for one thing or another, I was surprised when I saw the policeman put his arm around the homeless man, and with that the old man began to weep. The policeman was consoling him—a role that I did not associate with policemen. That day, in New York, I witnessed "policing through blessing". My heart is still touched when I recall that scene today.

In today's Gospel passage (Mk 9:38-40) we see the apostles stepping forward as "spiritual policemen". They notice a man who was casting out demons in the name of Jesus. Who did this man think he was encroaching on their ministry? John reported to Jesus, with pride, *"We told him to stop."* Instead of patting John on the back for guarding the ministry of Jesus, the Lord surprises the apostles by saying. *"Do not stop him...whoever is not against us is for us."* Jesus is not into the "control" business, but the blessing business. The Son of God did not need a group of secret service men around Him protecting Him from those who were trying to use His "trademark" illegally. Jesus chose the apostles to imitate Him, not protect Him. I wish I could have seen the confused look on John's face.

Then Jesus added a postscript message: *"I tell you the truth , anyone who gives you a cup of cold water in my name because you belong to Christ will certainly not lose his reward."* Let us remember that Mark was writing to a Church in persecution. We can imagine a

Christian being taken down the road to the Coliseum, and a bystander giving him/her a cup of cold water to ease his pain. In these cases those who bless the sisters and brothers of Jesus will be blessed in turn by the Lord Himself. We, as disciples of the Lord, have the power to bless others just by receiving the simple gifts they offer us out of love for God. We bless by giving, and we bless by receiving.

Jesus wants everyone to be connected to Him. He is not running around putting yellow tape around His church, protecting it from non-believers. He wants everyone to belong to Him, even the man who heals in His name but does not know Him, even the compassionate bystanders who show Jesus their love by giving a cup of coldwater. His blessing reaches out across the earth; all who are open to Him will be touched whether or not they fit the criteria that Christian leaders might expect.

As Catholics we have such a rich heritage that includes the sacraments, a system of Church authority, the teaching of the Church, the rich tradition of saints, the company of Mary, the love for God's word, an unusual variety and power of prayer. We may have a tendency to disrespect those followers of Jesus who do not participate in this fullness of blessing. We may even become arrogant about what we have and take it upon ourselves to judge and police others whom we believe are not as favored as we are. We may even take it upon ourselves to decide who's in the "in crowd" and who's in the "out crowd." Jesus' word to John is also meant for us. It puts us in our place, and makes it clear that humility, openness, and love are the characteristics that guide the disciples of Jesus as they relate to those outside their circle. We remember that it is not "all about us". We need to be ready to receive the gifts, even of non-believers, as we journey with Jesus toward the cross. Let us not become so self-sufficient that we start thinking we are the only ones that have something to give to the world.

We remember that we, like Jesus, are in the blessing business. There is not a circumstance in life in which Jesus-within-us is not capable of blessing other people with love, peace, and joy. Only our "closed-ness" of heart can deter this from happening.

"Great peace have they who love Your law, and nothing can make them stumble." (Ps 119:65)

"St John help us to learn the wisdom that Jesus taught you that day of which we read. St Polycarp, disciple of John, help us to be as generous in blessing others as you were in your many years of ministry."

Shocking Words

What are some of things we really value? One way of testing our values is by imagining our reaction if we lost them. Suppose you are shopping, and as you return to your parking lot you see two thieves driving off the property with your car. Would that upset you? Or suppose you are coming home and as you near your home you see a gathering of fire trucks in the neighborhood. Upon coming closer you realize your house is up in flames. How would that make you feel? We can take this deeper by thinking of how we react when we hear that one of our children or grandchildren has been involved in a tragedy. Some of us have been through these kinds of things.

In today's Gospel I believe Jesus is trying to be as dramatic as He can in impressing upon us the value of the human soul. (Mk 9:41-50) Words are limited in awakening us to truth; Jesus does the best He can to shock us out of our complacent thinking.

We are horrified if we find our car is stolen or our house has burned to the ground. We are even more horrified to hear the news that tragedy has struck a child that we know. These are losses we can hardly bear.

And yet what about sin? What about losing one's relationship with God? Is there anything more tragic? Jesus asked the question, *"What does it profit a man if he gain the whole world and lose his very soul?"* As I recall it was this word that so penetrated the heart of Ignatius of Loyola that he left everything to follow

Jesus. In time he founded one of the greatest Christian armies that ever existed—the Jesuits. He realized that nothing could be worse than spending his whole life gaining things and missing out on the one thing that counted.

Jesus stirs our imaginations with the image of a huge stone tied around a person's neck and the person being tossed into the sea. It sounds like something straight out of the Mafia world. Or think of the how we shudder when we hear of torturers gouging the eyes out of their enemies? How do we respond when we hear that in some Muslim states, a person has his hand chopped off if he is caught stealing? Jesus says that these things are minor compared to sinning or leading one of His little ones into sin. If a drug leader goes into a neighborhood and lures young children into taking drugs, wouldn't it have been better if that drug pusher had been killed in a car accident before he dragged children into this evil world of addiction?

Our society values things. It values eyes, hands, and feet. It does not value souls or see the horror of cutting oneself off from God. The world collaborates to keep our minds off this kind of thinking. If people stay caught up in the world of TV, entertainment, politics, and the rest, they will never have to stop to wonder *"what does it profit me if I get all of these things and lose my soul?"* They will be too busy buying and selling and pursuing illusory goals to wonder what life's ultimate purpose is.

Even the Church talks little about the tragedy of sin these days. I remember going to a meeting at Church some years ago and people chuckled when someone brought up the possibility of "mortal sin" - that is sin that cuts one off from God. John reminds us that, *"there is a sin that leads to death."* (1 Jn 5:16) Someone has tricked our whole generation into thinking that sin does not exist and losing one's soul doesn't really matter. What about us? Have we also been desensitized to such realities as sin, evil, and hell? Do we look around at our world and conclude that everyone probably loves God and is dedicated to serving Him? What do we see when we reflect on the values that drive our society today?

Does this mean we go around tossing people in the river, gouging out eyes, or cutting off hands and feet? Of course not. What good would this do in saving souls? It does mean that we let the words of Jesus so shock us that we dedicate ourselves to leading little ones into the truth, and intercede constantly for those who are headed toward a tragedy worse than having a hand severed. God has given each of us prayer weapons to combat the forces of evil that leads thousands into sin. How often and how well are we using these weapons?

"Blessed is the man...[whose] delight is in the law of the Lord, and on His law he meditates day and night." (Ps 1:1-2)

"Jesus, if I have grown complacent in my attitude toward sin or lost my zeal for winning souls, may your word shock me back into the truth as it did with St. Ignatius."

271

Divorce, Adultery, Marriage

In today's Gospel reading Jesus addresses topics that are extremely sensitive in our Church culture today— divorce, adultery, and marriage. (Mk 10:1-12)

The setting of this story is significant. Jesus had passed into Judea and crossed the Jordan River putting Him in the territory of Herod, the one who had John the Baptist beheaded. Divorce was a "hot" topic in this region, since Herod was in an adulterous relationship with his brother's wife and John had not minded confronting him on the issue. A popular teacher, like Jesus, would have been treading dangerous ground to address this topic—considering what had happened to John.

In the beginning of this passage we read that Jesus, *"as was His custom"*, was teaching the people. While healing and deliverance were the more spectacular ministries of Jesus, teaching was what He seemed to spend most of His time doing. He taught as one having authority and shared deep wisdom with a people who thirsted for the truth.

The Pharisees put a "legal" question to Jesus about divorce. Instead of "ruling" on the matter Jesus responded by teaching divine wisdom about the subject. When religion becomes a matter of legality instead of spirituality, it no longer has any power. We know what happens physically, financially, and legally when a man and woman get married. This is all about the outside. Jesus spoke about the mystery of what happens in the world of spirit—the reality that takes place inside. In effect Jesus says that the two become one though we do not understand how this can happen. God somehow intervenes with a new act of creation—making a new entity out of what used to be two entirely separate entities. And when God creates something, no mere creature can "uncreate it". I heard someone describe this with the example of pouring milk into coffee. Once this has been done, there is no way the two can be separated again—a new reality has been formed—lightened coffee. Jesus is not setting an arbitrary law but describing an unseen reality

I happened to open to chapter 5 of Proverbs today where the author shares wisdom about marriage and adultery. As we read this passage, we are not getting a set of "rights and wrongs" rather an exposition, by the Holy Spirit, of what is really going on with concrete situations of life. He knows what a powerful temptation adultery can be, and reminds men that the *"lips of an adulteress drip honey...but in the end she is bitter as gall."* (v.3) He talks about what he has observed in life, that if someone gets lured into an adulterous relationship, *"at the end of [his] life [he] will groan. "You will say, 'How I hated discipline! How my heart hated instruction.'"* These are words spoken from the loving heart of a Father.

Then the author shifts into a teaching about the potential beauty of a marriage relationship, and the joys that await the man of fidelity. *"May you rejoice in the wife of your youth...may you ever be captivated by her love."* Fidelity pays off in the end with inner joy and new depths of love, which are the opposite of the "groans" of the adulterer.

When we are confronted with life decisions, we sometimes want God to give a "yes or no" ruling. Instead He does like Jesus and the author of Proverbs did, He speaks words of deep wisdom to our hearts. He unfolds into our spirit the rich consequences of remaining in His will even when this requires discipline, and then He reveals to us the painful consequences of choosing a path that may seem more appealing at the present moment.

Jesus through the Holy Spirit is in the "custom" of teaching each of us daily the practical wisdom of God that relates to our current, real-life situations. John has reminded us that, *"his anointing teaches (us) about all things and as that anointing is real, not counterfeit"*, we must dedicate ourselves to remaining in Him. (1 Jn 2:27)

"Direct me in the path of Your commands, for there I find delight." (Ps 119:35)

"Speak Lord, I long to listen to Your voice."

Jesus is Indignant

What is it that makes Jesus indignant? One dictionary defines indignant as being angry about an injustice committed. We know Jesus expressed anger at money changers who were turning the Temple into a marketplace instead of a house of prayer. We know Jesus was angry at the stubborn resistance of the teachers of the law, who put rules ahead of God. Today we read that Jesus is "indignant" about the rights of children being violated. (Mk 10:13-16).

Children have a right to be close to Jesus. When the people were bringing their children to meet Jesus and receive His blessing, the disciples *"rebuked them."* Here they were again trying to take charge of Jesus' ministry and protect Him from people that they considered to be less important than they. Children were insignificant in that society—they had no power, no position, no political clout. To the disciples, the children had no business pestering the Messiah. Jesus was filled with indignation that the disciples were depriving children of the greatest of all their rights—the right to meet Jesus.

When the disciples got out of the way and the children finally reached Jesus, He took them in His arms, put His hands on them, and blessed them. Many artists, being touched by this beautiful moment, have tried to capture it in painting or in sculpture. Imagine the tenderness of the

**Jesus and the Little Children,
by Vogel von Vogelstein**

Son of God so openly manifest as He embraced each of these innocent children.

Jesus used this occasion to deliver a powerful teaching. *"I tell you the truth, anyone who will not receive the kingdom of God like a little child will never enter it."* This made no sense to the disciples. Their attitude indicated that they were not qualified to receive the kingdom of God, for a little child would not try to block people from meeting Jesus. Only after the crucifixion were the disciples rendered powerless, and being aware of their own sin and weakness they repented and became as little children who were open, for the first time, to receive the Holy Spirit at Pentecost.

Our life circumstances continue to remind us that we are powerless and need to continue receiving the kingdom of God as little children. When the events of our lives leave us broken, we become childlike again and need to go to Jesus, have Him pick us up in His arms, lay His hand on us, and bless us with His love. When we think we're too big for Jesus, then, as my mother used to say, we are "too big for our britches."

Fr. Al Lauer in today's reflection talks about how Satan is doing all he can in our time to keep children away from Jesus. He mentions, specifically the entertainment business, the education system, lukewarm churches, and confused parents as blocking children from being touched by Jesus. Do we feel the indignation of Jesus when we see the children of our time being "stolen" by the enemy? Sadly, I think too many of us have been lulled to sleep and blinded to the truth of what is going on today in our society.

We may feel powerless against the forces that seem to be luring our children away from the truth. The fact is, we are not powerless because we have the presence of the risen Lord within us and the power of the Holy Spirit. Jesus exercised authority in getting the disciples out of the way, so the children could come forward freely. Jesus within us has given us that same authority to get the obstacles out of the way that restrict our children from knowing Jesus. The enemy would have us believe that there is nothing we can do to combat these forces of evil. This is a lie. We have been equipped with all the weapons we need for breaking down strongholds, demolishing arguments, and capturing every thought making it obedient to Christ. (2 Cor 10:4-5)

When God filled us with the Holy Spirit, He equipped us with power to overcome the works of darkness. How well are we using this power?

"The Lord's love is with those who fear Him, and His righteousness with their children's children." (Ps 103:17)

"Jesus, we are reminded that You have given us weapons, and these are not the weapons of the 'world'. Build up our faith and our confidence in using these weapons more skillfully to defend our children against the assaults of the enemy."

Trust in Him

Did you ever ride in the front seat of a car that someone else was driving, and press your foot against the floorboard when you believed the brake pedal needed to be applied? Something in our brain tells us that we have the power to stop the car by pressing on the floorboard. Of course we have no such power, and the gesture on our part has no influence on the car at all.

Extending this kind of thinking to our lives, we sometimes act as though we are driving the car, and we go through various maneuvers to try to control what is going on. In faith we know that God is at the wheel, and He is perfectly capable of driving and stopping the car according to what He knows is best. Though we know that our lives are in His hands, we still have a tendency to keep "pressing our foot to the floorboard" or even "grabbing the steering wheel" when things seem to be getting out of control. Jesus calls us to practice the art of "trusting" in Him.

In today's Gospel passage (Mt 6:24-34), Jesus talks about trust, and worry. Even though we know that we are God's children and each detail of our lives is in His hands, we can still fall into the bad habit of worrying. How much of our thought life centers in worrying about food, clothing, health issues, dying? What about the worries that center around money—like worrying about losing our job or worrying about paying our bills or members of our families paying theirs? What about worries that focus on tomorrow and our futures? Jesus is clear in what He says to us: *"Do not worry about your life, what you will eat or drink"; "why do you worry*

about clothes?"; "Do not worry about tomorrow";
"Who by worrying can add a single hour to his life?"

What's going on when we worry? I think the root
cause is fear. We still entertain the subtle belief that we
are in charge, and our security depends on us. In a
society that serves the master called "Money", we begin
to believe that our safety and our security rest on our
bank accounts. This, of course, is a lie, and we need to
combat it with acts of faith. Whether we have enough
to eat, to wear, to live a long life, or to have a
prosperous future does not depend on our financial
circumstances. Jesus has reminded us not to store up
treasures on earth where thieves can steal, but to store
up treasures in heaven where no thief can touch them,
nor can moths destroy them.

When we get into the habit of worry, we have fallen
into the trap of thinking we are driving the car and
everything depends on us. What makes it especially
difficult to stay free of this illusion is that we live in a
world that is stuck in its belief that all depends on us
and that God is not even part of the picture.

Everything we have or will have can be taken away
from us, and we have little control of what's going to
happen to us tomorrow. Yes everything can be taken
except one thing. In today's first reading (Is 49:14-15)
we find out that God's care for us can never be taken
away. *"Can a mother forget her baby…though she may
forget, I will not forget you. See I have engraved you
on the palms of my hands."* God has made a solemn
covenant with us and will always uphold His part
of the covenant even if we waver in ours. The one

unshakeable truth is that God loves us and will never abandon us. All He asks us to do is to seek His kingdom first, and *"all these things will be given [us] besides."* Can the solution to life be any simpler than this? So there is no need to fear for He is always with us.

We don't have to watch the road and keep our feet resting on the imaginary brake pedal under our feet. Instead we seek first the kingdom of God, which means we keep our eyes not on the road, but upon the driver. As our union with God deepens, a childlike trust begins to overtake our entire being. We take on the simplicity of little children who are naïve enough to believe that their parents will take complete care of them, and so have nothing to worry about or to fear.

"Trust in Him at all times, O people; pour out your hearts to Him for God is our refuge." (Ps 62:8)

"Jesus, forgive me for the times I've worried, and deliver me from my tendency to worry. Help me to realize that God is in charge of everything—even the hairs of my head are numbered."

Missed Opportunity

Today the Church shares with us one of the saddest stories in the Gospels. It is the story of a man who said "no" to Jesus' invitation.

We make many decisions in life. The one fundamental decision that is more important than all the others is whether we will say "yes" or "no" to Jesus' invitation for us to follow Him. Since God wants all to be saved (1 Tim 2), it stands to reason that every human being sometime in his or her life encounters Jesus and He offers them an invitation. At the time of our baptism our parents spoke up for us and said "yes, I want to follow Jesus wherever He leads me." During the course of our lives we will have an opportunity to validate this "yes" or to say "no" to it. Sometimes the pull of other values is so strong that we are unwilling to let go of these and follow Jesus.

The story began (Mk 10:17-27) with a rich man (Matthew says that he was young) coming up to Jesus and falling on his knees. He knew that Jesus taught with authority and had deep wisdom; this led him to seek a practical answer to his spiritual quest. Wanting to make an instant impression on Jesus, the rich man addresses Him as, *"good teacher"*. This "buttering up" approach had probably worked many times before for the man, but it didn't work with Jesus. Jesus would not be manipulated and rejected the man's approach. We can imagine that this young man was one of the most popular and envied people in the community. He, perhaps, financed the local synagogue and had a large number of employees. Good chance he was the most "eligible bachelor" in town. Besides being wealthy, however, the man was unusually righteous, a trait that was not often seen among the rich. He kept all the commandments, and he wanted to do the right thing otherwise he would not have asked Jesus, *"what must I do to be saved?"*

What kind of answer was he expecting from Jesus? There was little that he, on his own power, could not do. If Jesus suggested that the rich man open up 10 more synagogues, open up a homeless shelter, or fund a pilgrimage to Jerusalem, he would have said "yes". Jesus instead asked him to do something that was outside the man's own power—*"sell all that you have, give to the poor, and follow me."* This stopped the man in his tracks, his face fell, and he turned away sad. His whole life was built on his wealth, his standing in the community, his freedom to do what he wanted. It was impossible for him to let go of all this. Later Jesus explains to His disciples that while it was impossible for the rich man to do, it wasn't impossible for God to do.

Sometimes God lets the bottom fall out of our lives to make it possible for us to say "yes" to Jesus. On our own we cannot surrender our status in life, our wealth, our reputations in the world. We need God to facilitate this for us, so that we don't pass up the opportunity to follow Jesus at that sacred moment when we meet Him.

Notice that there were three parts to Jesus' call. *"Sell what you have",* that is, let it all go. *"Give to the poor",* so you could not retrieve it at a later time. (Remember Ananias and Sapphira who kept a portion of their wealth as a "back up" plan in the early Christian community? (Acts 5:1-11)) And, finally, Jesus said, *"follow me"*. Giving things up and helping the poor is of little value, if it is not for the purpose of following Jesus. The kingdom of God is not about sacrificing ourselves so as to make the world a better place. It is about entering into a permanent covenant with Jesus Christ the Son of God. Selling all and giving it away is needed to remove all obstacles that stand in the way of our making a total commitment to Jesus.

Jesus, we read, looked at the man *"and loved him."* Jesus loved the goodness of the man and his desire to find the truth. He would have loved to have the man as a disciple, not because of **what** he had but because of **who** he was. In responding to the man's question, Jesus said to him: *"One thing you lack."* In time the rich man would lose his wealth, his power, his reputation. How sad that he missed the opportunity to give it up when he met Jesus.

Do we have the courage to approach Jesus today and ask Him what He wants of us? Are we willing ask Him if there is "one thing" that we lack—one thing that stands in the way of our going further down the road with Him? Our opportunity comes; we don't want to pass it up. And when we realize how weak we are, we remember that "all things are possible with God."

"Therefore let everyone who is godly pray to You while You may be found; surely when the mighty waters rise, they will not reach him." (Ps 32:6)

10,000% Interest Rate

It might be best today to start off with a short math lesson. Banks are offering about 1% interest on certificates of deposit. Which means that if someone puts $10 in the bank, after a year it will have earned an extra 10 cents. Imagine if a bank offered a 10,000% interest rate! In this case $10 would grow to be $1000. This would represent what is called "100-fold" increase. In the banking world this kind of return is preposterous.

Yet, this is exactly the return that Jesus is offering us in today's Gospel. (Mk 10:28-31). He promises that no one who has left home, family, or fields for His sake and the sake of the Gospel, *"will fail to receive 100 times in this age,"* without even considering what they will receive in the age to come. Jesus is not talking about heaven in this passage; He is talking about the returns available here on earth. Has even the most enterprising leader in the history of civilization ever made a better offer to anyone?

We, at some moment in our lives, made a decision to give up everything for Jesus. In some cases we were rejected by family members or friends because of our conversion, and in this sense *"left home and family."* In India if a young Hindu person converts to Christianity, his family disowns him, I am told, and will have nothing to do with him from that day forward. In some Moslem countries a Christian risks imprisonment and death by the mere fact that he professes faith in Jesus. The price we pay in our country when we line ourselves up with Christ is more subtle, yet just as real.

Each of us had to let go of something important to us when we said "yes" to Jesus and His Gospel. It could have been friends, wealth, reputation, position in life, or even a job.

What we forget is that the promise of Jesus about the "100-fold" return is real, and is happening now. If we have stayed faithful to our call, even now we are receiving new homes, new brothers and sisters, new mothers and fathers, new children, and new fields. If we aren't, then Jesus was not faithful to His promise. How is it, then, that we are receiving this abundance from the Lord? What about "100 new homes"? The first thing I notice is that Jesus said "homes" not "houses." In a loving, closely-connected Christian community, members open their homes readily to everyone else in the group. Each house becomes a "safe and loving haven" for each member of the community. What about new family members? The union of spirits that is brought about by God when a group meets regularly, prays together, ministers to one another, is deeper and more powerful than the "blood bonds" people experience in natural families. When a group loves each other "in Christ", it is the Holy Spirit within each that connects one to another. There are no human bonds that come close to this kind of union.

When a group is close in love, members become mothers and fathers to the younger people; everyone is brother and sister to everyone else, and children have many older members to look up to for example and guidance. Those who have been part of such a Christian environment testify to the literal fulfillment of

Jesus' "100-fold" promise in their lives.

And what about, *"fields"*? Does Jesus promise us that, as individuals, we will each own hundreds of pieces of property? No. But as a group we do. I have been to many cities in this country and in other parts of the world. In each of these places there are many Catholic Churches that belong to us. We can enter freely and partake of the Eucharistic banquet on a daily basis if we want. Think of the hundreds of thousand churches that we, as Catholics, own.

Why is it that we do not see, much less enjoy the *"100-fold"* that is available to us right now in this present age? Are we willing to give up our independence and open our homes generously to one another? Are we willing to reach out and build relationships with one another, so we can be brothers, sisters, mothers, and fathers to each other? Jesus' gift is there—are we free enough to receive it? Do we thank God daily for the fulfillment of this promise in our lives?

"For the Lord is a good rewarder; He will reward you seven times over." (Sir 35:10)

"Holy Spirit, open the eyes of my heart so I can see the fulfillment of Jesus' promise in my life. Stir within me a spirit of overwhelming gratitude."

Bartimaeus

Lent is just one week away. This is a time of "amazing grace" in the Church. It is a time of change and new growth, paralleling the transformation that we see in nature with the coming of spring. Lent is our spiritual springtime. Obstacles that keep us from getting deeper in the Lord are removed; new inspiration and new life are planted in our hearts. The Holy Spirit will be working overtime for us; let's not miss this season of grace.

If we are looking for a role model to help us move triumphantly through this season of grace, we might want to try the hero of today's Gospel—a blind beggar named Bartimaeus. (Mk 10:46-52)

Bartimaeus heard that Jesus of Nazareth was coming down the road from Jericho. Something in his spirit told him that this was the one chance he had been waiting for to be healed. He acted on his inner voice and shouted out to Jesus, begging for His pity. The bystanders, *"scolded him and told him to be quiet"*, yet the more they pressured him to be silent, the louder he got. Jesus, hearing the shouting, stopped and told the people to bring the blind beggar to Him. Throwing his cloak off (his only possession?), Bartimaeus *"jumped up and went to Jesus."*

What is this blind beggar teaching us? He wanted to go to Jesus and many obstacles stood in the way. Traditionally the three obstacles to our spiritual growth are the world, the flesh, and the devil. These are the influences that try to keep us from coming close to

287

Jesus. Notice how Bartimaeus dealt effectively with each one. The world (the people around him) tried to shut him down and discourage his frantic attempts to reach Jesus. He was not afraid of what the world might think; in fact, as a blind beggar, he had already lost his reputation with the world. He did not let the world hold him back from getting Jesus' attention. His flesh, his natural inclinations, would have him curl over in the street in defeat and give up. What power did a beggar have in getting the help of a famous preacher? Being blind he had no way to find his way through the crowd. He must have felt physically powerless, yet to our surprise, *"he through off his cloak and jumped up"* when Jesus called for him. Have you ever seen a beggar, or a blind person suddenly jump up? Such was the power of Jesus' call. Nothing is mentioned of Satan in this passage, however we know that this "father of lies" was working on the blind beggar's mind to discourage him from his quest. "Who are you, the lowliest of men, to expect God to do something for you?" "Your situation is impossible why bother to seek help?" "It's too much trouble; give up." We are all too familiar with the lies that Satan tries to plant in our minds. Bartimaeus did not fall for any of this "put down" thinking. He had his eyes fixed on his goal and nothing would stop him.

What does this have to do with Lent? Spring is at our doorsteps. Time to go out into the garden and pull up weeds, break up the soil, and get the ground ready for new life. If we are not willing to prepare the ground, we may not get the kind of new life we hope for. And still the object of our work is not creating a "clean ground", but making room for flowers and vegetables.

Spiritual Spring is also at our doorsteps; time to prepare the ground of our hearts and deal with the weeds and rocks—the world, the flesh, and the devil. Let nothing stand in the way of moving forward toward our goal.

But are we "blind beggars" who desperately need the touch of Jesus? If we are hanging onto prejudice, criticism, resentment, we are blind, because we are unable to see the real beauty in others. If we are hanging onto pride, self-sufficiency, low self-esteem we are blind to our own goodness and our own need for others. And are we beggars? A beggar is one who depends totally on the mercy of others. Spiritually don't we depend totally on the mercy of God each day of our lives? And if we think our spiritual safety is built on our own goodness or righteous deeds, we have missed the fundamental message of the Gospel. So, when our masks are removed, we are revealed as "blind beggars" who need to follow the example of Bartimaeus with all our hearts, minds, and strength.

Imagine how excited Bartimaeus was the day he met Jesus. Imagine how his life did a complete turnaround that day. Even when Jesus said, *"go on your way"*, this "healed" beggar chose instead to follow Jesus to Jerusalem. Jesus is walking down the street of my life this Lent. Will I let the world, the flesh, or the devil stop me from connecting with him in a new way?

"He spoke and it was created; He commanded and there it stood." (Ps 33:9)

"I once was lost, but now I'm found. I was blind but now I see."

289

March Madness

One of our local heroes this year is the University of Louisville basketball team. Plagued with multiple player injuries and having no "stars" on the team, they have played and defeated "superstar" teams this year. From being a team of "nobodies" they have emerged as a possible "final four" contender.

I wonder what kind of attitude they are sporting at this time. Are they approaching the "March madness" season half-heartedly thinking they they will probably lose early in the tournament. Or are they focusing on how less talented they are than their opponents? Though there will be many battles ahead, the team, I'm sure, is eagerly awaiting the first tournament game and is confident that they will pull upset after upset.

What does the attitude of the U of L basketball team have to do with us? We are just 5 days away for the Church's version of "March Madness"—we call it Lent (which means "Spring"). What is our frame of mind as we enter the spiritual tournament? Are we approaching our pre-tournament "practices" with laziness or even fear? Are we wondering if it's worth doing our best to defeat our opponent this year?

What a great opportunity lies before us. The entire Church around the world gears itself up this year to enter the Lenten game and hand Satan a major defeat as he prowls around the world reeking havoc. Each of us is a member of the Church "team", and when one of us lets up, other members of the body have to pick up the slack caused by our half-heartedness. Let's pray for the grace to enter into Lent with an attitude of confidence, eagerness, strength, and joy. March Madness is about to begin!

Jesus models an attitude of strength and confidence in today's Gospel story. (Mk 11:11-26) He is heading to Jerusalem to engage Satan in the greatest confrontation that history would ever witness. Knowing He was a "marked man", He walked resolutely straight into the Temple—the place where the priests and scribes hung out. He was neither half-hearted nor afraid. Then, almost as though He wanted to provoke a fight, the next day He walked back into the Temple and overturned tables, scattered money, and refused to let anyone carry anything through the Temple. In a dramatic way He shattered the idols that represented the Temple "economy". What had been designed a house of prayer *"for all the peoples"* had deteriorated into a cheap marketplace. Jesus acted with strength and authority in confronting the gods that blinded people from the presence of the Father.

He then calls His apostles to imitate Him by acting in strength. As they stood in front of the fig tree which He had cursed the day before, He exhorted them to be bold in the use of their spiritual gifts. *"Have faith in God"*, He told them. Command mountains to be thrown into the sea, believe that what you ask for in prayer is already yours, begin prayer with an act of forgiveness. What strength He is giving His followers, which includes us. Is He saying that we are powerful enough to move mountains? Notice that He begins with the exhortation to, *"have faith in God"*. Do we believe that the God who created the heavens and the earth has the power to lift a mountain and toss it into the sea? Remember this is the same God who brought down the mighty walls of Jericho, defeated the great Midianite armies, brought down the giant Goliath. Nothing is impossible with God. It is our faith and our prayer that accesses the very strength and power of God. Remember we are His children—not powerful on our own, but ones who have great influence over our Almighty Father. Remember God's only Son, Jesus, lives in our hearts. How can He refuse us?

We do not enter the "Lenten tournament" resting on our own talents and the power of our own wills. We enter leaning on the strength and power of God, using faith, prayer, and forgiveness as our weapons. Though we might seem as a team of "nobodies", we have the superstar of superstars as our team leader. We do not enter the wilderness alone; we enter hand-in-hand with Jesus.

Let's use this "pre-Lenten scrimmage" as a time to seek the lead of the Holy Spirit, and pray for new spiritual strength. Let us be equipped with faith and confidence in prayer, throwing off the cloaks of fear and laziness— and maybe a negative attitude. Let March Madness begin!

"For the Lord has been kind to His people, conferring victory on us who are weak." (Ps 149:4)

"Jesus, we repent of our weak-heartedness. Thank You for the gift of faith and the gift of prayer; help us exercise with confidence these gifts You have given us."

Flowers of Wisdom

When Spring arrives, my wife, Linda, gets excited about planting flowers and tomatoes. My main part in this project is digging up the soil and getting rid of the weeds. Linda gets focused on flowers, I get focused on dirt. Who do you think is more excited about the coming of Spring?

Lent, is our spiritual springtime—a time for digging and planting. We have a choice of focusing on the flowers that will soon come or of focusing on the dirt that has to be dealt with—the dust of Ash Wednesday or the new life of Easter. Which will it be?

In today's Gospel story we have another meeting of Jesus with the priests and Temple authorities (Mk 11:27-33) The Temple leaders were trying to "dig up dirt", and Jesus was planting seeds of life. The accusers of Jesus saw Him as a "threat" to their personal power. They saw Him as the one who just got rid of the corruption going on in Temple, and this scared them. On the other hand, the people saw this "spiritual Spring cleaning" as opening the door for a new age in Israel. A great teacher and healer was among them whose message gave them new hope. Perhaps this was the long-awaited Messiah.

The Jewish leaders threw the first punch by challenging Jesus as to who authorized Him as a Temple teacher. In effect they were saying, "We didn't give our approval; show us your credentials". They are accusing Jesus of violating the Law and their system of governance. Who was behind this "accusing approach" to Jesus? None other than the, *"persecutor who accused"* the early Christians as well. (Rev 12:10) Jesus, unlike Eve, did not get into a conversation with the adversary. Instead He rebuked His accusers with a question of His own.

"Did John's baptism come from heaven, or from man?" Jesus asked them. A short multiple choice question with two answers: "a" or "b". If they chose "a", they would be admitting their sin of rejecting a prophet sent by God, and would be challenged to humble themselves and repent. Their pride would not allow this. So maybe they should go with choice "b". This would get them in trouble too, because if they renounced John they would incur the disfavor of the people who knew that John was sent from God. Since the leaders were driven by a spirit of "people pleasing" they would be cutting their own throats if they opted for "b". This would mean they would be surrendering their power, which would have been another path of repentance. In effect Jesus said, "you have two choices: to repent or to repent." These leaders were experts at "playing it cool", so they replied with choice "c", "none of the above." His accusers were foiled again.

Jesus showed strength and authority in dealing with the conniving "father of lies". He did not waste His time playing games with the enemy; He had an important mission to carry out and nothing would stand in His way.

Jesus was the personification of wisdom. He could not be outwitted by the enemy, unlike our first parents who were tricked into the devil's trap. Today's reading from Sirach (51:12-20) speaks of this gift of wisdom which is now available to all believers through the Holy Spirit. Sirach talks about the delights of wisdom: *"from her blossoming to the ripening of her grape, my heart has taken its delight in her.", "By bowing my ear to her a little, I have received her, and found much instruction.", "Having my heart fixed on her from the outset, I shall never be deceived."* Wisdom brings delight, teaches our spirits, and keeps us from being deceived by the enemy.

Maybe "wisdom" is one the "flowers" God wants to plant more fully in our hearts during this "spiritual springtime". Let's work with him in getting the dirt ready, all the time rejoicing that we will see blossoms of wisdom come forth in us in this season of growing.

"His words are sweeter than honey, even the honey that drips from the comb." (Ps 19:10)

"Jesus, source of wisdom, may I deal wisely with the accusations of the enemy, and experience new growth during the Lenten season."

Checking Foundations

Before I received the Baptism in the Holy Spirit, the foundation of my life was work. It was good work—it was Church work, yet it was not a strong enough foundation to build my life upon. When floods came into my life, my sandy foundation began to collapse. Though in my imagination I thought Jesus was the rock of my life, in fact He wasn't.

I find it easy to identify with Peter who must have been proud of himself when Jesus named him "Rock". He boasted that he would stand by Jesus even if the rest of the apostles deserted Him. When the flood of testing came, however, Peter's house collapsed right within the view of Jesus. This "Rock" had left his business and family and followed Jesus enthusiastically. He knew Jesus' teachings by heart, went out on a mission, healed and expelled demons in His name, walked as the leading disciple of the Son of God. All this, and still his foundations were but sand. It wasn't until Pentecost that the "Rock" in Peter came into existence.

Today's reading confronts us with the importance of solid spiritual foundations. (Mt 7:21-27) As we move into the "Lent" of the Church, it is a good time to ask God to test our foundations. How much of my life is built on work still? How much is my security built on my bank account? Is family involvement my foundation? What about basketball? When the inspectors come to examine the strength of my foundations, do they find Jesus as the Rock on whom everything else in my life is built?

Let's listen to Jesus. *"When the day comes, many will say to me 'Lord, Lord! Did we not prophesy in Your name, cast out demons in Your name, work many miracles in Your name'?"*

Surely the great ministers who have prophetic words on a regular basis, or who have a successful deliverance ministry, or even have the gift of miracles, will be welcomed with open arms by Jesus when they come to the kingdom's gates. These were the superstars who impressed so many people with their charisms. How impressed is Jesus with these people? *"I shall tell them to their faces: I have never known you; away from me, you evil men!"* Notice at the start of this discourse Jesus says that "many" will approach Him with this kind of evidence. So "many" will be rejected, for Jesus does not even know who they are, and He tells this them this, *"to their faces."*

If ministers who perform great wonders in Jesus' name do not have an automatic ticket into heaven, what about the rest of us? Is there any hope?

So how do we win Jesus' approval and bring a smile to His face when we approach Him. How do we make sure we are not among those whom He doesn't even know? The secret, Jesus teaches, is listening to His words and acting on them. So simple! If we want favor with Jesus, we not only hear His Word but listen attentively to it. Then the fruit of our listening is action—we shape our lives according to His Word and His will.

Earlier Jesus says it is not the great "pray-ers" with

their *"Lord, Lord"* prayers who will enter the kingdom of heaven, but those who do the will of the heavenly Father. What impresses people does not necessarily impress God. Doing the will of God is what most moves His heart. Doing our "own thing" or doing what wins a following for us is not what it's all about.

God lets floods come into our lives, sometimes on a regular basis. There is a part of us that is usually shaken by these floods. And, if part of our lives are built on sandy foundations, we might begin to feel our lives beginning to collapse. Deep inside, though, as the sand washes away we will find "the rock of our salvation" resting soundly at the base of our hearts. This is our gift and our only source of security.

For the house built on rock "rain came down, floods rose, gales blew and hurled themselves against the house, and it did not fall; it was founded on rock." We need not be envious of those who seem to have bigger and better spiritual houses than the one God gave us. For it is not the size of the house, but the base on which it sits that counts.

"Be a sheltering rock for me, a walled fortress to save me. For You are my rock, my fortress; for the sake of Your name, guide me, lead me!" (Ps 31:2-3)

"Jesus is the rock of my salvation, His banner over me is love."

Rejection

One of the most fundamental needs of every human being is to be accepted. Perhaps the most painful of all experiences is to feel rejected by someone else, especially if that person is someone close to you, someone you trusted.

We would like to think that we can welcome Jesus into our hearts, turn our lives over to Him and not be rejected for doing so. We would like to think that in our generation people will be different from those of past generations, and they will accept the Jesus in us this time. We would like to close our eyes to the full truth of the Gospel.

Jesus was still having a "face off" with the priests, the scribes, and the elders as they stood together in the Temple area. (Mk 12:1-12) He began to speak a parable that they knew, *"was aimed at them"*. The parable was a two-edged sword that penetrated deep into their hearts and released the contents of hate that resided there. They were so angry that they wanted more than anything else to have Jesus arrested, and eventually killed.

The parable was a short history of salvation. A man went to much trouble in building a well-equipped vineyard, and then entrusted it to tenants while he was gone. We would expect that the tenants would be grateful for the privilege of working in the vineyard and making a living for themselves. We would expect that they would be eager to show their gratitude by cheerfully giving the owner his due share of their profit.

Instead, the opposite happened. When a servant came to collect the rent due the owner, the tenants, *"seized the man, thrashed him, and sent him away empty-handed"*. Another servant was sent and the tenants treated him even worse—they beat him in the head. Then they went even further in their hate and killed the third servant. The patient owner continued to send servants hoping that eventually the tenants would have a change of heart, but no they continued to reject and even kill the servants.

Jesus was giving the history of the Old Testament prophets, who spoke the truth before the people, calling them to turn to God and give Him the praise, love, and obedience that was His due. After all, it was only out of the generosity of His heart that He built the vineyard and leased it to the tenants in the first place. Time after time the prophets were rejected, abused, and many were killed.

In God's great love he made one last attempt to win a return from the tenants; He sent His "beloved Son". He thought, *"Surely they will respect my very own Son"*. Instead they treated him worse than any of the prophets. In rejecting God's own Son, they had no hope any more. This was their final chance. Jesus prophesied that the Owner would come and, *"make an end to the tenants and give the vineyard to others."*

The history of salvation is one of God pouring out His love and favor upon a people, and time after time His love is rejected. What happened in Old Testament history continued to happen even after the resurrection of Jesus. Stephen, James, Peter, Paul, and thousands of others were martyred because of the truth of Jesus that they bore within their hearts. Today is the feast day of Saints Perpetua and Felicity who with three other companions gave up their lives for Jesus. Tenants of every age continue to reject the sons and daughters of God whom He sends to collect the share of blessings that is His due.

It is naïve to think that if we have Jesus alive and growing in our hearts that we will not experience rejection. Revisit the promises of Jesus in John's Gospel, chapter 15. *"If the world hates you, remember that it hated Me before you."…"If they persecuted Me, they will persecute you."* Many this day (some readers of this message included) are experiencing painful rejection from family members, people at work, and even church members because Jesus lives within them. Jesus said, *"it will be on My account that they will do all this.."* (Jn 15:21)

If we are not going through this "fiery ordeal", maybe our moment has not arrived…yet. Because we are united to the body of Christ we suffer with our persecuted sisters and brothers. *"If one part is hurt, all parts are hurt with it."* (1 Cor 12:26) We all participate in the grief of those servants who continue to be rejected when they obey the Lord and address the tenants of our age. Our faithfulness to prayer and commitment to Jesus sends love and strength through the body so as to support those who are being rejected for Christ.

"It was the stone that was rejected by the builders that became the keystone; this was the Lord's doing and it is wonderful to see." (Ps 118:22-23)

"Jesus, let me be a servant who continues to bear the message of God's love and truth to my generation no matter the price I am asked to pay."

Freedom in Christ

It is fitting that today's Gospel is read at income tax time. Taxes was a touchy subject with the Jews of Jesus' era because they were under the domination of the Romans, and were being forced to support, through taxes, the godless system that had been imposed on them.

Yesterday we read of Jesus' confronting the Jewish leaders with a stinging parable. Today two other groups appeared on the stage, the Pharisees and the Herodians, a strange combination because they hated each other! They had a great plan for tricking Jesus into getting in trouble with the Romans, and it was a question about taxes. (Mk 12:13-17) Jesus was popular with the people, and He would lose His popularity with them if He supported the Roman taxation system. On the other hand if He catered to the crowd, He would speak up against taxes and thus get in trouble with the Romans. His enemies knew that He would not incur the disfavor of the people, for they thought that He, like they, was a slave to public opinion. Too cowardly to do their own "dirty work", they attempted to set Jesus up, so the Romans would arrest Him and do away with Him. Jesus responded with a wisdom that went far beyond the trickery of the Pharisees and Herodians. His famous one-liner: "give to Caesar what is Caesar's and to God what is God's" is known even today by Christians and non-Christians alike.

What freedom Jesus had! The Gospel says His accusers were "completely surprised" by Jesus' response. He was living fully in the kingdom of God and was in no way a slave to world or religious systems. On the other hand,

His accusers were enslaved to their own self-deception. Somehow they believed they could manipulate the plan and power of God.

In time, yes, Jesus would be arrested and done away with, but in "God's time", not man's time, and in God's way not man's way. No human coalition can force God's hand to act or have Him act according to their plans. Every attempt made by the enemies of Jesus served only to release more wisdom from Him and bring themselves into ever deepening conviction. Clearly they were under the control of the evil one, himself.

It is interesting to note that Jesus asked them for a denarius. He did not take one out of his own pocket, which meant He was not participating in the Roman economy. One of His accusers quickly withdrew a denarius which made it evident that they were compromising with Roman rule. How ironic.

When anyone plays the "power game" with God, they come out loser. The power of the Holy Spirit in believers is so much greater than all worldly power combined, that we always come out on top, as long as we choose not to play their game. As children of God who are temples of the Holy Spirit and operating in the power of the Holy Spirit, *"no weapon formed against us shall prosper."* (Is 54:17)

In giving us the Holy Spirit, God calls us to walk in the same freedom that Jesus had. The enemy no longer has power to trick us or trap us into being slaves again. Do we really believe this, or do we have a "victim mentality" which thinks we are controlled by powers other than God? And do we act on the knowledge of who we are, or do we, like the Galatians of old, fall back into a "pre-Pentecost" way of thinking?

The Church gives us a few short readings from the Book of Tobit these days (2 days only). I think the idea is to entice us into reading the whole book, the way the people in the food courts give us a piece of chicken mounted on a toothpick to win our patronage. This is a beautiful story of a righteous man, who like Job, had the entire bottom fall out of his life. Then it ends, miraculously, "happily ever after". Today's psalm reading speaks to those who have given their lives to Jesus, dedicated themselves to a righteous life, and still experience great troubles. The psalm gives us a list of the "returns" we will get for maintaining fidelity in the midst of tribulation. (Read Psalm 112)

Our children will be powers upon the earth, our descendants will be always blessed, their will be wealth for our families, we will shine like a lamp in the dark, we will leave an imperishable memory behind us when we die, we will never fear bad news, we will triumph over our enemies (as Jesus did) in the long run, and we will always be honored. What a deal!

"Happy the man who fears the Lord by joyfully keeping His commandments." (Ps 112:1)

"Father, as Your chosen children we share in the freedom of Christ. Let us not be duped to falling back again into slavery."

Someday

How many of us have ever said: "Someday I'll start losing weight." or "Someday I'll clean the basement", or "Someday I'll visit my sick aunt", or "Someday _____ (you fill in the blank)? "Someday" is not a real day, and it never seems to happen.

Today the Church tells us that "someday" has arrived! Paul steps up and proclaims, *"now is the acceptable time, now is the day of salvation."* (2 Cor 6:2). He urges us, *"not to neglect the grace of God"* that we have received. (2 Cor 6:1). We have been entrusted with the very life of the Holy Spirit. Have we, in any way, neglected this greatest of gifts? To make sure that we caught Paul's message, the Church has the prophet Joel step up, trumpet in hand shouting, *"Blow the trumpet in Zion, declare a holy fast."* (Joel 2:15). And then to put an exclamation point on the message, the Church takes us through the dramatic ceremony of putting ashes on our foreheads. We are getting a preview of what we'll look like 100 years from now. Knowing that life is amazingly short, presses us to make our "someday", now. Ash Wednesday is set aside by the Church to proclaim as loudly as she can "today is the moment to begin anew." Quoting Mark's Gospel, the Church announces to each of us, *"repent and believe the good news."* (Mk 1:15)

Today March 9, 2011, then, is the day we repent and believe that God is doing a new work in our lives. How are we to repent? Matthew steps up and writes the prescription for us: 1) give to the needy, 2) go into your room and pray to the Father, 3) fast.

"Do not be stingy in giving alms...almsgiving delivers from death...alms is a most effective offering for all those who give it...Never turn your face from a poor man and God will never turn His from you." (see Tobit 4:7-12).

"When you pray, go into the room close the door, and pray to your Father who is unseen...then your Father who sees what is done in secret will reward you...And when you pray do not keep on babbling..." (Mt 6:5-8). How can we develop a deeper relationship with God if we never spend personal time with Him? Communal prayer is not enough. And how can we improve our relationship with God if we do all the talking?

What about fasting? This is the least popular of Matthew's three prescriptions for me. Yet it may be the most powerful of all the medicines in dealing with our three enemies—the world, the flesh, and the devil. What is the most popular place in our neighborhood? You're right, Krogers. What is the most popular form of entertainment? You're right, eating out. What is the greatest health issue in our country? Obesity, you're right again. Fasting helps detach us from one of the world's most powerful forces—love of food. Our flesh, natural inclinations, does not like to be moderate in the use of food. Saying "no" to our appetites is a tough form of discipline. When we restrain our flesh, however, it gives the Spirit more room to grow within us. And when we fast, as Jesus did in the wilderness, our minds clear up so we can better recognize the lies of the devil. Also fasting strengthens us and enlightens us in how to use the Word of God to resist the devil's tactics. Though fasting is not popular, it is a necessary ingredient for spiritual growth.

If we look back on Jesus' Lent (Mt 4:1-11) we learn that He *"was led by the Holy Spirit"* into the wilderness. As we pray about Lent, it is important that we take specific directions from the Holy Spirit, and not just concoct a set of plans guided by our own imaginations and built solely on the power of our own wills. We need grace to do Lent.

Jesus also emphasizes "keeping secrets" about what we do. Matthew mentions the word "secret" about six times in today's reading. Alms are to be secret, prayer is to be secret, and fasting is to be secret. Not only are we to hide what we do but we are to "cover it up" with a clean face, a joyful disposition, and a huge smile. Secrets breed intimacy. What we do secretly with God draws us deeper into His heart. And isn't this what the wilderness was all about?---Jesus cut Himself off from everything but His experience of deep intimacy with the Father, which is the greatest of all joys. This is the "good news" that the Church tells us to believe in as we journey into the quiet wilderness with Jesus.

Let us rejoice and walk eagerly into the Lenten season, for our "someday" has arrived.

"The sacrifices of God are a broken spirit; a broken and contrite heart, O God, You will not despise." (Ps 51:17)

"Come, Holy Spirit, lead me into the wilderness where I will experience deep intimacy with the Father. Stir up wisdom and courage within my spirit as I set out to give alms, pray, and fast in a spirit of joy."

Saint Shabaz

Last week another martyr was added to our roster of contemporary saints. His name is Shabaz Bhatti. He was the only Christian in the Pakistani cabinet and a courageous advocate for the rights of religious minorities. In a country where blasphemy laws make being a Christian a crime, sometimes punishable by death, Bhatti was not afraid to bear the name and cross of Jesus. In an article this week in the Courier Journal (Tuesday, editorial page) he is quoted as saying: "These Taliban threaten me. But I want to share that I believe in Jesus Christ, who has given His own life for us. I know what is the meaning of the Cross, and I am following the Cross." On the morning of March 2 while on the way to work, Bhatti was ambushed and shot over 20 times, a martyr for his faith.

He was not afraid to lose his life in order that he might save not only his life, but that of thousands of his countrymen. The whole world will be blessed this spring by the heroic life and death of Shabaz Bhatti. We are proud to be part of the same living body of Jesus Christ to which he belongs.

Our Gospel reading this morning is from Luke (9:22-25). Jesus tells us that, *"whoever loses his life for my sake, will save it."* There is nothing we cherish more than our own lives, and the last thing our natural selves want to do is to die. Our natural self (Paul calls it the flesh) is unable to see that there is any more to life than what happens here on earth. To lose this life is to lose everything. Once filled with the Holy Spirit, however, we know that a new life has been planted in our hearts,

309

called "eternal life", and this endures beyond death. It is this presence of the Holy Spirit within us that gives us the courage to do as Shabaz Bhatti did and lose our lives for the sake of Jesus.

To be willing to gladly die for Jesus is either insanity or love beyond imagination. Jesus said that there is no greater love than to lay one's life down for one's friends. What empowers us to be willing to surrender all to Jesus, is that we are madly in love with Him and overflowing with gratitude for what He did for us at Calvary. It is said that the Jesuit novices in France longed more than anything to come to the new world, evangelize the Indians, and be martyred for the sake of Christ. They had become intoxicated with the burning love of Jesus within their hearts. And our country has been blessed with the martyrdom of Saints Isaac Jogues, John de Brebeuf, and their companions, all French Jesuits.

Let's read the words of Jesus closely. He said, *"if anyone would come after me, he must deny himself and take up his cross daily and follow Me."* These words are not meant for just a few heroic saints. *"Anyone"* does not mean 10% or 50%. It means 100% of those who choose to follow Jesus are called to deny ourselves daily, proud to shoulder the cross of Jesus.

The Church chooses this reading at the outset of Lent to stir up within us the love of Jesus that will give us the desire and courage to deny ourselves. This means that we, then, are also martyrs for Jesus Christ who are opting to lose our lives for Him. How will this "martyrdom" work itself out in our lives today and through the season of Lent?

Fasting is one way the Church puts before us. Our natural lives, our desire for food, drink and pleasures do not want to be denied. They rebel so strongly that at times they succeed in having us put aside the cross of Jesus for awhile. Yet the power of the Holy Spirit within us is stronger than the power of our appetites, and we see the witness of brothers and sisters who, out of love for Jesus, are giving up much more than a meal.

When our fasting gets difficult, let's unite the discomfort with the pain of those who are enduring direct persecution for their faith—and there are many. Remember we are part of the same living body of Christ as every other Christian in the world, and when one member suffers, so do all the other members. When one member denies himself or herself, even in a small way, a new wave of grace surges throughout the Body. Our acts of love and denial count.

"Now choose life, so that you and your children may live, and that you may love the Lord your God, listen to His voice, and hold fast to Him." (Dt 30:19-20)

"Jesus, may our acts of denial, empower the rest of our brothers and sisters to have the courage to witness for You in all circumstances."

Fasting to Feasting

Imagine someone walking into McDonalds, placing a five-dollar bill on the counter and then turning around and walking out. Or imagine someone walking into McDonalds and waiting to be served a "big breakfast" without paying for it. What's wrong with these pictures?

When we go to a restaurant, we give up something so we can get back something that we judge to be better. We give up 5-dollars so we can get a breakfast that we need more than we do the money. In a sense we "fast" from the money, so we can "feast" on the food.

Today's short Gospel passage is about "fasting" and "feasting". (Mt 9:14-15). The disciples of John approached Jesus and asked Him why His disciples did not fast the way they and the Pharisees fasted? Any credible rabbi would require religious fasting for his disciples. Why wasn't Jesus doing this?

Why did the disciples of John the Baptist and the Pharisees fast? They maintained this religious discipline so they could stay focused on their call which was to prepare the way for the coming Messiah. They fasted so that in time they could "feast" at the Messianic table. Well, hello! The goal had been reached; they were, in fact, talking to the Messiah. They had "spent" much fasting forgetting that the whole purpose was to prepare for the "feasting". It was as though they put down their 5-dollars, and then walked away just as the breakfast was placed on the counter.

312

And, as a matter of fact, the disciples of Jesus were fasting. They had given up jobs, families, and pleasures of life to join the bridegroom. What they had given up was much more than an occasional meal. Their type of fasting went far beyond the minimal religious fasting of other groups.

In fasting we give up one thing, to get something that we believe is far better. We give up a little food, so we can feast on a greater food, the Bread of Life. We give up a little time, so we can feast on the joy of serving others. We give up some of our "busyness" so we can feast on our love affair with the God who created us. If we "fast", and lose sight of the "feast", we fall into the meaningless religious routine exemplified by the Pharisees in today's reading. Our self-denial could work in reverse.

Isaiah speaks to this point today (Is 58:1-9). The people were dedicated to religious fasting, yet God was not impressed. Their religious activity was not working. Isaiah was saying "what about the feasting?" Give up bread so you can enjoy sharing it with the hungry. Give up some space in your home, so you can enjoy sharing it with the wanderer. Give up some of your money so you can enjoy clothing the poor person who cannot afford to clothe himself. Fasting without feasting makes no sense to God or to us. When we give up some of our comfort and pleasure, so that we can serve others, the joy we experience goes far beyond the few moments of satisfaction we would have had. We fast so that we can better *"rejoice in the Lord always."* The Church calls us to fast, so that we can better enjoy the bridegroom and serve His wedding guests.

"Yes," someone might argue, "but we are Christians who have the bridegroom with us already; why should we fast?" There are many reasons we can offer; here are three.

1. Fasting from some earthly pleasures, frees us to feast on a closer relationship with our Bridegroom

2. Fasting from some earthly pleasures, helps those who do not know the Bridegroom and have not come to His feast.

3. Fasting gives us the honor of freely participating in the suffering of our persecuted brothers and sisters throughout the world. It builds love and unity in the Body of Christ.

"In your good pleasure, make Zion prosper; build up the walls of Jerusalem." (Ps 51:18)

"Jesus, stir within me a desire to feast more fully on Your love, and free me to "fast" from some creature comforts so I am available to receive the comfort You offer."

Get Up, Leave Everything, Follow

Today we read the amazing story of Levi, thought also to be the apostle Matthew. (Lk 5:27-32). Jesus went out, saw Levi sitting at his tax booth, and said two words: *"Follow me."* In response Levi did three things:
    1) He got up
    2) He left everything, and
    3) He followed Jesus.

When, as a young child, I heard this story, it made complete sense to me. Jesus was the Son of God, He was full of love, He was wonderful; who wouldn't get up right away and leave what they were doing and follow Him. As I got older and became more jaded by the realities of life, this story began to seem more like a fairy tale.

Let's imagine it is one of us at our job, with a huge money box, and a book of tax records in front of us, and drawing a sizable income—one which enabled us to throw big parties at our impressive home. Jesus walks up to us and says, "Follow me". Would we be as eager to jump up and follow Jesus, as Levi was? Here are the thoughts that would probably go through my head: What will my wife think when I go home and tell her I quit my "6-digit income" job? What would happen to the big box of money that I was guarding at the booth? What about the meticulous records I was taking? How would I pay my bills? What would the Roman soldiers do to me when they came into town to pick up the taxes I had collected? Think of all the fears that we would wrestle with if Jesus approached us and called us as He called Levi. Fear of my family's reaction, fear of losing my job, fear of losing my money, fear of my work getting stolen, fear of punishment that the authorities might exact on me, fear of being laughed at if Jesus turned out to be a hoax. What a miracle of grace that Levi even got out of his chair in the first place, much less left everything.

This story is about us, today, as much as it was about Levi; that is why the Church presents it to us at the start of Lent. Wherever we are sitting right now, are we willing to get up and leave what we're doing behind to follow Jesus? Sometimes just getting up out of the easy chair to go to a prayer meeting or to serve someone in need is a major struggle for us. Leaving the table to eat less food, leaving our money for those who are in more need than we are, leaving our pet projects so that we can do God's project, all involve a level of pain and require that we allow our faith to overcome our fears.

Our reading from Isaiah today (Is 58:9-14) continues to throw light on what repentance and fasting are all about. *"If you keep from doing as you please on my holy day...and honor it by not going your own way and not doing as you please or speaking idle words, then you will find joy in your Lord."* Notice the *"as you please"*, *"going your own way"*, *"speaking idle words"*. Does this give us a hint at why getting up and leaving everything to follow Jesus is so hard? We are so anchored in doing our own thing and doing what pleases us that we do not find it easy to respond with enthusiasm to Jesus' call.

The call of Jesus is not some dramatic moment that occurred 40 years ago in our past. His call is alive and

316

is going out to us each day, in some way. Even today He is calling us to repent—to stand up, to leave something, to follow Him.

It would be impossible to do what Levi did, if it were not for the power of the presence of Jesus. Imagine the pull of Jesus' presence and His words, that made Levi forget about everything—family, job, money, safety, reputation. It is the overwhelming grace of God that sets us free to put Jesus first in our lives. He is worth more than all other treasures on earth, and saying "yes" to Him is all that, ultimately, matters.

God's call goes out to the Church in a new way, and this call falls upon the ears of each disciple or would-be disciple. Do we hear His voice? Is their an inner resistance that we need to detach from? Is He sending out small challenges, so we will be trained to meet the big challenges that lie down the road? In my life now, what is the "tax booth", what is the "chair" on which I'm sitting, how am I impacted by the living voice of Jesus?

"Will You not revive us again that Your people may rejoice in You?" (Ps 85:6)

"St. Matthew, pray for me that I will be as eager to follow the call of Jesus as you were, and so will be able to evangelize as you did."

Criticizing the Church

We live in an age of consumerism. Everyone, as a consumer, has the power to buy and sell, and so marketers have great respect for human opinion. Pollsters ask us our opinion on everything from fried chicken to the President's performance. It makes us feel important when someone asks us what we think.

In the spiritual life "consumerism" is not only of little value, it can be outright destructive. Did God consult us before He developed His plan for the Church? Does He need our critical input to have the Church be what He wants it to be? Many American Catholics have taken it upon themselves to stand on the pedestal of consumerism and make judgments about the Church. How many Pastors are plagued with parish "consumers" coming up to them after Mass telling them what's wrong with the parish and what the pastor needs to do to fix it? How many sins of gossip revolve around criticizing the Church or one of its leaders?

I remember when I was raising my children, trying to pay bills, take care of the house, and deal with 200+ teenagers a day at work, what a struggle it was. No one was more aware of my imperfect performance than I was. The last thing I needed was for an "expert" to step up, tell me how I was failing, and offer a quick and easy solution to my struggles. I remember reading an article written by a pastor who had pastored a church many years before he married. He said, in effect, "before I was married, I had five theories on raising children, and no children. Now I have five children and no theories." Our Church does not need our criticism, it needs our commitment to holiness.

Jesus explained it best when He said to focus on the "beams" in our own eyes rather than trying to pick the splinters out of the eyes of others. Criticism is not a gift of the Holy Spirit. One time I was talking with a Catholic friend and I was complaining about some of the things I didn't like in our parish church. He asked me "what about you? How well are you doing your job in the parish?" That caught me off guard. First I didn't know I had a job in the parish, much less was doing anything about it. Then I prayed, and received the word that my job was to intercede for the pastor especially at Sunday Mass. How well was I doing this job? I wasn't. Maybe the pastor was getting a 70% grade; I, however, was getting a flat zero. When I do my job well, I find the church leaders do theirs better as well.

The tendency to be a "Catholic consumer" and criticize the Church is a temptation. When we yield to it, we sin. Today's Gospel reading (Mt 4:1-11) is about Jesus dealing with temptation in the desert. Many of the allurements put to Him by Satan are the same ones Satan puts before the Church today, and puts on our minds as a way of criticizing the Church.

"Use your power to buy bread and feed the hungry of the world. Look how rich the Church is and how many people go without food." Or, "Be more spectacular, do something more exciting that will attract the crowds. Bring in some "stars" from outside town; God will fund the idea." Or, "take the easy way out; compromise a little here and a little there and everyone will want to join Church." From a consumer's point of view, all of these ideas of Satan make sense. The only catch is that when we follow these "great ideas", we give control back to the devil. Jesus refused to use His divine powers to solve world hunger, do the spectacular, or compromise with Satan as a way of winning control of the world. Jesus, instead, took the path of obedience; He committed Himself, even unto death on a cross, to doing it God's way.

Paul reminds us of God's tactics in saving the world in today's reading from Romans. *"...through the obedience of one man the many will be made righteous."* (Rm 5:19) Real power is not the cheap power of Satan, but the power of obedience to God; "one man's" faithfulness brought on the salvation of many. And today's reading from Genesis reminds us how the "old Adam" dealt with temptation. He chose to ignore the command of God and try the serpent's "quick and easy" way. We know the rest of this story.

"Have mercy on me, O God, according to Your unfailing love; according to Your great compassion blot out my transgressions." (Ps 51:1)

"Jesus, continue to impress upon me that humble obedience is the way to God's power, not arrogance and pride."

Why?

Momma says to Molly "when we visit Aunt Susan this afternoon, I want you to remember to be polite…saying 'yes ma'am', 'please', 'thank you'…" Molly responds, "Why?" Momma starts thinking of some good reasons like: 'because I said so', or 'everyone will like you better', or 'Aunt Susan won't gossip about us tomorrow', or 'I'll be proud of you'….or…..

God today (Lev 19:1-2,11-18) says to us: *"Be holy"*. We respond "Why?" God says, *"because I, the Lord your God, am holy."* What kind of answer is that? He could have said something like, "because this is one of my rules, and I am God", or "so you can be sure to earn a high place in heaven", or "because others will be impressed with you and respect you."

How wise God is. He appeals to the deepest desire that any human being has, to be like our loving Father. We love Him so much, that we want to be just like He is; we don't need any other reason. It was this desire to be *like God* that helped motivate Adam and Eve to sin. Had they obeyed God instead of giving into temptation, they would have, daily, become more and more like Him. Instead they chose Satan's "path to holiness" by disobeying, and they fell off the road to holiness.

Practical-minded as we are, the next question we say is, "Okay God, give me some specifics of how You are holy." In turn, God gives a list of twelve or more "do not's". Turning them into "do's", we get a glimpse of how God acts—He respects and gives generously instead of stealing; He always speaks the truth instead

321

of lying; He honors his own name and never profanes it, etc.

Was Israel able to live up to these commandments of God and thus, *"be holy"* as God is holy? No, their history gives evidence of their failure in this regard; they were still living under the curse of Adam. Why, then, would God command them to be holy if He knew that they did not have the power to do so? St. Paul teaches that the law was needed to convict His people that they were falling short and needed an intervention of God before they could be holy.

Jesus broke the curse of Adam and started a new race of *"holy people, people set apart to sing the praises of God."* When He sent the Holy Spirit into the hearts of His disciples, they received the power to, *"be holy as [their] heavenly Father is holy"* (1 Pt 1:15-16). God again calls His people to be holy not just in keeping commandments as the occasion arises but, *"in all you do."* This is possible, now, because the very presence of the Holy Spirit is within us creating us more and more into the image of our loving Father.

So let's get practical again. What are we to "do" if we want to be like God in all we do? Enter St. Matthew (Mt 25:31-46). Treat His children the way He treats them, and treat even His "potential children" the way He treats them. Why? We feed the hungry, clothe the naked, shelter the homeless, visit the sick and imprisoned because that's what God does! Moreover the way we treat the "least brother or sister" is the way we treat Jesus, the Son of God. Does God ignore the needs of His own Son? No. Neither, then, do we.

"The precepts of the Lord are right, giving joy to the heart. The commands of the Lord are radiant, giving light to the eyes." (Ps 19:8)

"Jesus, give me eyes to see You when You are hungry, homeless, sick, or imprisoned. Give me a heart of love to respond to Your needs as the heavenly Father does."

Daily Bread

Today's reading focuses on the "Our Father". (Mt 6:7-15) Matthew breaks Jesus' teaching on prayer into eight convenient parts, just as he did in listing the beatitudes. The first four parts are focused on God and His vision for creation. The second four parts focus on us and what we most need from God on a daily basis.

One of the dangers of reciting this prayer so many times is that it becomes just rote words without activating the deeper prayer of the Holy Spirit in our hearts. Sometimes we need to slow down and let these words arise from our hearts rather than from our mouths only.

I want to focus on the first line of the second part of the prayer: *"Give us this day our daily bread."* We might tend to think that this request is "outdated" because we don't really need God to give us our daily bread. After all we are grown-up, self-sufficient Americans. If we need bread, we just grab our money, hop in our cars, go to Krogers and buy our bread. We don't have to ask God for our bread - or do we? What about the underpaid workers who get up at 4:30 in the morning and take the bus from the other part of town to be there in time for the 6 A.M. shift. What if they decided not to show up? And what about the underpaid factory workers who help prepare and package the bread in some other part of the country? What if they decide to go on strike? We are not as self-sufficient and independent as we think we are. Few of us grow wheat in our backyards, mill it, and bake it ourselves. Our Father truly gives us each day our daily bread. Our mixed-up minds have a hard time seeing this way.

And what if we don't really need God to get the loaf of bread that sits in our cabinet? What about the bread of His love that sustains us with a purpose for living? What about the bread of His strength that keeps us moving forward in our Christian lives? What about the bread of His mercy and forgiveness that we cannot earn for ourselves or buy at the local grocery store? Do we realize how "poor" we are, and how much we depend on the goodness of God each day? Our daily bread consists of so much more than what we use to make our morning toast.

Our daily bread in its purest form is the heavenly manna we receive in the Eucharist—the risen body and blood of Jesus Himself. Certainly this is bread that we cannot earn or create ourselves, and this is the bread that gives not only strength but the promise that: *"whoever eats my flesh and drinks my blood has life in him, and I will raise him up on the last day."*

To get God's perspective on *"daily bread"*, let's revisit the Torah. *"He humbled you, causing you to hunger, and then feeding you with manna...to teach you that man does not live by bread alone, but on every word that comes from the mouth of the Lord."* (Dt 8:3) The bread of God's Word is so much more necessary than physical bread. God offered them "boring manna" instead of bread, so they would reach for something that fed their hearts not just their bodies. Moses went on to remind them that even when they were more independent and able to produce abundance of food, they needed to remember that it was not their power and strength, but the favor of the Lord who gave them *"the ability to produce wealth"*. (Dt 8:17-18).

When we remember how gracious God is to us in giving us our *"daily bread"*, and that we are poor children who cannot get our own bread, our hearts become filled with gratitude. When we remember the free gift of *"heavenly manna"* available to us daily, we will want to return thanks to God. We need to watch out that we do not take our daily bread for granted or develop the attitude of spoiled children as the Israelites did when they complained: *"But now we have lost our appetite; we never see anything but this manna."* (Num 11:6). Even if we feel spiritually "bored" with the daily portion God gives us, let us strengthen our faith to know it is exactly what we need, and all that we need. Gratitude and faith keep us from becoming "spoiled brats" in the family of God.

"Those who look to Him are radiant; their faces are never covered with shame." (Ps 34:5)

"Loving Father, give us this day our daily bread, and may our hearts be ever thankful for Your daily blessings."

This is a Wicked Generation

What if your pastor stood up this Sunday and began his homily with the statement, *"this is a wicked generation."* How popular would that be? How would we take it? Or what if a popular news person began his program with the statement, *"this is a wicked generation"*? How long would he keep his job?

Jesus was not into popularity; He was into speaking prophetic truth. At a moment when the size of the crowds was increasing, Jesus began His speech by saying, *"This is a wicked generation."* (Lk 11:29-32).

Why was his generation, *"wicked"*? Were they involved in abortion, or drug trafficking, or pornography, or other forms of sin? Were they skipping synagogue on Saturday, ignoring the laws of fasting, or not giving a full tithe at the Temple? What was it about that generation that led Jesus to label them, *"wicked"*?

It was wicked because it asked, *"for a miraculous sign"* from God. They wanted God to prove Himself by doing something spectacular for them. They wanted a God who was made in their image and likeness and who would perform for them according to their standards. They would not accept the living God present in His incarnate Son who came as a humble rabbi calling them to repentance and belief in his good news. And why did they ignore the hundreds of "miraculous" signs that Jesus had already worked in His ministries of healing and deliverance? They, indeed, were a stiff-necked people, a wicked generation.

What if a great king, full of splendor, like Solomon came and began building a new Temple; would that impress them? What if a great prophet, like Jonah came, with a doom and gloom message would that move them? Would they stop what they were doing and turn back to God? Jesus proclaimed that He was a king greater than even Solomon and a prophet greater than even Jonah. He reminded them that the Queen of Arabia traveled all the way to Jerusalem just to honor Solomon. He reminded them that the pagan king of Assyria, after hearing Jonah's message, threw off his robes, donned sackcloth, and called the whole city of Nineveh to stop everything they were doing and turn to the Lord. [Imagine President Obama putting on sack cloth and closing down the country so we could spend a day of repentance for the evils of our nation!] Two pagan leaders redirected their lives in response to God's presence; why wouldn't Jesus' generation do the same? What more could God do than to send His own son, the ultimate Priest, Prophet, and King? If they rejected Jesus, there was no hope for them.

"Wicked" is not so much doing bad things, as it is rejecting the presence and call of God's own Son, who alone has the power to set us free from "bad things." Jesus walks the earth today calling our generation to repent and believe in Him. He heals, He teaches, He offers salvation and forgiveness free of charge. How many give Him even the time of day? How many are so much in the "business as usual" groove, or even the "church as usual" groove to stop what they are doing, turn to Jesus and respond to His call?

Does our generation also qualify as "wicked?" We can

quickly come to the defense of our generation by pointing out all the good things that are taking place in the world, and there are. The bottom line criteria is how our generation is responding to the one who stands in our midst as a King greater than Solomon and a Prophet greater than Jonah. Are we willing to travel a long distance to see Him? Are we willing to stop everything and repent when we hear His voice?

Will we also insist on a miraculous sign? The generation of Jesus did receive a miraculous sign when Jesus rose from the dead, and some 40 years later they received a more dramatic sign when Jerusalem was destroyed by the Romans. Hopefully our generation will hear the gentle voice of the risen Jesus and not need a destructive earthquake or tsumani to get its attention.

"Against You only have I sinned and done what is evil in Your sight." (Ps 51:4)

"Praise You Lord Jesus, greater than Solomon. Praise You Lord Jesus, greater than Jonah. Your miraculous love is the only sign I need to want to surrender to You."

Everyone Who Asks Will Receive

In our cynicism we say, "there is no such thing as a free lunch." Jesus is here to tell us that there is. What God wants to give us is more than we can afford; the good news is that Jesus already paid the bill for us.

Today (Mt 7:7-11) Jesus tells us: *"Ask and it will be given to you...for everyone who asks will receive."* He doesn't say "Pay and it will be given you", or, "some people who ask will receive." Lest we be skeptical about the "free lunch" that God wants to give us, Jesus appeals to our parental instincts. Even with our limited love and aware of our sinfulness, we still want to do good things for our children. How much more does our loving Father who is unlimited in love want to pour out blessings on His children. His only requirement is that we "ask".

How do we ask? What do we ask for? Today's first reading (Esther C:12,14-16, 23-25) gives us answers to these questions. Esther was a Jewess who was in the unique position of being Queen to Persian king, Ahasuerus at a time when her fellow Jews were under persecution by that government. Her uncle Mordecai appealed to her to intercede for her poor relatives. Knowing that she was risking her life in approaching the king, Esther turned to the Lord in prayer. She was the only non-Persian in the king's household, and it had just been decreed that all Jews be put to death. Did Esther think of a strategy that would rely upon her own wits or her own seductive powers? No; her first action was to turn to the Lord and "ask". *"My Lord, our King, who alone are God. Help me, who am alone and have no help but You."* She acknowledged the presence of a listening God; she acknowledged her own powerlessness; her prayer was a simple "help me." As her prayer developed she asked God to manifest Himself and prayed, *"give me courage".* Then she prayed *"put in my mouth persuasive words...and turn his [the king's] heart."* Praying for her people she asked, *"Save us by Your power",* and exposed her poverty by reminding God that she was alone and had no one else but Him. (This is just a small portion of her powerful prayer.) In the events that followed Esther concocted an uncanny plan that flowed from the wisdom that only God can provide.

Let each of us think of the situations that we are in. God has placed us in certain positions in life just as He placed Esther in the king's household. We are there for a reason; God wants to use us to help "save" our people. But...we lack courage, we lack "know how", we don't know what to say, we are dealing with hardened hearts. Our first inclination is to throw up our hands and say, "the situation is hopeless." Esther visits us today to challenge our faith and to exhort us to "ask". Our own Father is Lord, King, and God. He is eager to come to us when we ask. He knows we lack courage, wisdom, and effectiveness. He also knows that He lacks none of these and is able to supply them even to the least members of Christ's body. Our Church history reeks with examples of how God confounded the strong by manifesting His saving power through the weak and the powerless. Facing impossible tasks, we turn quickly to our Loving Father and ask Him to make us something beyond what we are now.

331

Lent is the time we slow down, sober up, and face our own emptiness. Now is the time to focus on our mission in life and our inadequacy to carry it out. In face of this, now is the time to "ask". Through the ages, the Church has exhorted Christians to reduce their eating to one full meal per day during this season. (This incidentally is much more lenient than the fasting practices of the Muslims). The Church does not recommend an extreme practice, because the focus is not on our religious heroics but on the grace of God. To be honest, in our world filled with "creature comforts", we find it almost impossible to fast at all. That's the truth, and that's the point. Even in this area we need, like Esther, to admit our powerlessness and "ask". We need God to quell our appetites and stir within us a new spiritual hunger. We can't even give up a dessert without His help. Lent is all about Him and what He wants to do in our lives. It is all about becoming more deeply connected to Him in prayer, and yielding to deeper union with Him. So we keep turning to Him and "asking."

And each time we ask, we remind ourselves of Jesus' promise that "everyone who asks will receive." God is yearning to bless us with so many good things.

"When I called, You answered me; You made me bold and stouthearted." (Ps 138:3)

"Holy Mary, our Queen in heaven, we, like Mordecai turn to you for help. Knowing your great influence with the King we pray: 'Holy Mary, mother of God, pray for us sinners now and at the hour of our death.' "

God is not Fair

How many times have you heard a child say "that's not fair"? When one of their siblings gets something that seems better than what they got, they are quick to accuse parents of being "unjust" or "unfair."

This is exactly what the Israelites said as they complained about God: *"The way of the Lord is not just."* (from today's first reading: Ez 18:21-28). What was their complaint? God was too lenient with the wicked man, for He said, *"if the wicked man turns away from all his sins...he will surely live."* God was too strict with the righteous man, for He said: *"if a righteous man...commits sin...none of the righteous things he has done will be remembered."* I think we will agree that God is not being fair, at least by our definition of fairness.

We have this same issue in the New Testament. In the "lost son" story, the wicked, sinful, disgusting prodigal son gets the blessing of a feast, while the angry, resentful, self-righteous older brother gets nothing, even though he had been faithful in doing his father's work his entire life. And then, there is the one that really gets us—the parable of the workers in the vineyard where the fellow who worked for an hour received a full day's wage, the same that the "12-hour people" did.

What is going on here?

Jesus shocks everyone in today's Gospel reading (Mt 5:20-26) when He says that the righteousness of the Pharisees was not enough. We remember that the

Pharisees prayed daily, fasted regularly, were scrupulous in giving their tithe, were morally impeccable, as far as their behavior was concerned—yet this was not good enough for Jesus. In fact it seems the Pharisees were the guys wearing the "black hats" in most of the stories.

The rest of the passage hints at what Jesus is using as a criterion for defining "righteousness". It's the contents of the heart that counts. Harboring anger toward someone else in our hearts, putting people down in a hateful way, withholding love from someone who has offended us—these are the sins that indicate an unrighteous heart. We look at Ezekiel's audience and see people who considered themselves superior to the "wicked" and thus judged themselves "righteous" because of what they had done—they deserved God's favor; they earned it. And the elder brother, while looking righteous on the outside, held resentment, jealously, and anger in his heart toward his repentant brother.

God is not fooled. It is the contents of our hearts that counts. And which of us can declare that our hearts are pure, freed from resentment, pride, jealousy, criticism, superiority, self-righteousness, complacency, judgmentalism...and so on.

Through Ezekiel God calls us to repent. *"Repent! Turn away from all your offenses...and get a new heart and a new spirit...Repent and live!"* (Ez 18:30-32)

During Lent we enter into the desert with Jesus, so that we can listen again and see ourselves as God sees us.

He renews His love for us and shows us by the Holy Spirit what sin exists in our lives. As we open to Him in a spirit of faith He shows us the obstacles that keep us from entering into fuller union with Him. Then He gives us the grace to acknowledge this obstacle, repent, and allow Him to change our lives again,

Lent is an exciting period of grace because God is doing new wonders in our hearts. We do not achieve new growth through Lenten resolutions alone. Our efforts are actions that demonstrate the desire of our hearts to go deeper into God. The real work is done by the Holy Spirit as He creates a new Pentecost within our hearts.

"If You kept a record of sins, O Lord, who could stand? But with You there is forgiveness; You are to be feared." (Ps 130: 3-34)

"Holy Spirit, continue to lead me into the desert with Jesus, and there lead me to new freedom through the grace of repentance and a renewal of my spirit."

What is Repentance?
Do I Need It?

The Church is calling us to repent during this season of Lent. Are we sure what this means? If we are in serious sin and have severed our relationship with God, then repentance is clear—go to confession, confess our sin, and receive God's forgiveness. There may have been a time in our lives when we were in this kind of situation. Catholic charismatics have already repented many years ago, accepted Jesus into our hearts, and received the Baptism in the Holy Spirit. So, what's this idea of repentance as far as we're concerned?

Someone recently moved into a house they had just bought. It was filthy from top to bottom. Many hours of sweeping, scrubbing, and scraping were needed to get it back into a livable condition. Does this mean that the work is now over forever, and that they will never have to get a bucket and brush out again? While there was a dramatic moment when major work had to be done, there are less dramatic moments, now, when maintenance and further cleaning are needed. For most of us the initial cleanup is over; now the upkeep is necessary. And if we do not do the ongoing cleaning, soon we will find ourselves back to scratch again, the way we were when we first turned to Jesus.

How, then, do we go about repenting at this moment in our Christian lives?

Neal Lozano, the Catholic teacher on the ministry of deliverance, reminds us that repentance of itself doesn't work. Jesus preached, *"repent and believe the good news"*. Without the "belief" part, we do not have the power to change. We can make all kinds of Lenten resolutions, like I will quit gossiping, and our own will power will carry us through a few days. Then, as we well know, the gossiping returns again maybe worse than it was before. Forgetting the twofold nature of Christian repentance, we make resolutions and then watch them collapse in a few short days.

The short story of Matthew's conversion in the Gospels gives us insight into repentance and belief. First came Jesus' word to Him: *"Follow me"*. A grace was sent out by the power of the Holy Spirit working through Jesus. Then Matthew responded in two ways: he stood up, and left the tax booth. He took action and indicated that he was willing to leave what was keeping him from following Jesus. Finally his heart was pulled forward by the presence of Jesus, his feet began to move, and he walked close to Jesus. Matthew repented and believed— it was all a work of grace from beginning to end. Matthew repented and believed.

Let's apply this to our lives now. Do we do an "examination of conscience" and check off all the things that are wrong with us, all of our sins and failures, and then ask God to forgive our sins? There is nothing wrong with this approach. Another way of doing this is to let the Holy Spirit lead us into the desert of quiet, and there enter into a time of prayer. We ask the Lord to show us what He wants to change in our lives—not necessarily what we want to change. I might not like my habit of compulsive eating and want to change this habit. This may not be God's priority with me. Will God send an angel with a quick and concise answer to my question? Will He say "repent of sleeping in church during the homily"...or something like that? Usually He does not honor our time table, and we have to wait until He chooses to reveal something to us. He may respond to our prayer by reminding us how much He loves us, how happy He is that we are spending time with Him, assuring us that He will never leave us. We may get impatient that God will not cough up a list of our faults so we can "get down to work" eradicating them. We may get discouraged that God won't play by our "repentance rules".

We may quit looking for what's wrong with us and let the Holy Spirit lead us in our prayer. Then one day, when we least expect it, a still small voice within us says something like "pride". Hmm...is that all...just one thing to work on? What can I do with just one word?

Even if "pride" is not an item on my "confession list", I own up to it before the Father. And then I tell Him I want to change—I want to stand up and leave the pride, so I can better follow Him. This is repentance. I have acknowledged my desire to change, to leave something behind, and to be set free. Notice we are still in the beginning of the process. The Holy Spirit has taken charge, and the Holy Spirit has revealed an area of our lives where God wants to set us free.

Now comes the second part of the process. We "believe". No matter how hard I try, how long I fast, how much counseling I receive, I cannot free myself from "pride". There is only one way out and that is to "believe". Though I do not understand how God can do this, I believe that all things are possible to Him and that He can remove my pride. My faith may be shaky on this, but I make an act of trust that as long as I am willing to stand up and leave, God will step in and do the rest. This is a miracle of grace. It makes no sense to a world where people solve their own problems by applying the latest "self help" techniques. Poor in spirit, we depend completely on the mercy and intervening grace of God. We release ourselves to the saving, liberating power of the Holy Spirit.

I repent, I forgive anyone whom I hold something against, I renounce pride, I take authority over it in Jesus' name, and then let the blessing of God start to flow in a new way in my life. He may bless me with an understanding of what true humility is, and give me longing for it. In the days to come He may put me in situations where I can choose to act with humility instead of pride. He will help me not only change, but cooperate with His grace in taking up new behaviors that draw me closer to Jesus. I am now free to follow Him and follow His lead in various areas of my life.

Then I may seek out the Sacrament of Reconciliation, to celebrate what God has done for me, and strengthen the process with an infusion of sacramental grace. Because I believed and obeyed, I now begin to experience new growth in my Christian life and deeper union with God.

We all need the grace of repentance, just as we all need to clean our houses occasionally. Doing it our way may result in little fruit and much discouragement. Doing it God's way, under the lead of the Holy Spirit will result in much fruit and allow us to experience a new level of freedom in our lives. A great opportunity is ours now...repent and believe!

Happy Feast Day!

Today is our feast day, the feast of St. Joseph. For those who are unaware of this, St. Joseph is the patron saint of the Archdiocese of Louisville. It is a high feast day in Church as indicated by the fact that three Scripture readings are presented to us, instead of the ordinary three. If my opinion counts, I believe that St. Joseph was the greatest saint that every lived. Jesus was the Son of God and Mary was immaculately conceived, so they don't count. Joseph was just like the rest of us.

I know that Joseph was an extraordinary man because he was hand-picked by God to be the mentor for Jesus. The dad was the primary teacher of his son especially in matters relating to faith. Joseph was Jesus' teacher. My guess is that many of Jesus' parables and images were first told him by Joseph. Remember the one about "beams and splinters"? Moreover Joseph modeled "manhood" for Jesus. Chances are Jesus acted like Joseph, worked like Joseph, walked like Joseph prayed like Joseph. Could it be that these two men got up before dawn and went out to a "solitary place" to pray each morning? Or did Jesus first do that after He began His public ministry. What other saint can boast that he or she gave a "one to one" course to the Son of God?

Ironically we know almost nothing about Joseph except that he listened to God and obeyed. Mary makes a few remarks in the Gospel; Joseph is silent. We know he was righteous in the eyes of God and obedient to God's commands. Joseph was the New Testament version of Abraham, and that's whom the Church puts before us today in the reading from Romans. (Rom 4:13, 16-18,22).

What about Abraham? *"Against all hope, Abraham ...believed."..."he did not waver through unbelief in the promises of God..."He is the father of us all."..."he is the father of all those who believe but have not been circumcised...and he is also the father of the circumcised."* Can't each of these statements be made also about Joseph? Jesus is our brother and Joseph was His father (earthly)...for Mary, herself, said, *"Your father and I have been anxiously searching for you"* (Lk 2:48) when they found the pre-teen Jesus teaching in the Temple. God of course is our Father; Joseph, I believe, plays a fatherly role for us and the Church also. Jesus is our Brother of course; the saints are also our brothers and sisters.

Abraham's two great acts of faith were:
  1) when he believed that he and Sarah could have a son in their old age and,
  2) when he willingly took his only son Isaac up the mountain to sacrifice him.

When Joseph decided he had to divorce Mary, I believe it was as "heart crushing" as when Abraham was told to sacrifice Isaac. When Joseph believed that Mary's pregnancy was of God, and that there was no man involved, this took faith beyond that even of Abraham.

The Church chooses 2 Samuel 7:4-16 for the first reading. There is a way that what God promised to David, he promised to Joseph. Speaking to David of his son Solomon, God says: *"He is the one who will build a house in my Name, and I will establish his kingdom forever. I will be his Father and he will be my son..."* Earlier in the passage we hear God addressing David with the words: *"Now I will make your name great, like the names of, the greatest men on earth."* (7:9) During the lifetime of Joseph, the lifetime of Jesus, and maybe even the life of the early Church Joseph's name was not made great. Look, however, through the history of the Church, and today. How many of us men have Joseph as part of our name? (Even our Archbishop) How many churches are named after Joseph? How many streets and towns bear his name?

This great man of God slips quietly onto the Church's stage right smack in the middle of Lent. Then he quietly leaves, letting Lent continue. For one day we add an "e" to our fast and make it a "feast" to celebrate perhaps the greatest of all saints, and spiritual father to all believers. Joseph steps forth to remind us to rejoice and celebrate God's new work even if we are in the middle of some tough times. He reminds us of what he did, so we have an example to follow.

"I will establish his line forever, his throne as long as the heavens endure." (Ps 89:29)

"St. Joseph, just man of God, the new Abraham, mentor of Jesus, model for men, patron of a happy death, patron of the spiritual life, terror of demons, and patron of our archdiocese, pray for us today."

Join with Me in Suffering

St. Paul invited Timothy to join with him in suffering (from today's reading: 2 Tim 1:8-10). Can you imagine using this as a recruiting slogan? What if the army said, "Join the army and get shot at"? Or a church advertised itself, "Come join and suffer with us"? Who in their right mind would want to be part of a "suffering club?" Does the Church advertise Lent as the "season to suffer?"

I pulled a Scripture trick and did not give you the full quote. Paul was in prison when he wrote to Timothy, and the whole piece was: *"join with me in suffering for the Gospel, by the power of God, who has saved us and called us to a holy life."* Anyone in history who has been committed to a great cause and inspired by a great vision has had to suffer. Thousands, maybe millions, of Christians have been imprisoned, just as Paul was, for the sake of the Gospel. Paul situates suffering in the context of the greatest of all causes—the Gospel of Jesus Christ—the cause above all causes. He reminded Timothy that it is the power of God that gives us the courage to suffer for the Gospel and the sustenance we need to endure it. Paul finishes his exhortation with a reminder of the infinite treasure of salvation that we have been given, and the call by God to live a holy life. Inspired by the vision of Paul, we gladly raise our hands and volunteer to join Paul and Jesus in suffering for the sake of the Gospel.

Suffering by itself leads only to depression, discouragement, and even despair. Even Lenten penance, apart from God's vision, can have a negative effect on us. Maybe that's why the Church feeds us with the stories of Abraham's call and the Transfiguration. (Gen 12:1-4 and Mt 17:1-9).

Listen to the vision and promise God spoke to Abraham: *"I will make you into a great nation and I will bless you...I will make your name great...and you will be a blessing."* It was only in the light of this vision that Abraham would have the courage to leave everything behind and head toward a strange land.

Now let's join Peter, James, and John on the mountaintop, close our eyes and watch the Transfiguration take place. In the brilliance of a heavenly light we see Jesus, Moses, and Elijah having a conversation, and then they are enveloped by a bright cloud that throws them to the ground. Caught up in this taste of heaven we hear the voice of God telling us to "listen" to Jesus. In this mountain top event, Peter and the rest received a vision that would eventually carry each of them (except John) to shedding their blood for the cause of the Gospel.

Let's not forget how Paul began his journey: *"Suddenly a light from heaven flashed around him. He fell to the ground and heard a voice..."* (Acts 9:3-4) This was Paul's personal "transfiguration" that empowered him to preach, suffer, and die for the sake of the Gospel.

Suffering makes sense only in the context of transfiguration. Maybe that is why the Church takes us with Jesus to the top of the mountain today. Each of us who are reading these words have had a personal transfiguration; maybe this happened at the time we were baptized in the Holy Spirit. Expect other transfigurations. Expect that sometime during this Lenten season, maybe while we are in prayer that the Holy Spirit will lift us up and carry us to the top of the mountain. Expect that there we will be surrounded by a glorious light and hear the voice of God. Expect, also, that because we have been saved and called to be holy that suffering will be part of our spiritual "menu". And remember what Paul said: it is only, *"by the power of God"* that we can drink this cup. That is why more than ever before in our lives that we need to take time to develop a more intimate relationship with our loving Father.

"May Your unfailing love rest upon us O Lord" (Ps 33:22)

"Jesus, as Lot followed Abraham and Timothy followed Paul, so we decide again to follow You even if at times it is through the valley of suffering."

Your Last Confession?

When is the last time you received the Sacrament of Reconciliation? If it has been over a month, your homework assignment is to make arrangements today to receive the sacrament before the week ends. Now that is a bold and perhaps intrusive statement!

Archbishop Kurtz, Fr. Al Lauer, and other of our spiritual leaders have repeatedly suggested that we develop the habit of receiving the Sacrament of Reconciliation monthly. Please do not kill the messenger; I am only reminding each of us what we already know.

I have a mild heart condition for which I take medication. If I am not consistent with the medication, I increase my chances rather dramatically for becoming a stroke victim. To monitor the effect of the medication, I am required to get my blood checked out about every three weeks. A couple of years ago I decided that I would skip the "blood checks" because it had become too inconvenient for me, and I didn't like sitting around the waiting room with a bunch of old people. When my doctor learned what I was doing, he quickly set me straight and reminded me of the risk I was taking. I think he cared about my health more than I did.

Going to confession is inconvenient and at times uncomfortable, so we either skip it or put it off. Do we realize how we increase the chances of a "spiritual stroke" when we get careless about our sacramental lives? The "old time" pastors used to sit on us and remind us sternly about frequent confession. The "new time" pastors turn the responsibility over to us to remind ourselves and one another.

One of the excuses that I use is that we don't have weekly confessions at our Church any more. Being honest, I must confess, when we did have weekly confessions, I seldom went nor did other members of our parish. Truth is, the Sacrament of Reconciliation is almost as available these days as is daily Eucharist. Numerous times I have called priests about meeting with them for confession, and 100% of the time they say "yes", and set up a convenient time to meet. We are blessed with the Franciscans at Mt. St. Francis, the Passionists at the Sacred Heart Monastery, and the Dominicans at St. Louis Bertrand—there is always someone available. And, to put in a plug, I have gone to various priests in this area, and each one has been kind, gentle, and wise in ministering to me.

"Well", we say, "I don't really have much to confess." Human nature as it is, the longer we put off confession, the more we become convinced that we have nothing to confess. Our spiritual eyesight weakens as we procrastinate. And if I have nothing to confess, then I don't need forgiveness anyhow. Welcome to the spirituality of the "good old" Pharisees.

In today's gospel (Lk 6:36-38) Jesus presents us with "five commandments" (shorter than Moses' offering). These might provide a short list for examining our consciences today.

1. Be merciful...then the kicker...as our heavenly Father is merciful.
2. Don't judge...or else you will be judged.
3. Don't condemn...or else you will be condemned
4. Forgive....then you will be forgiven
5. Give....then God will give back to you generously

The reader who is "perfect" in all five categories gets to throw the first stone.

Today's reading from Daniel is a model prayer for confession. (Dn 9:4-10). To show how desperate he and his people were, Daniel turned to God with prayer, fasting, sackcloth [do they sell that at Dillards?], and ashes. He got down to business with God and confessed his sins and the sins of his people. We all share in some way the sins of the people. Have, we, for example, prayed and fasted regularly to put an end to abortion in our city? Yes, we all need to be cleansed by the blood of Jesus. And we have a sacrament in which Jesus does exactly that—He applies His saving and healing blood.

"...May your mercy come quickly to meet us, for we are in desperate need." (Ps 79:8)

"Bless me, Father God, for I have sinned. I have not approached You often enough to receive Your merciful love and forgiveness. I repent."

Come Now Let Us Reason Together

Through the words of the prophet Isaiah (Is 1:10, 16-20) the Lord rebuked the Israelites. He was fed up with their "multitude" of sacrifices (v.11) and even told them to, *"stop bringing meaningless offerings"* (v.13). He said, *"Your incense is detestable to Me"* and *"when you spread out your hands in prayer, I will hide My eyes from you; even if you offer many prayers, I will not listen."* I'm sure these words came as a shock to Isaiah's listeners. Apparently their culture abounded in "religious stuff"; when they gathered together, they assumed that God was pleased with them and that their religious efforts won the favor of God. They could not have been more wrong.

What tough words from God—when they spread out their hands to pray, God actually hid His eyes. I wonder what God's honest opinion is about all the religious gatherings that take place in the Church today? How much of it is "going through the motions"? How much is meaningless in the sight of God? Are our hearts in it?

What was missing with the people of Israel? They were ignoring the oppressed or maybe even contributing to the oppression. They were so wrapped up in their own interests that they did not devote themselves to defending the orphans and the widow. So into their comfortable culture, they kept the needs of the poor and the outcasts outside their scope. Did this reflect the heart of God who was close to the brokenhearted, and stepped in to save those who were crushed in spirit? Once again God was not so much interested in ceremonies as He was the content of hearts.

There must be at least a tinge of "conviction" in our hearts as we hear these words spoken by Isaiah. A prophetic word is a grace from God, for it pierces our hearts and releases a spirit of sorrow in us. It moves us to want to turn to God and get back on His track.

How do we respond to God's word? Listen. *"Come now, let us reason together,"* the Lord said. As disgusting as Israel's behavior was to Him, God, as a gracious Father, appealed to His children with the simple invitation to "come, sit down, let's have a talk." Were they willing to let go of their pride and sit down to have a talk with God?

If they were willing to make this simple, humble gesture, God would make their *"scarlet"* sins *"as white as snow."* And what stain is tougher to deal with than "red"? Yes, He would step in, though they did not deserve it, and do the impossible—even the deep scarlet of sin would be eradicated and made white as snow once more.

Jesus, in today's Gospel reading (Mt 23:1-12) talks about the sin of pride that was reflected in the teachers of the law. Their life styles were built on a spirit of superiority. Their self-esteem was rooted, not in their relationship with God, but in the belief that they were better than other people and deserved special treatment. Pride is a block that keeps us imprisoned in our own stubbornness, and does not allow us to respond to God when he says, "come, let's sit down, and talk about what's going on." Why would they need to sit down and have a talk with God? Why would they need to submit to the teaching of Jesus? People called them "father"; why would they need to be childlike and sit down with their true Father?

An interesting line in today's psalm (Psalm 50) has God saying: *"These things you have done and I kept silent; you thought I was altogether like you."* God does not jump on us when we sin; this is not His way. And why do we believe that the way we think is the way God thinks—that He is like us? In repentance we release everything to the Lord, including our theological notions of who He is and what pleases Him.

Where do we start in responding to God's invitation to "sit down and talk"? *"He who sacrifices thank offering honors Me…and prepares the way…"* (v.23). When we release thanksgiving from our hearts, we humble ourselves admitting that we deserve nothing of what we have, especially the forgiveness that God pours out so generously upon us.

"He who sacrifices thank offerings honor me." (Ps 50:23)

"Father, thank You for inviting us to sit down and have a talk with You. Thank You for the humility You give that allows us to admit our sins and seek the action of grace that makes us 'white as snow' and pure 'as wool'."

Saint Toribio

Do you know anyone named "Toribio?" Do you know who Saint Toribio is? Do you know that today is his feast day?

Toribio is the first canonized saint of the new world. He was Archbishop of Peru in the last part of the 16th century, built chapels, schools, hospitals, convents, roads, and established the first seminary in the Americas. As Archbishop he traveled (often alone and on foot) the 18,000 miles of his archdiocese three times, end to end. It is estimated that he baptized and confirmed half a million Peruvians during his 25 years ministry. Doing some quick arithmetic, I figure he baptized on the average of 50 people a day, 7 days a week, for 25 years. What a track record!

One of his favorite sayings was: "Time is not your own; we must give a strict account of it." From his "superhuman" accomplishments, it is obvious that he practiced what he preached.

Toribio was an extremely talented person. He was of noble birth, a law professor at the University of Salamanca, and appointed as chief justice of the supreme court by the king. Knowing the wealth of talent and opportunity God gave him, Turibio must have realized that, *"to whom much has been given, much will be expected."*

As Turibio was ambitious, so were the apostles mentioned in today's Gospel reading. (Mt 20:17-28) James and John wanted to have top positions in

Jesus' kingdom, and were smart enough to use their mom to plead with Jesus and melt His heart. Maybe their ambition was well-founded. They saw how Jesus helped so many people and perhaps they had visions of helping all of Israel and maybe the whole world. Though they are depicted as "self-seeking", who knows, their intentions may have been noble. In time, after they drank the cup that Jesus drank, they did have top positions in the kingdom.

Jesus wants all of us to be ambitious for the kingdom. He wants us all to use our time, talent, and money as generously as Turibio did. In the Gospel story Jesus did not reprimand James and John for being ambitious; instead He redirected it. When ambition is converted into service, it can be powerful for changing the face of the earth. Maybe we will not lead "50 people a day" to Christ, but it is reasonable that we can pray for "50 people a day" by name. It is reasonable that we find a prayer partner and agree to spend 5 minutes together (by phone? by email?) to pray for a list of people daily. Remember the promises Jesus made when two people come together in His name? (Mt 18:19-20)

God expects us to be ambitious for the kingdom. As Catholics we are used to following our priests and waiting them to tell us what to do. Since the second Vatican Council, it has been made clear that "waiting for the priests" is no longer an option. When we receive the Holy Spirit we are prompted from within on a daily basis to move forward in service for the sake of the kingdom. Are we ready to give a "strict account of our time?"

Lent is a time of regrouping for us. We fast, pray, give alms, repent, and try to get our lives in better order. Do we do this so that we will be more spiritually perfect (which can be self-centered), or do we do it so that we can be of more use in the service of God? Lent is not a self improvement exercise, but a "boot camp" preparing us for new ventures and new battles.

Let's add to our Lenten program a prayer to the Holy Spirit that He will show us new ways to use our time and to be enterprising in building up God's kingdom. Most of us are in privileged positions as was Turibio. We have education, freedom, and a reasonable amount of money. In addition we have all the wealth of our Father at our disposal. What can hold us back? Remember, you seniors, life begins at 70! Ask Caleb if you don't believe it.

"I trust in You O Lord...my times are in Your hands." (Ps 31:14-15)

"St. Turibio, pray for us that new ambition stir within our beings, so that we will have the courage to begin new works for God and use our time as you did."

Animals Rescue

Bible Quiz. Where in the New Testament is a dog presented as the hero of a story? Answer: in today's Gospel reading (Lk 16:19-31)

Jesus tells a story of two men: a rich man whose name is not given, and a poor beggar who does have a name, Lazarus. What does that tell us? One didn't even have a name worth mentioning; the other had a name and was therefore a "somebody" in the eyes of God. We know the story. The man without a name was dressed in purple and fine linen, and lived in luxury every day. He imagined himself to be a king living safely and comfortably within his "gated community" (see vs.20) Lazarus was hungry and covered with sores. He would have considered it a feast if could eat the scraps of food that were thrown in the rich man's garbage can.

Now enter the heroes of the story. It is told that little dogs came up to Lazarus and licked his wounds. They loved Lazarus and were sent by God to comfort him; they showed compassion toward someone in distress by licking him. They were not afraid of catching a disease or of what people might think of them for associating with a poor beggar. The little dogs followed their hearts and ministered to the suffering Lazarus. The rich man had no heart; busy about building and protecting his material resources, the rich man didn't have time to notice Lazarus, much less offer him something to eat. We can imagine the wealthy man telling his servants: "it's okay to feed the dogs, but don't give a crumb to that disgusting beggar; if we feed him he'll keep hanging around the property and people will begin to talk."

I wonder who was happier, the rich "nobody" or Lazarus? As Lazarus sat by the gate begging, he dreamed of the day when God would take him into the bosom of Abraham. There his sores and his pain would be gone, and he would have all the luxury he'd every need. When he went to bed at night, he fell quickly asleep, for he trusted in God to take care of him in the short run and the long run. The "poor" rich man was too busy tending to his affairs and ordering his servants around to even discover that he had a heart. At night time he tossed and turned worrying that he might lose his wealth or have his property confiscated by the Romans. When the thought of death and the "hereafter" crossed his mind, he went into a panic and tried to switch his mind to something else. Lazarus trusted in God, the rich man trusted in his wealth. Who was happier?

Jeremiah, today, talks about trust. (Jer 17:5-10) *"Cursed is the one who trusts in man, who depends upon flesh as his strength...but blessed is the man who trusts in the Lord, whose confidence is in Him."* Listen to the benefits that come to the "blessed" man. He will be like a tree planted by the water which doesn't fear when the heat comes and never worries when drought comes. His *"leaves are always green,"* and he *"never fails to bear fruit."* Picking up on the same theme, Psalm 1 tells us that the one who takes delight in the Lord "prospers" in whatever he does. The one who trusts in himself, in time, will be like a, *"bush in the wastelands...he will not see prosperity when it comes...he will dwell in the parched places of the desert."* Read the rest of the Gospel today to get a concrete description of what happened to the rich man

356

who refused to trust in the Lord.

Now let's have a show of hands. Who would rather trust in the Lord instead of herself or himself? Trusting in the Lord wins by a landslide. The fact is however, we still get bogged down with fears and worries. Deep inside we still have this belief that our security lies, somehow, in the things we can control. Trusting in God with all our hearts is still a challenge for us, especially if we have been brought up to be "self-sufficient" and "independent". Is it possible that we might trust more in our prayers and "religious practices" than in the God to whom these are to be directed?

We repent this Lent of placing our trust in ourselves, our skills, our money, and even our families. Look again at the little dogs of today's story who were not involved in fear and worry. They trusted God for their needs and went about their business showing love and compassion to those who were hurting.

"For the Lord watches over the way of the righteous, but the way of the wicked will perish." (Ps 1:6)

"Loving Father, once again I let go of my self-reliance and place my trust in You."

Eat Meat Today

In the midst of the "desert" of Lent, the Church steps in and surprises us with an unexpected banquet which includes "eating meat". No abstinence today because something much greater than the season of Lent is being celebrated—the Feast of the Annunciation. When something extraordinary is taking place in the spiritual world, the Church has the responsibility of catching our attention so we don't miss it. Earthy events like an earthquake disaster or the "Final Four" event quickly grab our attention because the media is out their taking pictures. Spiritual events cannot be seen, and do not usually carry a "sensational" impact and so are missed by the world.

What is the spiritual event that we participate in today? (Lk 1:26-38) A moment in history occurred in which three "impossible" things happened. One of God's top-ranking officials in the spiritual world, the Angel Gabriel, visited and talked with a human being. This is so rare that the Bible cites just 4 such visits over a 4000 year span. Secondly a humble "hillbilly" girl from God-forsaken Nazareth (remember the popular opinion in those days was *"what good can come out of Nazareth?"* (Jn 1:46) is promised that her son would inherit great King David's throne and rule over Jacob forever (remember even David's reign was only for 40 years). And thirdly, another impossible thing happened; a virgin became pregnant with no man involved. No wonder the Church is getting excited today and dispensing with its rules!

Does the "Final Four" even come close to matching this event?

When the Church celebrates a mystery, like the Annunciation, it is not just to recall a great event in salvation history or to honor the Mother of God. It is about the present, not the past. When we enter into a mystery, we become present to the very action of God as it occurred in a past event. The visit of an angel, an unimaginable promise, the incarnation of the Son of God in human hearts are all taking place at this moment. We are not just watching Mary interact with the angel; we are connecting with her as the same act of grace takes place for us today. And by the power of the Holy Spirit within us, we have the courage to say *"let this* [also] *happen to me according to your Word."* And the Word does become flesh again within us as it did within Mary.

The other New Testament reading (Heb 10:4-10) tells us about another impossible event in which we are invited to participate. A way was opened by God to set us free from sins. The greatest religion that had ever existed, established by God through Moses, did not have the power to remove sin. *"...it is impossible for the blood of bulls and goats to take away sins."* Man at his best could not do what he most needed. Yet while God was not pleased with sin offerings, He was pleased with the offering of His only Son, who said He, *"came to do Your will, O God."* So powerful was this offering that the impossible happened: *"We have been made holy through the sacrifice of the body of Jesus Christ, once for all."*

The Annunciation event tripped off a "witnessing" expedition. Led by the Holy Spirit, Mary went quickly to Elizabeth to share the good news. What God is doing for us as we enter into the mystery of Jesus within us, is so significant that we too, are called to go forth and witness to the great work God is doing in our time. The institutional Church is doing its part today; are we doing ours? We are called to take the lead in the "new evangelization" efforts announced by the Pope and as well as by Archbishop Kurtz. [The author's bishop, ref: *The Record*, diocesan paper for the Archdiocese of Louisville, KY USA.] In our Lenten prayers of repentance we might consider not just "what we have done" but "what we have failed to do". Have I used every opportunity God has given me to evangelize my world?

Let's listen to the Angel Gabriel tell us at this moment *"For nothing is impossible with God."* Let these words stir our faith each time we present a request before our heavenly Father or witness for Jesus.

"I speak of Your faithfulness and salvation, I do not conceal Your love and Your truth." (Ps 40:10)

"Mary, show me how to feast with you today on the mystery of the annunciation in my life. Show me how to continually invite others to celebrate God's saving love in our midst."

360

American Idol

A nationwide search for the best "idol-god" was conducted and the three finalists were: 1. the god of money   2. the god of fame and 3. the God of Christians.   Each of the "gods" had a representative make a presentation to convince the judges that their "god" was the best.

First, Warren Buffett took the microphone and praised the advantages of choosing "money" as the nation's best "idol". He brought in a truckload of $100 bills and talked about everything that money can buy—cars, property, vacations, recreation, clothes, and things of all kind.   Then President Obama came forward and extolled the benefits of "fame".   He told the audience how great it feels to walk on stage in any country of the world and get a standing ovation.   He talked of when people see him, they run up to him and seek his autograph.   Finally Pope Benedict came to the podium with his Bible in his hand.   Opening the Bible he shared with the audience the kind of God he believes in.

First he opened to the prophet Micah (7:14-20) and read the following passage: *"Who is a God like You, who pardons sin and forgives the transgression...You do not stay angry forever and delight to show mercy...(You) will hurl all our iniquities into the depths of the sea."* Buffett and Obama began to squirm in their chairs. Their "gods" didn't know how to forgive or show mercy; nor were they able to pick up our sins and throw them into the depths of the sea.

The Pope continued by telling a story about God, the

forgiving Father. (Lk 15:11-32). An ungrateful son took half of his Father's wealth (Buffett cringed when he heard this) and went off to a big city and squandered every penny of it. When people saw him tending pigs and dressed in rags, they wondered what kind of Father would let his son live this way (Obama was visibly upset to think the Father had lost his good reputation). When the son "hit bottom" and decided to apply for a servant's position in the Father's house, the Father not only allowed it but embraced and kissed his son, and instantly reinstated him as an honored son. No one in the audience could believe that a Father would bend this far for a rebellious son. Not only did the Father accept the son unconditionally, he bought the most expensive clothes he could find and threw the biggest party ever to celebrate the return of his son. Never had he treated any of his other children this way. The judges challenged the veracity of the Pope. No one can possibly have this much love for someone who in effect "spit in His face". Pope Benedict agreed with their statement...and added "no one except the God whom I represent here tonight."

In closing, the Pope sang a song written by someone who actually met and knew God. The man was David, and here is what he wrote. *"Praise the Lord...who forgives all our sins, heals all our diseases, redeems our lives from the pit, crowns us with love and compassion, satisfies our desires with good things, renews our youth like an eagle's."* And that was just the first verse. *"He does not treat us as our sins deserve...His love for us is great as the heavens are as high above the earth...as far as the east is from the west, so far does He put our transgressions from us."* Before the Pope had time to sing the third verse which told about God sending His only Son to die for all people that we might have eternal life, the people in the audience were all standing, cheering. "We want God", Buffett and Obama walked sheepishly off the stage, and the three judges marked their ballots, stood up, and joined the cheering crowd. The contest was decided.

America began to believe the truth that, *"there is no god like our God."* With that the Pope smiled, blessed everyone, and quietly left the stage.

The sad part of this story is that the two other "idols" receive more attention, time, and enthusiasm from their "worshippers" than the true God gets from His. In fact many of us are quick to put our God "on hold" when "money" or "popularity" knock at our doors. So the Church continues to repeat the message "repent". As we read the Scripture selections from today's liturgy, let us linger with them for awhile, until we are overwhelmed with the kind of God whom we love and profess. Let us repent for not returning to Him the love, attention, and praise He deserves.

"Praise the Lord my soul, and forget not all His benefits." (Ps 103:2)

"Loving Father, each of us at one time was a prodigal child who came back home to You and received Your loving embrace. Stir within us a zeal to bring the other "prodigals" of the world to know You and Your infinite love for them."

Dying of Thirst

Once while listening to a talk on weight reduction, I heard the speaker say that many people grab something to eat when they are thirsty. Our brains can get so mixed up that when we desperately need a glass of water, we eat a cookie instead.

I believe our "spiritual brains" get mixed up too. What ails us, so often, is spiritual dehydration. We are dying for a drink of the "living water" that Jesus speaks of today in His conversation with the Samaritan woman (Jn 4:5-42). Rather than going to our inner well for a drink we might go to the kitchen and grab a snack, do some busy work, or play with our computers. When we finish our diversion, we are even thirstier than we were before, so we seek another useless solution.

The fact is we are spirit-body creatures. Our spirits need to be watered as much as our bodies do—even more so. When we neglect our spiritual needs, every part of us—spirit, soul, and body—suffers. Jesus surprised the apostles by saying "I have food that you know nothing about." He was energized and nourished by the Holy Spirit who guided Him in eating the "spiritual food" of doing His Father's will. We are surprised in the Exodus reading today (Ex 17:3-7) that when the Israelites demanded water Moses saw it as "testing God". It seems perfectly normal to want a drink when they were in the desert. God was feeding their spirits with His loving kindness, and their focus was on their bodily needs instead. God's love was not enough for them.

The Gospel story today takes place at a town called Sychar where Jacob's well was located. Isn't this amazing that a well used by Jacob was still releasing water 2000 years later?. There seems to have been an unending supply—a well that never ran dry. In that setting Jesus set the stage for releasing a new well that would never run dry. In fact this "living water" would spring not from the earth but from the inner depths of the human heart that surrendered to Jesus. We know from personal experience that this living water is the Holy Spirit that God has planted within us.

Every human being thirsts for the living water that Jesus alone can give. Many have sought it by going to church or doing volunteer work or maybe by reading religious books, and have come up dry. Feeling spiritual thirst and not knowing where to find the water that quenches that thirst, people learn to live with it or try to find a substitute that doesn't work. Many addictions arise from seeking spiritual relief through a physical substance or activity.

Could it be that we charismatics have forgotten how to tap into the inner spring of the Holy Spirit that we have received? Has the enemy tricked our "spiritual brains" into thinking that we are not spiritually thirsty at all? We have become like dry sponges that need to be immersed once again in a pool of water to come back alive. Our busy lives try to keep us from slowing down and becoming still enough to let the living water rise again from the springs in our hearts. Paul reminds us today (Rm 5:1-2,5-8) that, *"God has poured out His love to us by the Holy Spirit."* Yes he is "pouring" out His water even at this moment. It would be tragic to let this season of grace pass us by.

"Today if you hear His voice, do not harden your hearts." (Ps 95:8)

"Jesus, thank You for the fountain of living water that You have placed at the center of my heart. Today, I take quiet time with You to allow this living water to rise up again and flood my being with the Holy Spirit."

Unsung Hero

Someone once asked me, "Who do you think made a bigger impact on the world, Pope John Paul II or Pope John Paul II's mother and father?" My answer to this is, "It's a tie." The Pope represented the harvest of the lives of two holy people who did the planting and nurturing of his faith. Yet how many people know even the name of John Paul's parents?

In today's first reading (2 Kgs 5:1-15) we read the remarkable story of how Naaman, the commander of the Aramite army, was healed miraculously of his leprosy by God through the intercession of the prophet Elisha. This story was so significant that Jesus used it in preaching to the people of His own town. What is easily missed in the story is the fact that a slave girl evangelized Naaman's family with the good news that Elijah existed and had miraculous powers.

We learn that, *"bands from Aram had gone out and had taken captive a young girl from Israel and she served Naaman's wife."* Isn't this the same as human trafficking? Imagine how the Israelites and the young girl must have hated Naaman and the whole Aramite nation. Imagine her ongoing grief and depression. Could an Israelite have had even a grain of compassion for anyone connected with Naaman?

How could the young girl from Israel even think of doing Naaman a good deed? Yet that is what she did. She said to Naaman's wife, *"If only my master would see the prophet who is in Samaria! He would cure him of his leprosy."* Even in her state of captivity the slave girl was able to do God's work and even have "love" for her Aramite master. When Naaman took the young slave girl's message to his master, the King of Aram said, *"by all means, go."* How did this girl from Israel gain such credibility that the leaders of the country honored her advice?

I want to believe that this young Israelite girl, *"worked as unto the Lord."* (Col 3:24). She accepted her circumstances, believed that God allowed her to be put there for a purpose, and sought to be His instrument among those Gentiles. She learned to love her master and to seek his good. At the same time she did not forget her own faith; she knew that Elijah was a prophet of the living God and had powers beyond the medical experts of Aram. Though she was the victim of a horrible kidnapping, she chose to rise above a "victim mentality." Being part of God's plan, she knew God had a purpose for her position in this Gentile family.

If we read on to the end of the Naaman story, another remarkable event takes place. After being healed, Naaman asked Elijah if he could take a huge cart load of soil back to his homeland, so they could worship the true God in his home country. He promised that he would never worship any god except the God of Israel. God made a way for the young slave girl to worship the Lord on a plot of soil taken from Israel. She could not return to Samaria, so God brought the land of Samaria to her. We can imagine that this young girl began to teach Naaman and his household the truths and ways of the God of Israel. She was truly one of the unsung heroes in salvation history.

Many Christians today are God's unsung heroes. Locked into unpleasant situations that do not support their faith, they choose to rise above a "victim mentality", continue to trust in God, and believe that He wants to use them where they're at. Like Queen Esther, they know that in time they will be used to promote the salvation of their people. Sometimes our job circumstances, our family situation, our church environment, or even our marriage relationship may not meet our expectations. Instead of being discontent, we can trust in God and be available to Him as instruments in His plan of salvation for those among whom we live. No credit may be given us; we may go down in history as one of the millions of unsung heroes that God used to accomplish His work. We can rejoice in whatever circumstances we are in because we *"work as unto the Lord."*

"My soul thirsts for God, the living God. When can I go and meet with God?" (Ps 42:2)

"Loving Father, forgive me for my grumbling and my feeble faith. I trust in You and know that no matter where my circumstances take me, they cannot take me from You."

Back to School

Have you wondered what Jesus did when He was out in the desert for 40 days? I believe He went to school. Jesus had just been filled with the Holy Spirit at the Jordan, and the Holy Spirit needed time to reveal to Jesus all that He needed to know.

We are half way through our Lenten desert under the guidance and tutelage of the Holy Spirit. What have we learned so far? What else does the Holy Spirit have in store for us? Have we taken sufficient time to be still and listen, or have we been one of those squirmy students who pay little attention to what the teacher is presenting to him?

Our fasting quiets our bodies. Our prayer opens us to listen. The sacraments feed and sustain us. We have the unique privilege of participating in a Holy Spirit "crash course".

Jesus is seen today teaching His disciples. (Mt 5:17-19). He had taken them up a mountain, and there Jesus, the new Moses, began to reveal the New Law to them. He reminded us of Moses saying: *"Hear, O Israel, the decrees and laws I am about to teach you...See I have taught you decrees and laws as the Lord commanded me."* (Dt 4)

Jesus made it clear that He was not undoing anything of the Mosaic Law but fulfilling it. What does this mean? I have a lilac bush in the backyard. All winter it sits with its many intricate collections of branches awaiting the coming of spring. Spring "fulfills" the lilac bush by letting buds, blossoms, and leaves burst forth through its branches. Jesus was not tearing down the revelation that God had carefully built through the ages. He and His kingdom were the buds, blossoms, and leaves that sprung from the Law.

Jesus also instructed them to *"practice and teach these commands."* Moses told the people to be careful so that they would not let the decrees of the Lord "slip" from their hearts. *"Teach them to your children and their children after them."* Both Jesus and Moses tell us that we are all both students and teachers. As I read Moses' exhortation, we are to teach our children and grandchildren the ways of God. How do we do this?

First, we are students. Jesus promised that the Holy Spirit will come and, *"teach us all things"* (Jn 14:26) In John's first letter he reminded those who were dealing with false teachers that the Holy Spirit, *"teaches you about all things."* Our teaching is the overflow in our lives of this ongoing, daily teaching of the Holy Spirit in our hearts.

"What other nation is so great as to have their gods near them the way the Lord our God is near us whenever we pray to Him?" (Dt 4:7) What nation is so great as to have a god who dwells in their hearts and teaches them His decrees day by day? In our efforts to teach we do not have to "brow beat" or try to "force feed" others. We just tell others about how wonderful our God is, and how privileged we are to have such a loving Father who always watches over us and cares for us. [I was struck by the long list of things that God does

as listed in today's psalm (Ps 147) It is a nice way to praise him today.]

"He has revealed His word to Jacob, His laws and decrees to Israel. He has not done this for any other nation" (Ps 147:19-20)

"Jesus, through the Holy Spirit You continue to teach us as You taught the disciples. Let us have docile minds and hearts to absorb even the 'smallest letter' and 'least stroke of the pen' that You reveal to us."

How to Make God Mad

Moses met God personally and was able to describe His "personality". Here are some of the adjectives Moses used about the Lord: *"compassionate and gracious, slow to anger, abounding in love and faithfulness, maintaining love to thousands...forgiving wickedness, rebellion, and sin."* (Ex 34:6-7)

Is it possible, then, to make God really angry? Today's Gospel reading tells us it is. (Mt 18:21-35). Jesus told a parable about a servant who owed his master 10,000 talents (equivalent to an infinite amount of money) which the servant could not repay him. Jumping quickly to the end of the story, we read the terrible ending: *"In anger the master turned him (the servant) over to the jailers to be tortured until he should pay back all he owed."* And since he owed an infinite amount of money (the footnote in my Bible says that even the wealthy Herod raised just 900 talents of revenue per year—so imagine owing 10,000 talents—over 10 years worth of national revenue), this means he would be tortured forever. Now that is some kind of anger. Of course, we might think, this is just a story; certainly God could not be as angry as the master was in the story. Wrong, according to Jesus. *"This is how my heavenly Father will treat each of you unless you forgive your brother with all your heart."* (v. 35)

The master was rightly upset over the debt the servant had incurred. Servants collected taxes, and apparently this particular servant had stolen the money he collected. Yet the master was infinitely compassionate, and when the servant asked for mercy, his master conceded. He didn't just reduce the debt; he cancelled it completely and let the man go "scot free". Now there is a compassionate man! What happened next would get anyone angry. Instead of being grateful for the cancellation of his debt, the angry servant went out and found a fellow servant who owed him 100 denarii (maybe one talent), and insisted that he repay him. When his fellow servant begged for time to pay him back, the heartless man refused and had the man thrown immediately into prison.

It wasn't the size of the debt, the theft, or the dishonesty that brought out the deep anger of the master; it was the unforgiving heart of the servant. He forgave the servant 10,000 talents, and in turn the servant would not forgive another man even one talent."

Our sins do not stir the anger of God for He is rich in mercy. Our unforgiveness does!

Each of us owes God much more than 10,000 talents. One sin against such a loving Father, one ingratitude, requires more pardon than we deserve. Yet time after time, he cancels our debt. We might say, "I just can't forgive that person who harmed me." And we are right; it is not within our power to do so. What is within our power is to "consent" to the grace of God which does give us the divine power to forgive even the worst perpetrator. If we ask, we will receive.

Lent is a time to examine our hearts. If there are remnants of unforgiveness stuck inside us, let us go immediate to our merciful Father and ask Him to give us the power to forgive all those who have sinned against us.

"Remember, O Lord, Your great mercy and love, for they are from of old." (Ps 25:6)

"Father…forgive us our trespasses as we forgive those who have trespassed against us."

Faithfulness

Shortly after the "9-11" tragedy I was talking to a saintly Christian woman who worked in the cafeteria at school. I told her how wonderful it was that in the wake of this catastrophe many people were returning to Church. With a knowing smile she replied, "for awhile". And that's exactly what happened. Faithfulness is a rare treasure in our world and our Church today. God is calling us today to be faithful

The number of people who continue to be involved in the charismatic renewal has shrunk considerably. The enthusiasm for the renewal that once existed is hard to find now. When God gave us the gift of the Holy Spirit, He entrusted to us the greatest of all treasures. We have been taught over the years that we need "four pillars" to uphold this new life, or otherwise it will collapse. A daily personal prayer life, a daily study of God's word, frequent Christian fellowship, and evangelizing are all necessary to keep our life in the Holy Spirit healthy. I wonder if those who no longer participate in the prayer meetings are sustaining this "4-point" program in other ways, or if they have let their enthusiasm die and have retreated into a "pre-renewal" life style?

Jeremiah rebuked the people (Jer 7:23-28) for their lack of faithfulness to their covenant with God. *"They went backward, not forward...they did not listen or pay attention to (God)...They were stiff-necked and did more evil than their fathers."* Earlier we read that their religion had degenerated into the minimal observance – a "burnt offerings and sacrifices" approach. No longer did they obey God.

When the excitement dies down, do we die with it? Do we let our life in the Holy Spirit fade away to a "Sunday observance" approach to the spiritual life? If this is all that remains, we are in deep trouble. Jesus says in today's Gospel reading (Lk 11:14-23), *"He who does not gather with me, scatters."* None of us would consider ourselves to be "scatterers"; but are we "gatherers?"

What is going on here? Let's listen to the whole story in today's Gospel. Jesus cast out a mute demon. His enemies tried to discredit Him by saying, *"By Beelzebub, the price of demons, he casts out demons."* They wanted to honor Satan for exercising a charism of the Holy Spirit. *"Others tested Him (Jesus) by asking for a sign from heaven."* Imagine the arrogance of putting the Son of God to a test! What greater sign could Jesus work than setting a man free from the grip of an evil spirit? These signs were worked not to help the people feel "excited" but to call them to conversion. *"But if I drive out demons by the finger of God, then the kingdom of God has come to you."* Like the people of Jeremiah's time, they were a stiff-necked people who chose to go backward instead of forward.

We live in a time of great testing. It is difficult for us to take steps to remain faithful. Voices around us continue to discredit the work of God by writing it off as "religious fanaticism" or the work of Beelzebub. These voices have gotten into the heads of many of us as they tell us to discount the wonders God has done for us and regress to a more lukewarm version of the Christian life. Satan loves lukewarm Christians. Are people still "testing God" by sitting around waiting for Him to give them another, *"sign from heaven?"* Hasn't He given us signs enough? Where is our faithfulness?

"Today if you hear His voice, harden not your hearts, as you did at Meribah, as you did that day at Massah in the desert, where your fathers tested and tried Me, though they had seen what I had done." (Ps 95:8-9)

"Come, Holy Spirit, let the fruit of faithfulness ripen among all Your people."